In memory of Coyne Steven Sanders

ALWAYS FOR JUDY:

Witness to the Joy and Genius of Judy Garland

Joan Beck Coulson

Always for Judy © 2014 Joan Beck Coulson

In line with Judy's caring for handicapped children, a percentage of profits from this book will be donated to Autism Speaks.org.

Published by Yarnscombe Books, PO Box 577, Elmira, CA.95625
Printed in the United States of America

ISBN 978-0-9913739-0-1

Cover designed by Betty Lucke

Cover photograph by courtesy of Photofest, also photographs on page 93, 174 and 177.

TABLE OF CONTENTS

ACKNOWLEDGEMENTS

This book would not have been possible without the help of so many people. My history with the fan club in Great Britain gave me access to their records and I am grateful to all those who, through the years, sent Lorna Smith their own reviews of concerts and television performances along with newspaper cuttings. This information is in the archives of the International Judy Garland Club preserved by Gary Horrocks and Dr. Justin Sturge.

Occasionally I referred to Scott Schechter's book, *Judy Garland, The Day-by-Day Chronicle of a Legend,* (2002) and other books.

After I left employment at CBS in 1963, I lost contact with Judy's activities. When I re-connected with Lorna Smith in 1997 and received copies of her 1960's club records, I immersed myself in this history, I wrote my first piece trying to capture the six months Judy lived in London in 1964; subsequently published in the Club magazine. I began to think about Judy's life and how she became the icon, she was. I researched her background: parents, life in vaudeville, Grand Rapids and Lancaster. Kate Russell helped me with these early chapters. As I wrote, I began to understand the damage, done to her as a child in Lancaster, and I thought back to the *7up* documentary, which I had seen many years ago in England. I contacted Michael Apted in 2011 and asked him if I could use his study as a basis of my book and he readily agreed.

As the young fans seemed to like to hear about my meetings with Judy and witnessing her perform, I retrieved my records and included many of the write-ups I did for the club for the Dominion 1957, Palladium 1960, *I Could Go on Singing* and shows at CBS *The Judy Garland Show.*

As I had no first-hand knowledge of her work across the country in the years 1965-1969 I have included stories that my friends have shared with me. Particularly I want to thank Lorna Smith, Brian Glanvill and John Theaker from England, Gordon Stevens from Canada, and Nancy Bar-Brandon, Sonny Gallagher, Eleanor Lyon, Wayne Lawless, Jon Perdue, Bill Seibel, Jack Wood and Kenneth Young. They have helped me recreate those years by sharing their stories about seeing Judy perform and talking with her.

If there were such a thing as a Research Assistant, it would have to be Amelia Armijo who was always there to look up information for me and champion me on in moments of doubt.

Gary Horrocks, Lauren McShea, Frank Labrador, Peter Mac, Jon Perdue, Les Pack, Elizabeth Rublein, Heather Siebert, D.j.Schaefer, Clayton Schiebel, George Sunga, Christopher Ward and Bobby Waters have always been there to help and encourage me on in many different ways.

I then there are my children, Carolyn and Adrian, who have lived with Judy Garland and maybe have the lives they have because of my love of Judy and the marvelous movies of MGM.

By far my main inspiration to continue with this book was Coyne Steven Sanders. He constantly encouraged me and felt I had something worth contributing to the history of Judy. I was devastated when he passed early in 1913, but Martha Wade Steketee gave me the guidance to finish this project. _2013_

I doubt I would have completed this endeavor without my local writing group. the Town Square Writers sponsored by our local library and particularly Deni Harding, who did the first edit for me; Terry Murray and Dotty Schenk for their artistic talents; Betty Lucke, who has become an expert in the self-publishing field and Joseph Whitson from Adventure in Personal Computing who helped me with formatting the book.

This book is in no way a pictorial exploration of Judy's life; there are so many books more beautifully done by others. I only use photographs to illustrate a point; many I took or are from my collection, which I acquired over the last seventy-five years, and many shared with me by my friends. The following people have generously allow me to use their photographs; Amelia Armijo, Nancy Barr-Brandon, Daniel Berghaus, Mickie Esemplare, Jan Glazier, Gordon Gush, Gary Horrocks (the International Judy Garland Club), Steve Jarrett, Eleanor Lyon, Jon Perdue, David Price, Bill Seibel, Gordon Stevens, Jack Wood, Michael Siewert, Brent Phillip/John Fricke, Heather Siebert and Charles Triplett. Sadly, I could not use all of them.

INTRODUCTION

So how and why did I decide to write a book about Judy? Judy has been in my life since I was about six years old, but it had never occurred to me to write a book about her. Sometimes I feel that life is a path we meander down, people we meet, ideas, which are exchanged (rather like *The Celestine Prophecy*), and suddenly one is doing something which a few months ago would never have occurred to one. My endeavors to write this book are in this category, and I think it is important to document them.

In October 1996, my son and I are in New York State for my  daughter's wedding, and we spend a few days in Manhattan. While in the Theatre Circle shop, I noticed someone is buying the shop's last copy of the famous poster for the Judy Garland's April 23, 1961 concert at Carnegie Hall—I had had one of those once, now lost along with many of my Judy press clippings—and so I look ruefully at the item. The woman who was making the purchase told me of the Grand Rapids Judy Garland Festival the next June. She urges me to go because it would be the celebration of Judy's 75th birthday. The person behind the counter asks if we had been out to Ferncliff Mausoleum, where Judy is at rest.

"No," I say, "Can we find it?" I ask my son. We are leaving the next day for Monroe, fifty miles from Manhattan, and it appears we would go past Ferncliff—that is, if we could find it! Time is of the essence because we have to be in Monroe by 5 p.m. for the wedding festivities to start. I begin to get very anxious.

"I know we won't get to Judy," I wail.

"Oh, yes we will," my son, insists.

It is a beautiful October day in New York City, and we have Frank Sinatra singing "Autumn in New York" on the car stereo as we leave. I search the map as we drive, and suddenly my son, is the one actually driving, sees a small sign: "Ferncliff". I would never have seen it. We turn quickly and drive through the beautiful grounds. We are videotaping, so the moment is captured. I go to the search desk to find her gravesite. There are a few people ahead of us. I expect to feel a fool, asking, "Where is Judy Garland?" But just then my son rushes up.

"I found her, I found her!" We run through the quiet halls to where she lies. Sadly I realize that in the rush to leave I have not brought any flowers! Everything has been too unexpected, but two vases of flowers stand there with messages of love. (I learn later that the UK Judy Garland Club regularly collects money to send flowers, and I always contribute to their fund now.) We take a few photographs, and my son asks if I want to be alone, but I just want to see it, and I am content.

GRAND RAPIDS 1997

The next spring I think about going to the big Judy Garland Festival in honor of Judy's 75th birthday and start trying to find out about it. I called the Michigan Tourist Office first (there is a much larger Grand Rapids in Michigan, another Midwestern state) before I find my way to the Minnesota Grand Rapids that is Judy's birthplace. I manage to locate the site and plan to attend, but my life becomes very confused as there were other demands on my time and an opportunity to work in an archaeology laboratory in Mexico, and it appears that the dates clash. I decide I will do both activities and my travel plans ultimately involve a night flight to Minneapolis, a rented car and four-hour drive to Grand Rapids for the weekend, and a four-hour return rush back down to the airport on Sunday night for a Monday flight to Mexico City.

I am a little apprehensive about attending a Festival on my own, being rather shy. As I am checking out the rental car, the woman at the next counter asks about the route to Grand Rapids and I catch her eye. It takes one to know one and I meet my first friends, Bill and Carolyn Seibel.

After the long drive to Grand Rapids, I check into the Sawmill Hotel, where most of the Judy activities were taking place. The first people I meet are five or six fifteen-year-old girls and one boy from Holland of a similar age. They are all wearing "Judy" tee shirts and I want to know how they became friends—from the internet club they tell me. They all live in different parts of the country and have met for the first time that day and they are very excited. (I have kept in contact with one of the group, through the years and later met another last Easter in New York, and really, these young people are the reason I am writing this.) Moments later Sid Luft and son Joey Luft come down the stairwell and go into the indoor

Jacuzzi. The young people run screaming after them, "We know it is Sid from his baggy eyes." I have not forgotten how to be a fan and I am not going to be left behind. I leave my suitcases in the middle of the hallway and follow the girls. Sid is shaking hands with the girls and after they leave, I say, "Hello Sid, do you remember me from the recording studio in London, with Lorna Smith, in the 60s?" "Of course," he says (what else could he say?) "And what are you doing here dear?" "I'm here for the same reason you are, here for the 75th Festival. Isn't it wonderful about all the young fans?" We talk of this and how the last time I had seen Joey was when he was eight years old at the CBS Television Studio. Joey does not seem very impressed with this memory, but later we will have several delightful conversations about  his mother, and Sid and I talk more.

In one conference presentation, Sid talks of the early days in Hollywood and, of course, answers questions about Judy. One comment stands out in my memory, **"I consider the greatest moments of my life were when she was my wife."**

 Judy's daughter, Lorna is also present that year in Grand Rapids and both she and Joey talk about the thrill of working with their mother in the summer tour of 1967 and performing at the Palace in New York. They both loved their mother's serious work in movies, such as *A Star is Born*, *Judgment at Nuremberg*, and *A Child is Waiting*.

During one of my private conversations with Sid, we talk of both our survival of cancer. He says encouragingly, "We will beat it, we'll still be here when everyone else is gone" and I could imagine him telling Judy, "Don't worry, we will deal with those agents, managers, and studios." I could understand the confidence he must have given her at times of doubt and uncertainty. His relationship with stepdaughter, Liza Minnelli was good. He had come into the Judy life when Liza was about 3.1/2 years old and become her Poppa. He appears to be obviously exceeding fond of Liza and by all accounts, the feeling reciprocated. Liza recently appeared at a theatre near to me and I have a good newspaper review with me, which I give him to pass on to Joey. He comments. "She was always good girl."

The days in Grand Rapids were full with meetings with other fans. I am on a panel, trying to explain what it was like to attend one of Judy's concerts and this experience leads me to dig down deep into my memory to articulate them. I realize that I had experiences; which others had not had, and that I should share these memories. People come up to me and ask me for my autograph! I am no one, why do they want my autograph. This is when I start using the expression, "Always for Judy." The UK Fan Club organized this panel and they urge me to attend their next meeting, which, coincidentally, would occur two days after my next planned trip to England. I am going to be there for three months and a second club meeting would happen before I left in October. So suddenly, I am in the middle of the "Judy World." I am meeting so many old friends and meeting so many new young fans of Judy.

LONDON 1997

For 35 years, after moving to the United States in 1962, having and bringing up a family, I had no contact with other Judy fans. I

have no idea how or why I lost contact with Lorna Smith, who ran the British Chapter of the US Judy Garland Club in the 1960s, but trying to survive in Los Angeles as new immigrant was not exactly easy. It was not that I had forgotten Judy, she was always in my thoughts and I listened to my LPs, but I just did not meet anyone to talk with about her.

While in London I am able to re-new my contact with Lorna Smith and our friendship continues where it left off. Lorna had written two books. The first is a straightforward biography, *Judy, with Love*, which came out in 1975 along with Anne Edward's *Judy Garland* and Gerold Frank's *Judy*. Perhaps as a result, Lorna's book did not get much attention but now when a copy comes up on e-bay now it sells very quickly. The second book is about some psychic experiences Lorna had with Judy. Now I have to explain that Lorna was a very serious person, a government official

before she retired, and not someone to become involved in bizarre activities so I was interested to hear about how this book had come into being. All this is in Lorna's book, *Over the Rainbow*. Lorna gave me a copy of the book and I thought the words in it were beautiful. She told me that many copies of the second book were sitting on the patio of longtime fan Sonny (Francis) Gallagher in Pennsylvania and I determined to try to get the books out to the public. (Sonny was ill with cancer and, sadly, eventually left us, but he was such a charming, kind and sensible man.) I advertised the book on the internet with Judy Fan Club sites and got to speak to even more young fans. People still say to me about Judy Garland, "but she committed suicide," and

suddenly I understand why Lorna felt she had to write her books. I met other fans of Judy at this time. Beverly Shields bought one of Lorna's book she introduced me to Frank Labrador, who came out to my house in Palm Springs to interview me. (Frank started his video career then!) I also met many other fans; Wayne Lawless, Meredith Ponedel (niece of Judy's make-up artist, Dottie Ponedel), Eleanor Lyon and Maureen Case Davis (members of the famed Bench Wenches-fans who waited outside CBS), and Kate Russell. During the next few years, we often met up, attended parties and shared our love of Judy. Just before I leave England that summer, I visit two clinical psychologists I had met on a vacation in Europe. In discussing my recent activities, I mention

Judy and my thoughts of her life and one of the women says, "of course, she was an abused child." After I discuss my life and my mother's marriage, they classify me as an abused child also. There is always the reason, we go somewhere and meet someone; they are to lead us to the truth. Well time goes by, five grandchildren are born, several house moves occur, various medical problems had to be overcome and I continue to wander the world seeking out strange and magical places. But Judy is always with me—I spend many weeks with Lorna Smith hearing first hand her experiences with Judy, write articles for the fan club; attend several London club meetings and then the advent of Facebook brings more young fans into my orbit.

I attend a concert by Richard Glazier on April 7, 2009 in San Rafael "A Salute to Judy Garland" and Jan, his lovely wife, incorporates me into her Judy Family of Garland fans and encourages me to tell some early fan club stories.

In April 2010, Jan organizes a *Judy in Hollywood* function over three days visiting many of the sites where Judy performed, including CBS where I worked many years ago and MGM, now Sony studios. Again, I meet more young fans and realize that Judy's magic will go on forever, 100, 200 and even 500 years. Young people will hear her voice somewhere, or see one of her old movies on television and will become captivated and want to learn more about her. I would like there to be a book out there, which is not sensational but looks at Judy's life sensibly.

PREFACE

My background in social science and anthropology enables me to look at Judy Garland's life from a different perspective than most of her other biographers. My master's degree covered the life of a Chinese woman who spent 17 years attempting, and finally succeeding, to escape from Communist China, "Daughter of the Landlord." [1] Exploring women's lives are my interest and passion. As most of my writing has been in the academic field, I have chosen to use the Chicago Manual of Style in this book indicating showing Endnotes with a digital number.

Digging back into my anthropology theory, in "The Personal Document in Anthropological Science," Clyde Kluckholm points out, "life events have meaning only in their context. This context is, in part, created by the contemporary situation of the subject and by the sequence of experience which are peculiar to him as an individual." [2]

It is necessary to place the life of Judy Garland into the era in which she grew up: in the vaudeville stages where she witnessed hundreds of acts and performed herself, the sound studios where she recorded songs, MGM sets where she sang, danced and acted as she grew up. I want to understand why and how this special person evolved, her challenges, how she dealt with the chaos of her life, what motivated her loves. Most importantly, I wanted to understand the damage, done to her in those years by being continually forced to audition as a child. I hope to explain some of her actions and incorporate my experiences at concerts and meeting Judy.

As we will see from Judy's life, she knew the drugs, which had been introduced into her system by her studio, MGM, and she was addicted to, were not good for her. Many times, she admitted herself into hospitals trying to get free of the drugs and get well. However, because she was programmed by the age of seven, to entertain, regardless of health or personal issues, she was not able to break this pattern. We also understand now that childhood drama is the root cause of many adults' drug use.

Now it is easier for young actors to control their careers because they are not restricted with five-year contracts with studios. They are able to further their education, learn to analyze their job opportunities, gain confidence in dealing with people in positions of power such as heads of studios and defend their choices about what type of work they want. Judy Garland never had these opportunities. She was the breadwinner and did as she was told.

I have included many stories, related to me through the years from people who met her and witnessed her perform. I want to capture her charm, grace, wit, artistry, and most of all show how she was a thoroughly nice woman.

Judy loved her audiences and fans, and they became part of her life towards the end, when other friends turned their backs. The fans asked, "Can I do anything for you?" Sonny Gallagher drove the children to and from the theatre and took them swimming. Nancy Barr-Brandon, longtime fan and photographer paid her bills and kept her company. Wayne Martin, another longtime fan, called her and sympathized. Lorna Smith acted as her dresser for five weeks at *Talk of the Town*. Brian Glanvill, devoted fan from London, was set to be a companion to Judy a few days before she died.

I share my memories of seeing her films first hand at the time they were made, mostly during World War II, and what she meant to the British people. As I have lived on both side of the Atlantic, I have a unique perspective with which to view her life. I want to capture her essence, energy and unbelievable talent. As

I was present at many of her concerts, I will try to explain her effect upon audiences.

This book is for the fans who cared for her in the past, for those who love her now, and for those who will fall under her spell in years to come.

I am particularly grateful to Michael Apted filmmaker, who graciously allowed me to use his documentary *UP Series,* which looks at lives of people over the years, as a framework for my analysis of Judy's life. Also, to prove the Jesuit saying, "Give me the child until he is seven, and I will show you the man."

PART ONE

Chapter 1

Carnegie Hall

Little did Judy Garland know when she crooned, "The Joint is Really Jumping Down at Carnegie Hall" to Jose Iturbi in the movie, *Thousands Cheer*, that one day she **would** be making the joint jump? On April 23, 1961, Judy Garland created her own

event at Carnegie Hall, which has gone down in show business history.

A recording was made of the concert and a long-playing record issued titled: "Judy at Carnegie Hall." As technology evolves and CDs are re-mastered in different formats, there is a multitude of material for the public to enjoy. A recreation of this show with her musical arrangements and film clips is appearing all over the country. Some artists try to recreate that evening, but of course, no one can. There was only one Judy Garland and a documentary is underway of this important event, titled *Stay All Night* under the guidance of Steven Lippman.

Essayist, critic, editor and anthologist Clifton Fadiman captured Judy's essence when he talks about her performance:

carnegie Hall

As we listened to her voice, with its unbelievable marriage of volume and control, telling the most delicious jokes with arms, legs, head, and eyes, we forgot—and this is the acid test—who she was, and indeed who we were ourselves. As with all true clowns (for Judy Garland is as fine a clown as she is a singer) she seemed to be neither male nor female, young nor old, pretty nor plain. She had no "glamour," only magic. She was gaiety itself, yearning itself, fun itself…She wasn't being judged or enjoyed, not even watched or heard. She was only being felt, as one feels the quiet run of one's own blood, the shiver of the spine.…And when, looking about eighteen inches high, sitting hunched over the stage apron with only a tiny spotlight pinpointing her elf face, she breathed the last phrase of "Over the Rainbow" and cried out its universal unanswerable query, "Why can't I?" it was though the bewildered hearts of all the people in the world had moved quietly together and become one, shaking in Judy's throat, and there breaking.[1]

This historic evening might not have happened if Judy had not traveled to London in July 1960 to recover from her serious 1959 illness. Judy made some recordings and spent time with her friend, Dirk Bogarde. She was contemplating doing a concert and Dirk encouraged her to forget about the opening act structure she had been using for years and just SING herself on stage with a big orchestra. Judy was initially was apprehensive about this idea and went

to Rome to discuss the idea with another friend, Kay Thompson. She came back, put together a program, and tried it out one Sunday evening on the stage at the Palladium. That evening was August 28 and I had a seat in the front row center.

One may ask why the Palladium and why London? This is where Judy felt most comfortable and at home. She had revived her career on the stage at the Palladium in April 1951, had a successful month's run at the Dominion in 1957 and now she was there among friends again. At the end of this first concert she said, "I must say that it is lovely to see you. It is lovely to be home (and a little shyly) because this is my new home." This did not prove to be precisely true but this is how she felt on this night.

It is one thing to experience Judy singing in a recording studio or an empty theatre, but it is quite another thing to be present at one of her performances in front of a live audience. The theatre feels as if it would burst with excitement and electricity in the air — it is quite unbelievable. Judy transforms into an entirely different being. Her body moves as she uses all her talents as an actress, dancer and singer and pours her soul (and humor) into each song. The people who are sharing this experience with her affect Judy; this seems to make her feel she wants to give more and more to the audience. Finally, there is a joining of these two entities, Judy and the audience. Her performing presence and personality are overpowering, one knows that this is the only place on earth to be just then.

About twenty minutes into the show on August 28, 1960, Judy knew she had succeeded. After a chat with Norrie Paramor, her conductor, Judy dances or skips back to the front of stage and I saw a glint of excitement in her eyes, as if to say, "I have done it – it works – I can do it!"

This was the evening of a lifetime and I am glad I can share details in Chapter 15.

To put this in historical context of Judy's life, at the time she performed at Carnegie Hall in April 1961, Judy was in the midst of her concert years, which had started at the London Palladium in 1951, and continued until her death in London, 1969. She performed more than eleven hundred concerts, theatre and nightclub performances, on occasion singing over thirty songs in one performance. Every conductor and arranger loved to work with her, and musicians in her orchestras commented on her professionalism and had great respect for her. During these years, she toured all over the United States, Canada, Great

Britain, Europe, Scandinavia, Australia and Mexico. Many conductors traveled with her: Gordon Jenkins was with her in London 1957, and Mort Lindsey, who had conducted her television series, traveled to Australia with her in 1964.

Judy had an amazing life working with many of the talented performers and artists in the world. Every composer loved her to sing their songs, and she had close friendships with Arlen, Mercer, Gershwin, Porter, Rodgers, and Hammerstein. Johnny Mercer carried a torch for her for years. She had many romances with the beautiful men she met, including Tyrone Power and Joseph Mankiewicz. She had close friendships with Bing Crosby, Bob Hope Noël Coward, David Niven, Humphrey Bogart, and later his wife, Lauren Bacall as well as Kay Thompson, Lana Turner, June Allyson, Debbie Reynolds, and make-up artist Dottie Ponedel.

With the memories of many friends who also witnessed her perform; I hope to capture her charm, genius and joy of being with her audiences.

Chapter 2

The Early Influences

Michael Apted - Filmmaker

Jesuit saying: *Give me the child until he is seven, and I will show you the man.* Attributed to Francis Xavier

Judy Garland's first venture onto the stage was as Frances (or Baby) Gumm was in her father's theatre in Grand Rapids, Minnesota at the age of 2.1/5 years, and later in Lancaster, California. She continued performing and auditioning until her discovery at the age of twelve by MGM. During these formative years, she came to love entertaining audiences and the applause, but bitterly disliked the auditions her mother insisted she attend. Perhaps we can try to understand this conflict and see how it played out later in her life. The two sides of the conflict were happiness and joy at performing under the gentle guidance of her father in one of his family theatres, as opposed to the stress of the long drives into Los Angeles from Lancaster by her mother to audition before unresponsive agents and managers. This happened between the ages of five and eleven years of age. The seeds of this conflict would be played out repeatedly on movie sets and concert stages during the years. Additionally, Judy would always be caught up in her love of performing and the demands of the movie studios, agents and managers. These people ordered her to work when she did not feel she had enough energy to give her best; as she always wanted to please, she relied on energy boosting drugs supplied by her mother and the movie studio.

As my background is in the social science and anthropology field, I am always interested in how early influences affect a child. I am intrigued by the award-winning television documentary of filmmaker, Michael Apted who explores the Jesuit saying, *Give me a child until he is seven, and I will show you the man.* Apted was born and raised in England and now resides in Los Angeles. He directed *Gorky Park, Gorillas in the Mist,* and recently, *Chronicles of Narnia: The Voyage of the Dawn Treader.* In 1963, he started his training at Granada Studios for a career in television. He was assigned to do research for Australian journalist, Tim Hewat, and for Paul Arnold, who directed the first documentary, *7Up.* They were curious to see if the social revolution (changes to the rigid class English system) had actually made a difference in people's lives. To do this, they question and view this study from the eyes of a cohort of seven-year-old children from different social backgrounds. This study has been shown on British television since 1963, and has been made into several full-length documentary films in subsequent seven-year periods following the same group of children as they age--the latest being *56 Up* made in 2012.[1] These later documentary films are in cinemas and on PBS television in the U.S. [2]

I first saw and was profoundly affected by the initial Apted documentary when I lived in the U.K. in the early 1970s. I had young children and already understood the importance of the early years on the development of a child and his or her future, especially the type of education the child receives—education that can help the child reach its full potential without unnecessary pressure.

One would think that this was basic, but how do we ensure that our children are encouraged without pressure? In addition, I was aware of the damage, done to Judy and other child performers—damage which, once done, is hard to eradicate. Right or wrong, my method when bringing up my two children was to emphasize a balance of education and the arts, which interested both my children. They enjoyed the old MGM  musicals I would watch. My daughter wanted to be a dancer, and my son loved music, so they both had music or dance lessons, but schoolwork had to be kept up and homework done. I was neither concerned with making stars of them nor pushing them into show business. My daughter obtained a theatre arts degree and was originally a dancer and actor for several years in London and California, but finally decided she missed the academic life and went back to graduate school and obtain a Ph.D. She is now a Professor of Theatre at a university on the East Coast. In addition to her scholarly work, she teaches movement and acting, directs plays, and occasionally performs. She has a very full life. My son is a jazz musician who combines his work as a band director at a high school in California with playing professionally with big bands, Latin and jazz bands. I am grateful to Apted's study for making me aware of these influences.

Apted's study *7-Up* is an enquiry into whether the social revolution, which was happening in the U.K., had actually made a difference to people's lives. The original project used fourteen seven-year-old children from different social and economic backgrounds. Apted questions them about their interests and opinions on life. As already noted, the exploration has continued with new interviews and a new film every seven years to see if the patterns that were present at seven years old changed as the years went by. His study focuses on the effects of the economic background of the children, but I am more interested in seeing the thoughts and ambitions which are in the children at this early age, how these to develop in the teens and mid-life, and if this formula can be applied to Judy's life.

Apted proves that the earliest influences on the children of his study make them the adults they become. Those children from affluent backgrounds all go into the professions planned for them by their parents. Those with parents who are less determined or have less financial means struggle with their lives, and some are reasonably content. One boy brought up on a farm in the beautiful countryside of Yorkshire in the north of England says he would like to find out all about the moon and "If I could change the world, I'd change it into a diamond."[3] He ends up as a physics professor at University of Wisconsin. Another boy wants to go to Africa and help poor people and ends up teaching math to immigrant girls from Bangladesh and Pakistan in the east end of London, after a stint in Pakistan himself. The study shows that often what is in the heart of a child at aged seven stays with him or her always.

On the surface, this study may not appear to apply to Judy, as she was not born in the U.K. during the time of the study, but the results, which apply to one study, are relevant to another. If we consider that her early years were spent performing in her father's theatre, or traveling to other locations to perform, we can see that she could not act in any other way. I will look at what had happened in the life of Judy Garland, or Frances Gumm, to the age of seven, and what opinions, feelings, and ambitions she had at that early age.

Little Frances Ethel Gumm was born into a very musical and show business-oriented family. She would have heard more music than talking as she was waking up. Ethel, her mother, was always playing the piano and practicing songs for the theatre, and teaching the two elder sisters to sing and dance. Frank, her father, would burst into song and entertain anyone who might visit, so there was always music in the house. [4]

The early years when Judy performed with her family in her father's theatre, or traveled with the family to other locations, were happy. The performances done in the midst of her family to warm audiences thrilled her and she enjoyed herself, but the times, later in childhood, particularly in Lancaster, when her mother dragged her off to auditions against her will, had a profound effect upon her. This led later to the hostility she felt toward demanding and critical directors. Judy hated to sing before the unsmiling managers and agents whom she felt did not like her. Added to this was the confusion Judy felt because it appeared she was only of any value if she was singing or performing. She ended up not feeling she had any worth unless she was performing.

Towards the end of her life, many of those who loved Judy wished she did not need to go on performing because she was so ill. But as we see from this study, those who are programmed at an early age to act one way, and who do not have opportunities to develop in other directions, are unable to come out of the mold and act any differently. We need to know how this happened, and then perhaps this will help us understand why she appeared difficult and uncooperative later in her life.

Judy was given musical and performance influences; but later when she wanted to stop performing, no one would allow her. There was no particular emphasis on college or work, although her father had been to college. Her mother's opinions were the most important. Judy loved to sing when she felt like it but hated to be made to sing to unresponsive people.

Judy wanted to open a hospital for sick children; even before she encountered handicapped children. However, she was not able to stop and go down other paths because the work machine of MGM felt it had invested money in her and she had to work for it.

Judy's first adventures on the stage are important to me because they laid the cornerstone for the rest of her life. As we will see in the segments on Lancaster and Los Angeles, great damage was inflicted on Judy by continual trips into Los Angeles from her home in Lancaster.

PART TWO

BABY GUMM

Chapter 3

Parents and Vaudeville

Some young people may not feel vaudeville is important to the story of the life of Judy Garland, but if we are to understand Judy, we must understand her background and her early training and the influence her vaudevillian parents had upon her.

Vaudeville (or Variety in Britain) had been the main form of family entertainment in Britain and America since the 19th century. It really became popular at the turn of the 20th century and remained so until the 1930s. Typical shows would include Irish tenors, bold flirtatious female singers with loud voices, dancers, comedians, acrobats and jugglers. Every town had a theatre—and if there were not enough theatres, warehouses were converted. As this was the main entertainment for the family, the entrance fee was a modest five cents.[1] A different feature in America from Britain was the inclusion of minstrel shows with white performers blacking their faces and hands and imitating black performers. Al Jolson was a well-known example of this style.

The movie, *Babes in Arms (1939)* features Mickey Rooney and Judy in this kind of minstrel act.[2]

Vaudeville singers always needed new material, and songwriters kept turning out new songs. The audiences could buy a sheet of their favorite music and play and sing in their own home. Judy's parents Frank and Ethel Gumm grew up in this atmosphere, and they were both enamored with show business.

JUDY'S FATHER

Frank Avent Gumm was born March 20, 1886, of mixed Northern European decent. Judy considered him an Irishman, but the family may also have had German ancestry. Frank was born in a little town called Murfreesboro, Tennessee, about fifty miles southeast of Nashville; he was named for a prominent lawyer in town, Frank Avent. Murfreesboro had been an important location during the Civil War era, but when Frank was born, the town was a sleepy southern community of about 5,000 people. Frank was one of five children born to William T. Gumm and Clementine Baugh; the others were Mary, Robert, William and Allie. The Gumm family had been part of the original settlement in Tennessee, and many Gumms are in the cemetery in the small village called Gumm.[3]

The Gumms were lucky enough to have some influential friends in the town. One of them was George Darrow, who became Frank's godfather. George Darrow had married well and become wealthy, but he did not forget his poor childhood and enjoyed helping young people who had talent. Frank had a lovely voice and sang in the choir at St. Paul's Episcopal Church, which Darrow had helped to establish. Darrow persuaded William Gumm to allow Frank to attend Sewanee Grammar School, about sixty miles south of Murfreesboro, and obtained a scholarship for him. In June 1899, thirteen-year-old Frank entered the new school on the Cumberland Plateau in a particularly beautiful location. The grammar school was a prep school for college, with classical education in Latin, Greek, history, math and private voice lessons for Frank. Frank enjoyed school, performing in plays and singing in the choir, and he appeared to be a good student; he was good-looking and very popular.[4] He graduated in June 1903 and entered the University of the South for a year. Frank said that these years were "six of the happiest, the most beautiful years of my life."[5]

Frank's father, William T. Gumm, was a merchant, but he does not appear to have been very successful. They were able to live comfortably due to an inheritance his wife Clementine received from her mother, Mary. They had a fine house on East Main Street, Murfreesboro, near the town square, and they appeared to neighbors to be a happy family enjoying music and singing. They enjoyed the traveling vaudeville shows that came into town, and at one time Frank ran away for a while with a minstrel show.

After Clementine's mother Mary died in 1902 and her house was sold, William, Clemmie and the children moved into a small cottage Mary left to Clemmie. Clemmie had been an invalid most of her life, even though she had given birth to five children and died in October 1895. At this point, the family fortunes seemed to deteriorate. A fire destroyed the cottage and William Gumm asked the Rutherford County Chancery Court for permission to use his children inheritance's to buy a house for them. Later he was at court again and pronounced insolvent.[6]

When Frank's father died in 1906, his sister tried to keep the family together and Frank left college and returned home, presumably to help support the family. In 1909, siblings Mary, Allie and Frank moved to Tullahoma, a small town half way between Murfreesboro and Sewanee where Frank found work first as a bookkeeper and then as an office manager. He continued his singing in the church choir and at the local vaudeville house. His sister, Mary, also had a beautiful voice; later she became depressed when she became crippled, and threw herself off a bridge. One wonders if she had inherited the same health problems as her mother.

There was plenty of work for those who loved show business—managing theatres or performing as song illustrators. Song illustrators would have to be great showmen, for they were singing songs to encourage the public to buy the sheet music.

Frank moved around learning the business, and by September 1911, he bought the Bijou and Diamond theatres in Croquet, Minnesota. Then he decided, for whatever reasons, to move on, and he passed them to his older brother, Robert.

Frank moved to Lake Superior, Wisconsin in 1912, which had a population of 45,000 and many theatres with plenty of work for entertainers, particularly in the summer time. Ray Hadfield, who ran several theatres in Lake Superior, liked Frank and gave him a job as a song illustrator at the Orpheum Theatre. [7] Frank rotated and worked at other theatres. At the Parlor Theatre on Tower Avenue, he met the pianist, Ethel Milne, and later rented a room from her parents. Frank did not stay very long, though, moving on to Portland, Oregon. He found work at the People's Amusement Company, managing the theatre and singing in the intervals. In the autumn of 1913, Frank returned to Lake Superior. Ethel was still playing piano and singing at the Parlor on Tower Avenue, and they renewed their friendship and decided to marry.

JUDY'S MOTHER

Ethel Marion Milne was born in 1893 in Marquette, Michigan. She was the eldest of seven children born to John Milne, son of Scottish Protestant immigrants from Ontario, Canada, and his Irish wife, Eva Fitzpatrick. Eva's family lived in Massena, New York, for several years, and by 1890, they moved to Marquette, Michigan, where John and Eva met and married. John was a railroad man and worked his way up from a laborer to engineer. They moved to Michigamme a small town with less than six hundred people around 1903 and remained there until 1910. [8] The Milne family was at the center of the town getting involved with concerts; John could play the violin and Eva sang and played the piano. John was an agnostic and "John, who was perhaps too fond of the bottle, seemed to enjoy making it hot for his dear old Episcopalian wife" [9] Even so they managed to enjoy themselves singing, playing and performing. In the movie, *Meet Me in St. Louis* (1945), depicting an American Midwestern family in 1903 and 1904, we see the type of entertainment that families engaged in at the turn of the century. There was no radio or television, so families provided the entertainment themselves.

While Judy often referred to her father as a laughing Irishman and he obviously enjoyed singing. On the other side of the family, the Fitzpatrick family passed on their love of song and storytelling on to their children and grandchildren. Grandma Eva had no problem encouraging Baby Frances, at two-and-a-half, to get up on stage with her sisters. Ethel played the piano by ear but learned to read music. This enabled her to play, sing and sell sheet music in stores, rather the way that Judy did in the movie, *In the Good Old Summertime* (1949) set in Chicago in the late 1800s. One of Ethel's jobs was to play songs and sell sheet music, and Frank was the Irish tenor.

Ethel was petite; Judy commented that they were the same height, 4' 11". Although Ethel was not actually pretty, she had a strong personality with bright, flashing black eyes and she could be charming, energetic and determined. She persuaded Frank that they could share a life together since their interests were the same. Ethel was ambitious and wanted to get on in life, and one can guess she thought that marrying a theatrical manager would be the first step on the way to success.

Ethel was twenty and Frank was twenty-seven when they were married on January 22, 1914.[10] Within two months, Ethel had persuaded Frank to move to Grand Rapids, Minnesota, and take over management of the New Grand Theatre with Ethel playing the piano in the intervals.

The silent movies came along and would eventually bring about the demise of vaudeville, but for several years the two media worked side by side, and this is where Judy's parents thrived. Many of the new movies were short, ten or fifteen minutes in length, and vaudeville entertainment was included to fill out the program. They needed a person to play the piano; this was ideal for Ethel because of her experience playing for the family at home. While the reels were changed, another person entertained the audience. Hence, the position of song illustrator came into being. This was a perfect job for Frank, with his fine voice. Jack Warner, who later founded a movie studio with his brothers, had done this in his father's movie house as did Eddie Cantor and Al Jolson. In addition, there were still photographs projected onto the screen by Thomas Edison's Vitascope.

Many of Judy's movies contain examples of vaudeville performances. In *Ziegfeld Girl* (1941) Judy as Susan Gallagher performs with her father are a vaudeville act, and when Susan auditioned for the Ziegfeld Show, her father tries to show her how to punch out a number in the old style. Susan manages to get the orchestra to play slower tempo and we see and hear the beautiful, "I'm Always Chasing Rainbows." There are many more examples in the movies *Little Nellie Kelly* (1940) representing the Irish immigrant experience into New York in the late 1800s and *For Me and My Gal* (1942) set just prior and during World War I, as in her movies with Mickey Rooney.

The popular English singer Julie Andrews came out of a Variety background in England and toured for many years as a child with her parents prior to her career on Broadway and motion pictures. I remember hearing her on the radio in the 1940s and 1950s. In the United States, many well-known entertainers came from a vaudeville background, such as Bob Hope, Burns and Allen, Mickey Rooney and Donald O'Connor. George Burns wrote in his book, *Gracie: a love story* about life on the vaudeville stage, and being on the road performing three or four shows day. Although they were earning $125-$250 a week, by the time they paid their agent, transportation, food and hotels, there was little money left over. Of course, they were doing the work they loved. Burns and Allen did not really begin to be financially solvent until they found their opportunities in radio, movies and eventually television.[11]

Ed Sullivan's television shows in the 1950s and 1960s were structured like vaudeville show with a wide array of acts. Eventually folk and rock music came into being in the late 1950s and 1960s and influenced the music of those eras. We see the remains of vaudeville performers on the cruise lines where singers, dancers, jugglers, comedians and musicians are needed to entertain their many passengers.

This vaudeville background gave Judy "the edge" and polished her ability to be comfortable and handle an audience. Judy was most at home on the stage and interacting with any audience. These skills she learned from performing in her father's theatre as a child. She loved giving them pleasure. She felt of herself as an entertainer; this was her role in life, to make people happy.

I was lucky enough to be present at many of her performances in London in 1951, 1957 and 1960 and witnessed her recording four songs in London at EMI in 1960. I remember once being at CBS when Count Basie was a guest on her television show. Some of

the numbers had been pre-recorded, so the audience was watching monitors. Judy obviously felt they were being short changed not to see a live performance, so she dragged Mel Tormé out with her and they did their songs with the monitors. So we had two Judy Garlands and two Mel Tormés; we certainly were not shortchanged!

Judy had seen and witnessed so many acts from her vaudeville years (as she was to amuse audiences in her

later television appearances) and was able to incorporate these aspects into her performances. Many of the musicals of the 1940s and 1950s made in Hollywood had a vaudeville theme because this was the background of most entertainers. Judy incorporated vaudeville into her movies. Think of "Be a Clown" from the movie, *The Pirate (1948)* "We're a Couple of Swells" from

18

Easter Parade (1948) and the beautiful and haunting "Clown" number and "Here's to Us" recorded but not originally broadcast from the last episode of her 1963-1964 CBS television show. Finally, one cannot forget "Swanee" from *A Star is Born* (1954).

Chapter 4

Grand Rapids

In 1915, Grand Rapids, Minnesota, was a small lumber community of 2,500 people near the Pokegamma Falls--a beautiful area with lakes surrounded by pine and newly planted forests, but enduring many harsh winters. The main industry of the town was a local paper mill called The Itasca Paper Mills, still active today.

Moving to Grand Rapids and being the wife of a theatre manager might have been enough for some women, but it was not enough for Ethel, who was determined to be a star. She and Frank put together an act, calling themselves Jack and Virginia Lee, the Singing Sweethearts from the South. When the first winter came, they persuaded some relatives of Ethel to look after the theatre so they could try to break into vaudeville. They were not very successful and Ethel became ill with influenza and had to recover at her mother's house in Superior.[1]

When Frank and Ethel returned to Grand Rapids a couple of months later they found that Ethel was pregnant. They settled in Grand Rapids and Frank bought half ownership in the theatre. Their first child, Mary Jane, was born in September 1915, and they rented a house on Pokegamma Avenue. Frank enjoyed his role as theatre manager and singing in the intervals between reel changes. To bring in extra money he also worked as a reporter for the Grand Rapids Itasca County *Independent* newspaper. The newspaper reported many of the family's activities, including Frank's social functions, which presumably had Ethel's blessing as she did the catering. She would have been six months pregnant with their second child when this event appeared on March 24, 1917:

> A surprise party was given at the home of Frank Gumm Tuesday evening, the occasion being the twenty-first (?) birthday anniversary of Mr. Gumm. Mrs. Gumm had assembled some 16 young men friends of her husband and when Mr. Gumm came home from the show he found "some crowd at the house." The evening was spent in cards and music, after which delicious "eats" were served.[2]

Another entry reported:

> Frank Gumm entertained on Sat. evening with prettily appointed six o'clock stag dinner for the young men who were home for the Easter vacation from the university. Covers were laid for ten and Mrs. Gumm, assisted by Miss Katherine Gilbert, served a sumptuous three-course dinner

Frank seemed to enjoy the company of young men, and this might not seem so odd if we remember he had experienced six very happy years at a preparatory school and college in a male-oriented environment.[3] To a certain extent, the couple led independent lives with Ethel regularly visiting her family in Michigan, some hours away. When their second daughter, Virginia, was born on July 4, 1917, they bought a house for their growing family. Frank had a lovely baritone voice, an engaging personality and performed in regular vaudevillian shows singing, "The Old Rugged Cross," "You Made Me Love You" and "Danny Boy." "Through the Years" was a particular favorite.

When looking at the lives of Frank and Ethel Gumm during the Grand Rapids years, one would say they appeared to do well: they were successful in town, active in community affairs, had a busy social life and a maid. For all the negative things said later about Ethel, one could not call her lazy or slothful. She was the ideal wife and mother--cooking, making everyday clothes as well as costumes for her and the girls, and teaching the girls to play the piano and dance. She also organized bridge games for the

21

neighbors, played the piano at the theatre contributing to the family income, and played the organ at the church. At this time Ethel was in the midst of a family life, a busy wife and mother, so what went wrong and why did they decide to move? Why did Ethel become disenchanted with her life? We have to consider that Ethel was a northern girl and added to this she was the eldest daughter and very determined. Frank was a southern gentleman inclined to take the easy road and let his wife run the show. This difference in their styles must have caused some friction.

Marc Rabinowitz (later called Rabwin) was a family friend in these early years. He met Frank Gumm when Marc was trying to earn extra money selling independent movies during his summer break from medical school at the University of Minnesota. His father owned and ran a theatre similar to Frank Gumm's, so he understood the business, and they struck up a friendship. Marc was included in the Gumm family activities when he was in town. He enjoyed Ethel and their two girls and often stayed for dinner.

Frank had a dislike of the big distributors. It is ironic that, later, it would be MGM, one of the biggest film distributors, who would treat his daughter so badly (prior to the lawsuits of the mid-20th century that broke up the movie studio monopoly on distribution their own product).

When Ethel found she was pregnant for the third time, it was to Marc that Frank went. Ethel tried to obtain an abortion and even told stories to friends, with Frances present, about trying to get rid of the baby by falling down stairs. One can only imagine how this made Frances feel, to know that she was so unwanted. It was illegal to obtain an abortion at that time, although it did not stop women from trying to terminate a pregnancy. Marc Rabwin warned Frank about how it would endanger Ethel's life if they tried anything.[4] Therefore, Frank and Ethel accepted the fact that another child would join their family, and they hoped for a boy. On June 10, 1922, a little girl Frances Ethel Gumm was born and they forgot about not wanting her

Ethel's determination to abort this pregnancy was an odd action if the couple were still happily married. Ethel came from a large family and finances were not the reason. Explanation that is more logical is something was not right in the marriage and her unhappiness made her not want to add to the family.

There were already rumors in Grand Rapids about Frank's homosexual activities and even though it is unclear whether there are any police records of any irregularities, these rumors would have been enough to upset Ethel and make her uncomfortable.

When Frances was about a year old, something happened to bring Ethel and Frank together again, their precious baby came down with a serious illness, with high fevers and stomach upsets and dehydration. When nothing seemed to help, Frank and Ethel drove her two hundred miles to a Duluth Hospital where she stayed for over a month (Grandma Eva lived in Duluth). We must remember there were no antibiotics or penicillin then. Frances was to have a similar re-occurrence of this illness after they reached Los Angeles, and these experiences in hospital make Judy very sympathetic to hospitalized children.

Joey Luft told me in 1997 at the Grand Rapids Judy Festival that his mother liked looking after sick children. She would fuss over any of his friends who were not well while at their house. These children were surprised to realize that "Judy Garland" was looking after them.

Frank and Ethel were busy working at the theatre much of the time, so the children would have spent time there with their parents. Often tiny Frances Gumm slept in a drawer in the evenings while her mother played piano.

Judy later insisted the family was very happy in Grand Rapids and told stories about snowball fights and making angels in the snow. She recalled a big burial ceremony for a bird in one of her father's cigar boxes and being chased by a neighbor because they were gathering apples from a

23

farmer's land up near a lake. Judy often said, "The beginning of my life was terribly happy. Everything that represented family, clean, old-fashioned beliefs, not frightening and a gay good home." She also said, "That's the only time I saw my parents happy."[5]

Some members of Ethel's family considered her bossy, but this is often usual for the elder daughter. Ethel was certainly the disciplinarian in the family, as Judy became the disciplinarian in the Luft family. Lorna and Sid Luft confirmed this in their discussions about the family life in June 1967, in Grand Rapids. They all laughingly agreed that Judy had been the one who had laid down the rules.

Mendel's theory of genes and inheritances informs an understanding of how the three Gumm children evolved. Both Mary Jane and Virginia appeared to have inherited adequate musical and singing talent from their mother, while Judy inherited Frank's magnificent voice, which was supposedly like that of Al Jolson. Frank enjoyed the music and singing more than anything else, and this magic he passed on to his daughter. Judy also inherited Frank's romantic love of ballads, poetry, and a way with the audience. From her mother, Judy inherited the enormous black eyes,  which missed nothing, charm, sociability, and most of all her drive and determination. (Monk and scientist Gregor Mendel proved in the mid-1800s through experiments with peas and bees that inheritance "was particulate rather than blended." This work confirmed in 1900 with the discovery of deoxyribonucleic acid (DNA) in the makeup of genes.[6]

By 1924, Mary Jane and Dorothy Virginia were performing regularly with their parents. In December 31, 1924, they decided to add little Frances to the act as shown in the announcement in the newspaper.

AT THE NEW GRAND

Thursday and Friday

PECIAL FOR CHRISTMAS, "Through the Back Door" with MARY PICKFORD, America's sweetheart, in the leading role. One of the nicest pictures Miss Pickford has appeared in. You will enjoy every bit of it. A two-reel comedy "Motor Mad" will also be shown. Added attraction for Friday evening: the three Gumm girls will entertain in song and dance, featuring Baby Frances, two years old, Virginia, seven and Mary Jane, nine. The little girls will appear between the shows at 9 o'clock" [7]

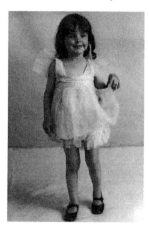

There are many stories about just how Frances Ethel Gumm got onto a stage for the first time, but I think the one Judy tells is probably closest to the truth. It was not the spontaneous event she sometimes described, the wiggling toddler escaping her grandmother, or Grandmother Milne sending the child up to sing. She was, in truth, sitting on her grandmother's lap watching her sisters on stage, wanting to be up there with them. She ran up to her mother, who was playing the piano, begging to be with her sisters. Her mother reportedly said, "No, not now Baby; next week." Ethel made a lovely white dress for Baby's debut. [8]

The two older girls sang, "When My Sugar Walks down the Street" and Baby came in on the last chorus. Then Baby Gumm decided to continue singing and she went into "Jingle Bells," which her sisters had taught her earlier in the year. She loved the reaction she got from the audience and she did not want to leave the stage, singing three choruses until Frank walked on stage and carried her off, laughing. From then on Baby Gumm was included in most shows. Judy said that "My father gave me my first singing lessons; they started about the same time I learned to walk. When I began playing vaudeville engagements with my sisters, he helped coach us. He told me to put all my enthusiasm into a song. Doing that would make the audience like me, he said, even if they didn't like the song."[9]

The Herald Review reported on Dec. 31, 1924:

> The three young daughters of Mr. and Mrs. Frank Gumm delighted a large audience at the New Grand Theatre last Friday night with twenty minutes of singing and dance. Mary Jane and Virginia, the two oldest girls, are becoming accomplished entertainers while the work of Frances, the two-year-old baby, was a genuine surprise. The little girl spoke and sang so as to be heard by everyone in the house and she joined in the dancing both alone and with her older sisters. The audience expressed their appreciation of all three girls by vigorous applause.

Frank was not slow to promote his daughters, as this notice shows:

TONIGHT

EXTRA ADDED ATTRACTION MISSES DORIS SMALL AND PEARL TROMBLY OF NASHWALK IN "THE VALENTINO TANGO" and other novelty dances and song specialties. These clever girls present a near up-to-the-minute VAUDEVILLE attraction which will surely be a big hit. Between their changes MISSES MARY JANE, VIRGINIA and FRANCES ETHEL GUMM will entertain with a novelty song and dance skit.[10]

In March, Frances was a solo performer at a Zane Grey western. The announcement stated, "Baby Frances, the 2-year-old daughter of Mr. & Mrs. Gumm, will entertain between shows and there will be a vocal solo by Frank Gumm. The little girl will appear only on Sunday evening."

Why did the Gumms decide to leave their successful life and take off for California? One wonders if they had stayed in Grand Rapids, would their daughters have had a different life? *Even Joe Luft wondered about this when we talked in June 1997 at the Judy Garland Festival in Grand Rapids. Joe liked Grand Rapids and had to muse about what his mother's life would have been like if the family had stayed there.*

Judy always said that she loved working on her father's stage. It was not the touring vaudeville as many others like the O'Connor and Yule (Mickey Rooney) families did. The majority of the time she performed on her father's stage at theatres in Grand Rapids and Lancaster, except when they worked on the vaudeville circuit on the visiting trip to Los Angeles. She was comfortable there among the loyal local audience who supported them. It was home to her, and she considered her family the aristocracy of vaudeville because they had their own theatre.[11]

There seem to be several reasons for the move to California; to get away from the Minnesota harsh winter. Frank had continuing ear infections and Baby Gumm had been very ill with a high fever for several months. Was it just for the better weather? Marc Rabwin had been writing letters advocating the merits of the California coast.

Was it the weather and health issues, or was it something else that caused them to move? For all their social activity and acclaim, Ethel was still as unhappy as she had been before Baby's birth, by the very fact of wanting to terminate the pregnancy. Was it the hint of Frank's homosexuality? I feel that as the old saying goes, "There is no smoke without fire." My gut feeling is something had gone on in that regard, particularly as Marc Rabwin, who became the family doctor, confirmed this in later years. Apparently, there were rumors about Frank in Lake Superior, Wisconsin, even before Ethel and Frank's marriage. Perhaps Ethel felt he was a good catch and she could change him, as many women have tried to do before. One has to consider these rumors in context of the time in which this happened. People did not talk about homosexuality openly then, but in a very hushed manner. Frank was an established and well-liked businessman and probably many would not have believed these rumors. However, it is highly likely that Ethel heard the talk, and she was mortified and embarrassed, not to mention angry. It would have been very difficult for a woman to leave her husband and support herself and three young daughters on her own. She did not have many options open to her. In addition, the children adored their father and there is no question that

Frank loved his family. All he could do would be to promise it would not happen again and have them start over again where no one knew them.

In the summer of 1926, the family decided to take a long trip, traveling and working through Minnesota, North Dakota, Montana, Idaho, and Washington. The performing engagements were necessary to finance the trip. Initially Frank and Ethel were intending to make the trip on their own, but the girls looked so disappointed that they were included, and four-year-old Judy retained wonderful memories of the trip. She would tell great stories of the fun they had as a family. They traveled by train and some engagements were booked ahead of time by an agent, but mainly Frank would go ahead to the next town to sell the talents of "Jack and Virginia Lee, the Singing Sweethearts from the South." He carried large photographs of the family, and the ones of the girls helped them obtain engagements. They were billed as two acts: the parents and then the daughters. In this way they could be paid twice and cheer each other on, "California, Here I Come" was one of Frank's favorite songs. They mainly played in small towns and Judy would later say that they were not very good. They visited friends, and it took them six weeks to reach Washington State. It was during this trip that Frances started to perform the Egyptian dance while her sisters performed "In a Little Spanish Town." Frank often sang "I Will Come Back," which Judy insisted Frank wrote and she used later to end her television programs.[12] On arrival in July in Los Angeles, Marc met them and showed them around, and they loved it. There were no freeways at that time, just clusters of small towns with beautiful flowering bushes — oleanders and palm trees. The added attraction was the growing new movie industry. They spent a month at a hotel and decided this was the place for them. They drove quickly back to Grand Rapids and informed the town they were leaving. By October, they had sold their possessions, and they were ready to leave. There were many goodbye parties; it seems the town could not have disapproved or disliked the family too much.

Chapter 5

Los Angeles and Lancaster

After the family sold their possessions and interests in the New Grand Theatre in Grand Rapids, said farewells to relatives and friends in the area, they went straight to Los Angeles. Frank was anxious to get his family settled, so he went ahead and rented 3154 Glen Manor in Atwater, near Glendale. Frank looked around for a theatre he could afford, but times were difficult and vaudeville was declining, people did not have so much money to spend on entertainment.

In 1926, Ethel enrolled the girls in Ethel Meglin Dance studio, a training school and booking agency. Ethel became good friends with the owner and a neighbor, Peggy DeVine. The girls first performed in Los Angeles at the Biltmore Hotel, and in the Meglin's Christmas show called, "100 Clever Children in the Twinkle Toe Kiddies Revue" at Loew's State. The Duncan Sisters were the headliners in black faces in *Topsy and Eva*. The sisters were very kind and encouraging to the Gumm girls.

When Frank could not find a suitable theatre in Los Angeles, Marc Rabwin suggested the Antelope Valley Theatre in Lancaster. Marc was aware of because Lancaster was on the outreaches of the area he covered from his position as doctor at the Los Angeles County Hospital. Lancaster is about 80 miles northeast of Los Angeles and was a three-hour drive before the advent of freeways. Antelope Valley, named for the antelopes that used to roam the Mojave high deserts, was a small town with a population then of 1,000. It supported the outlying ranchers and farmers. There was a railway station, banks and stores, and a modern theatre with screen and stage that seated 1,000 people twice the size of the old Grand Rapids venue. Ethel was disappointed about having to leave Los Angeles, where she felt there were more opportunities for the girls, but Frank was trying to recreate what he had had in Grand Rapids—a stable home base for his family.

I visited the town on my last drive north from Palm Springs after my final move to Northern California, and I could understand why Frank found the town attractive: high desert with Joshua trees, sagebrush, wheat, barley, fruit trees, and accented by the beautiful Tehachapi Mountains on the north.

In March 1927, the family moved to Lancaster and first rented a house on outskirts of town, but they quickly moved to a more central two-story wood-framed house on Cedar Street,

within walking distance of schools and the theatre. The inland farming areas of California are very cold in the winter and scorching hot in the summer (sometimes 120 degrees) as anyone can attest to who has visited Palm Springs, Las Vegas or Sacramento. The more pleasant California temperatures are along the coastlines where the ocean keeps the land cool in the summer and temperatures warmer in the winter. The family was to live six years in Lancaster, but much of that time was spent in trips to Los Angeles for auditions, so it was a very fragmented and confusing period for the young Frances. She developed hay fever from the dry desert, and her mother would drive her out during the nights to relieve the symptoms—or perhaps to relieve her frustrations after an argument with Frank.

The years from 1927 to 1933 when the Gumm family lived in Lancaster, and sometimes Los Angeles, is a difficult period for me to consider. Being the mother of two performing arts children myself, I am fully aware of the amount of time needed for classes, rehearsals, and the reluctance of the children to practice when they would rather play with their friends. So when I realized just how much time little Frances Gumm, or Baby Gumm, spent performing, I was horrified and could quite understand how Judy would complain later that she had been working all her life.

Baby Gumm performed over fifty times while the family lived in Grand Rapids in the years 1924 to 1926, but in Lancaster these figures increased to approximately sixteen times in 1927, thirty times in 1928, and an average of fifty times between 1929 and 1933. That totals over 300 performances in the seven years between the critical ages of five and eleven.[1] These performances do not take into account dance and voice lessons and rehearsals for these performances or the time for travel. Of

course, Frances loved to perform in front of audiences and make people happy. The times when she was with her parents and sisters together as "Frank and Virginia Lee and Kiddies" or "3 Lees" or "Gumm Sisters", life was not bad for Frances: show business was what her family did. However, Baby Gumm did not like being dragged by her mother to audition for movies and unfriendly booking agents. This would build up resentments in the child, which would continue in her soul for the rest of her life.[2] As we see from the Apted study what a child is and feels at age seven remains with them for the rest of their lives.

Judy often said she was not born in a trunk, but she lived out of one practically from birth, if one counts sleeping in a drawer as an infant. From the time they hit Lancaster, it was a long, hard journey to the discovery of Judy Garland.

A man named Whitford B. Carter had built the theatre in Lancaster the year before and leased it to vaudevillian Sam Claman, who was unsuccessful with running a theatre and was glad to sign the lease over to Frank. Frank made some improvements, including installing a better cooling system, and re-named it The Valley Theatre. On May 20, 1927, the local newspaper ran a piece announcing, "Mr. & Mrs. Frank Gumm and Daughters will present a cycle of songs and dances between shows." He started his program with the words he had used in Grand Rapids, "It Pleases Us to Please You." The program started at 7:15 p.m. with a movie, followed by Frank and Virginia Lee, the Southern Singing Sweethearts, and then their three daughters singing "Bye, Bye Blackbird" and "When the Red, Red Robin Comes Bob Bobbing Along." Popular songs of the day were "My Blue Heaven" and "Bye, Bye Baby." *The Ledger Gazette,* the local newspaper, welcomed them and gave them a good write-up. Frank introduced an amateur night to get the local people involved with the theatre, as he had done in Grand Rapids. He sold discounted ticket books and instituted vaudeville in between shows. The girls spent most of the first summer sitting in the cool of the theatre watching the movies of Bessie Love, Norma Shearer, Lon Chaney, John Gilbert and Richard Dix. Judy would often say later that she learned from the greats.[3] (The theatre was destroyed by fire in 1953—LA Times Feb. 23, 1953)

Frank wanted his family accepted by the local people. However, in some senses this acceptance was more difficult because the farmers and ranchers of Lancaster were more conservative and suspicious of the vaudeville background of the family than the Grand Rapids people, who were from an industrial background. The family joined the Episcopal Church where Frank became the choirmaster, Ethel played the organ, and the girls sang in the choir.

In December, Frank was showing the Duncan Sisters in the movie *Topsy and Eva,* and the elder girls performed in blackface doing Duncan songs. Frances wanted to join in and sang "Mammy," in blackface in a very loud and exuberant minstrel style.

By 1928, the family became the center of social activities as they had in Grand Rapids of the town, playing bridge and entertaining. Ethel kept up her energetic piano playing at the theatre, school activities, weddings and any other activity where she could earn money. She organized a quintet to play for the Saturday night dances. Frank joined the Rotarians and other business organizations. Frank was jolly and sociable, and Ethel was always ready to help at any functions. She was 31 years of age then and still full of energy, teaching the girls new songs and making clothes and costumes. She wrote songs and played for the school plays—one being a Gilbert and Sullivan in which Frances performed.

The Gumm family also met some relatives of a friend from Grand Rapids, Laura and Will Gilmore, who were living in Lancaster. Will, was an engineer working on irrigation systems getting water into the valley from the Mojave River. They had three children around the same ages as the Gumm girls and the families became good friends. Later Laura had a stroke and be was confined to a wheelchair, and Ethel and Will spent time together while Frank worked at the theatre and became romantically involved.[4]

When Frances was six years old in 1928, she became very ill again with acidosis, with high fever, dehydration, and inability to keep food or liquids down, so Frank called Marc Rabwin and he managed to get her admitted to the Los Angeles County General Hospital where he was a resident.

The illness lasted for several weeks. Ethel and Frank spent much time in Los Angeles staying with their friend, Peggy LeVine. Grandma Eva came out from Minnesota to look after the family in Lancaster. The attending pediatrician was Dr. Oscar Reiss. Judy never forgot his kindness, and later when Liza was born, she asked him to be Liza's doctor.

In later years, Judy remembered every detail of this stay in hospital, just as she did the earlier stay in Duluth. This may have led to her fear of hospitals and pain as well as her continuing sympathy for sick children.

When Frances recovered from her illness, the real disintegration of the Gumm family started. Ethel wanted to become independent of Frank and out of her marriage and to do this meant obtaining work for her daughters in Los Angeles. She re-enrolled the girls in Ethel Meglin Dance Studio with lessons on Saturday and Sunday. This started the weekend routine of the 5 a.m. haul into Los Angeles over the rough roads of the San Gabriel Mountains in the old Buick. They drove through whatever harsh weather came through the Mint Canyon Highway: rain and windstorms, blinding heat—through hell and high water—nothing would stop Ethel. Frances would have preferred to stay in Lancaster with her father and play with her friends but she had no choice but to go with her very strict mother to perform. This began the period when Frances became aware of the unresponsive movie agents and managers, and life was not fun anymore. She would have been happy to sing for people who responded, but these auditions frightened her.

The audition process is overwhelming enough when the participant is in late teens or early adulthood; but to inflict this constantly upon a child of six or seven years is cruel. To understand this process imagine getting your child ready (fixing the hair and deciding upon dress) for a visit to the annual portrait studio and multiply that by 20 times will give you an idea of the stress level involved with preparing a child for an audition. *I have observed several auditions at the music conservatory where my daughter teaches. These students have come into the university through an audition process and have received three years training in stage techniques, voice, acting, dance, movement and performance. These young artists are in the age range of 20-21 and are as ready as they can be, but even with this training, they are apprehensive about auditions. The agents, casting directors and theatre managers who come into the university on these visits are pleasant professionals who are eagerly looking for new fresh talent. They are helpful, encouraging often-suggesting different material, which will help the young artists, quite different from the hard eyed and probably unpleasant managers and agents who Frances met back in the 1920s. In effect, an audition is a job interview. The students at the university are told to remember: "Your job to audition and you must love it to succeed."*

The trips back and forth to Los Angeles continued for any gigs they could get—luncheons and small events at places like Kiwanis, American Legion, theatres in Los Angeles and surrounding area. Taking into account costumes and transportation costs, there was little profit.[5]

During the summer vacation from school in August 1928, Ethel took the girls to stay in Los Angeles for a few weeks. Big broadcasting companies, such as CBS and NBC were just forming at that time. The girls performed on *The Kiddies Hour* produced by Kennard Hamilton at KFI radio. They were asked to return and perform every Wednesday at 5.00 p.m. Frances sang, "You're the Cream in My Coffee." [6]

At Christmas break, Ethel enrolled the girls, now thirteen, eleven, and six, at the Meglin Studio again and they performed in the Christmas show: "All Star Benefit with 100 Meglin Kiddies," at the Shrine Auditorium in Hollywood. They followed that with a week's long run at Loew's State Theatre. The children were not named in the program, but the *Los Angeles Record* reported "special praise for the precocious youngster who sang, 'I Can't Give You Anything But Love.' ...One small miss shook the well-known rafters with her song *a la* Sophie Tucker." Later, Judy told a funny story about how she had a frizzy perm, a sty on her eye, and a nosebleed in that performance.[7]

Frances's screen debut was in an eighteen-minute two-reeler, *The Big Review* (1929) produced by Mayfair Pictures featuring "Ethel Meglin's Famous Hollywood Wonder Kids." Frances sang "I'll Get By" along with "That's the Good Old Sunny South" with her sisters.

As an additional feature, in the *Meet me in St. Louis* DVD (2-Disc special edition including Vitaphone Kiddies) issued in 2004 there is footage of *The Land of Let's Pretend* in the segment called 'Bubbles'. Here we see little Frances standing and singing her heart full out. Most of the other children look like a usual bunch of amateurs one sees in children's shows, but little Frances is different. It is obvious from the clips that Frances had enormous talent, which most of the other children, including her sisters, did not possess. These strip Technicolor shorts, were produced to show off aspiring stars of the day.

After the success of the previous year Ethel optimistically decided to take the three girls to live in Los Angeles in March

1929 where she thought there would be more opportunities for the girls. The local newspaper Ledger-Gazette in Lancaster announced they would return on weekends for her to play at church and see their father.[8]

This move was most unsettling for the girls; they were aware of the quarrels between their parents and here suddenly was the first break with their father. Ethel got an apartment on South Orchard at the junction of Washington and Vermont, near the theatrical district where the girls were in a few Meglin shows.

By May, the adventure was over and they were back with Frank Gumm in Lancaster. The highlight of their return in May was the *Second Annual Minstrel Show* at the Valley Theatre with Cousin Joe, Frank, Uncle John, and several other men who enjoyed banjo strumming along with bass and piano accompaniment and wisecracking men wearing blackface makeup.

Life was not all bad for Frances: the times with her father at his theatre were wonderful, and she often commented later in

life that she came from the aristocracy of Vaudeville. Everybody loved the child; she had charisma, charm, was anxious to please, and wanted to make everybody happy. She was as hard to resist then, as she was later in life. [9]

In 1929, the Gilmore family moved to Los Angeles and consequently Ethel wanted to follow.

The girls continued to perform in various parts of California. In November, they joined Flynn O'Malley's "Hollywood Starlets" when they worked on the Big Brother Ken's Kiddies Show on KNX (KFI). The girls made three movie shorts, "The Vitaphone Kiddies" for Vitaphone Pictures, a subsidiary of Warner Bros. One of the shorts was the eighteen-minute two-reeler "Holiday in Storyland" premiered on August 14, 1929 at the Fox Belmont Theatre in Hollywood, and

Frank was able to show the movie May 9 and 10, 1930, when the girls performed live at the theatre.

The girls performed in their grammar school plays, and in February 1930, Mary Jane was in a production of "Gypsy Rover." The music teacher at the high school, Miss Kinnamon, who knew the family well, thought that Frances would have a good voice for opera. Frances had "a long voice, with great volume and capacity," but she did not think the family was interested in this form of music.[10]

I remember thinking the same thing when I heard Judy singing, many, many years ago, "When You Walk Through a Storm" from the musical show, Carousel. I thought then that this sounded like opera. Her voice was not like any other pop singer. Judy recorded this material in New York when on honeymoon with Vincente Minnelli and hoped to stay there and perform in musical theatre.

Harry Pleasants discusses the unusual and distinctive voice of Judy Garland his book: *The Great American Popular Singers*. Unfortunately, this book is out of print but I did obtain a copy of his book: *The Great Singers: From Jenny Lind and Caruso to Callas and Pavarotti* and the writer is an expert on voices. Luckily, Christopher Finch includes some quotes in his book, *Rainbow: The Stormy Life of Judy Garland*. In talking about Judy Garland Harry Pleasants said:

> She had the most utterly natural vocal production of any singer I have heard. Probably because she sang so much as a child, and learned to appreciate the appeal of her child's voice, she made no effort as she grew older to produce her voice in any other way. It was an open throated, almost birdlike vocal production, clear, pure, resonant, innocent. One keeps coming back to that word innocent, again and again. It was not just an innocent sound, it was a sound innocent of anything that smacked of artful management.

> This almost certainly explains a conspicuously limited vocal range. . . . I can think of no other singer whose top was so low. One reads of Judy's occasional troubles in reaching for high notes. Those notes were not so very high, no more than Cs and Ds, and not a soprano's high Cs and Ds, but the Cs and Ds an octave lower. She never extended that range by recourse to head voice or falsetto as other popular singers have done. She just sang naturally and purely as far as she could go without vocal expertise, and that was that.

The highlight of 1931 was in July, when Maurice Kusell, who ran a talent school, put the girls in his "Stars of Tomorrow" show at the Wilshire-Ebell Theateer in Los Angeles. The girls performed several routines, including Irving Berlin's 's "Puttin' on the Ritz." Judy continued to sing these early songs throughout her life.

The girls performed through the rest of 1931 with Kusell in Lancaster and the surrounding area, although the two older girls were beginning to show reluctance. Ethel continued with her trips to Los Angeles, and when the two older girls would not go, she took one of Frances' friends, Ina Mary Ming (called Muggsie), to keep her daughter company and happy. Muggsie, who was three years older than Frances and performed in Frank's theatre, observed that Frances loved performing before audiences, but she disliked harsh directors and hard-eyed publicity agents and managers. Muggsie also felt that Ethel was cold, and not one to embrace or coddle Frances.[11]

Ethel was still attempting to be financially independent of Frank and was glad when Kusell hired her to lead his eight-piece orchestra and teach popular singing at his school at the end of 1932. Ethel got a five-year contract for Frances with the talent agents, Frank and Dunlap and re-named the child as Frances Gayne, but her father Frank revoked the contract saying Frances, at nine years old, was too young to go out on her own. He wanted Frank and Dunlap to take on the other two sisters but they were not interested.[12] This action by her husband made Ethel even more determined to get her younger daughter discovered.

In January and March 1932, Frances performed at the Cocoanut Grove, the Ambassador Hotel nightclub in Los Angeles at a tea dance with Jimmie Grier and his orchestra. (Judy later reminisced about these tea dances during her *Cocoanut Grove* concert performance shows in 1959, the closing night of which was recorded and released by Capital Records.)

A busy summer continued, and in August the girls did a twenty-minute routine at the Paramount Theatre in Los Angeles, five times a day, with an extra performance on weekends, and

Frances received her first review from *Variety* "...Selling end of trio is the ten-year-old sister with a pop of a lowdown voice.."[13]

On December 31 1932 Ledge-Gazette announced that Mrs. Ethel Gumm plans to spend the greater part of her time in Los Angeles, where she will be associated with Maurice Kusell, producer.[14] Ethel, Frances and Jimmie (as Virginia was now calling herself) [15] moved to Los Angeles early in 1933 and lived in a house in the Silver Lake district of Los Angeles. Mary Jane stayed behind in Lancaster with her father so that she could graduate from high school among her friends. Frances's general education must have been very fragmented moving back and forth between Los Angeles and Lancaster. From all appearances, it appears that Ethel did not consider general regular school as important to theatrical training.

The girls performed at the Golden Gate Theatre in San Francisco August 2 to 8, 1933 and received their second *Variety* review. It was a complete family show with Frank Gumm opening for the girls and Ethel at the piano.

George C. Warren wrote in the *San Francisco Chronicle*, "[they]...have a strong-voiced small woman, who imitates and sings in a big way." [16]

In October, Ethel enrolled daughters, Frances and Jimmie in Lawlor Hollywood Professional School, or Mrs. Lawlor's Professional School for Children, or Mom Lawlor's. Other students at the school were Donald O'Connor and Mickey Rooney. Frances was to come home and say, "I met Mickey Rooney. He is just the funniest....He clowns around every second!" [17]

Depression was causing changes. People could not afford lessons for their children if they were out of work. Kusell had to close his studio and Ethel lost her job. Frank's business in Lancaster was also failing. Frank had given up the lease on the Lancaster Theatre and Marc helped him find a theatre in Lomita he could afford.[18] The family was back together again and moved into a house at 842 Mariposa Avenue, Los Angeles.

The girls were on the program at the Orpheum in Los Angeles in from February 8 – 13 1934. Starting on February 16 Ethel took the girls on the Paramount circuit appearing in Portland, Seattle and Vancouver. They performed several one-night stands on the way back south and finished with a week in San Francisco. Memories of these years were potent: Judy and Donald O'Connor later talked about performing in San Francisco when they were children when he was a guest on one of her CBS television series in September 1963.[19]

There were other performances in San Diego, Long Beach and Los Angeles.

At this point memories of the show, Gypsy come into my mind with Mama Rose dragging her children around the circuits in the 1920s in vaudeville.

Ethel planned another tour and took off with the girls June – October around the northwest in theatres in Denver and Colorado Springs in Colorado, Washington and Idaho to the World's Fair in Chicago. They were also to perform in a nightclub in Chicago. Frank was opposed to this and insisted they take some travelers checks in case something went wrong. Of course, something went wrong: the nightclub closed,  they were without money, and they had to cash some of Frank's checks. But they met people; they got to know the Andrew Sisters and a trumpeter called Jack Cathcart. They were out of work and Cathcart called to say there was an opportunity for them at the Oriental Theatre, so they rushed over to fill a vacated spot.[20]

From the confusion in Chicago, young Frances "Baby" Gumm became Judy Garland. George Jessel, the Master of Ceremonies for the Oriental Theatre realized when he

40

introduced them as the Gumm Sisters that this was not a good show business name and suggested they use Garland from his friend the drama critic Robert Garland. It was about this time that Mary Jane decided to change her name to Suzanne, and Frances thought, if her sisters could change their names, why couldn't she? She hated her names—first, middle and the despised "Baby" not befitting of an adolescent. She loved Hoagy Carmichael's song "Judy." By August, the girls became "The Garland Sisters." Jessel helped them again by arranging for the William Morris agency to represent them and they found work for the rest of the tour until October. Ethel was having Judy sing, "Bill" in the Helen Morgan style with a shawl in the way Helen sang the song. [21]

They got a week's booking at the Paramount and held over for four more weeks. Judy also received lessons from Cantor David Blanko and was taught "Eli, Eli" (My God, My God) for a B'nai B'rith benefit. These lessons by the cantor enabled Judy to expand her vocal technique and enabled her to become a singer rather than a belter. She sang in Yiddish and later she would later record another Yiddish song, "Bei Mir Bist Du Schoen."

The family was now using the name of Garland. The two elder girls, Suzanne and Jimmy, were becoming less interested in performing and more interested in dating. When Ethel and the girls returned from their trip, Marc Rabwin had married Marcella, who worked as executive secretary to David Selznick. (Selznick was a big movie producer and married to the daughter of L. A. Mayer) Marc had told Marcella about the Gumms, and later in the spring of 1935, Marc got a gig for the girls to perform at a party in front of medical professionals and movie business friends. Their performances went well, but no screen offers resulted. The Rabwins then told their friend, Joseph L. Mankiewicz, a screenwriter and director at MGM, about Judy and encouraged him to see the Garland Sisters at the Wilshire Ebell Theatre. Twelve-year-old Judy sang, "Be Still, My Heart!" and Stormy Weather" Twenty-five-year-old Mankiewicz went to see Judy perform, went backstage to meet her, and thought to himself, "This child has a strange and rare beauty. She is like something out of a forest...." [22]

The girls went up to the Cal-Neva Lodge at Lake Tahoe for a week's run. Again, some special forces seemed to be at work for the discovery of Judy Garland. Suzanne had fallen in love with a saxophone player, Lee Cahn, and Ethel was furious considering a musician unreliable. Just why Ethel was annoyed does not make any sense because the men the girls met were musicians due to the lifestyle the mother pressed upon them.

As they were leaving after the last show, Suzanne realized that they had left their hats and music behind, so Judy ran in to collect them. The manager of the club insisted that Judy and family come back because he had been telling some important men about the little girl who could sing. The men involved were Harry Cohn, head of Columbia Pictures, Al Rosen, an agent and two songwriters, Lew Brown and Harry Akst (Al Jolson's songwriter and accompanist). Ethel sat down to play and started "Zing! Went the Strings of My Heart" and several other numbers. When "Dinah" came up Akst asked to accompany her because he had written it. They all appeared pleased with the show and Al Rosen and Ethel exchanged phone numbers. The family returned to Los Angeles to make a short movie, *La Fiesta de Santa Barbara* (1935) the last performance of the three Garland girls together before Suzanne married Lee Cahn. [23]

The discovery of Judy Garland was eminent. Mankiewicz was working on behalf of Judy, and he told Ida Koverman, Chief Assistant to Louis Mayer about Judy. He had little faith in Mayer's judgment, who was more interested in Shirley Temple. He worked through Koverman to bring Judy in for an audition. Al Rosen, had also told Ida about Judy and suggested Mayer see her. [24]

There are several versions of how Judy's contract was signed with MGM, and probably there is an element of truth in all of them. Two weeks after the Lake Tahoe performances, Frank Gumm received a phone call at home asking Judy to get down to MGM immediately for an audience with Ida Koverman and Sam Katz. As Ethel was out, Frank drove Judy down to MGM in her play clothes. Ida did not feel Frank's piano playing was very good and called Roger Edens to come down and accompany Judy. She called Mayer in and Judy sang several songs. Bill Grady was there. The next day Rosen called again and Ethel dressed Judy up and they went into Stage One and Arthur Freed was there. Ida asked Judy if she knew "Eli Eli," and Judy said she knew it very well. He asked her to sing it. One version is that Judy was signed without a screen test, but George Sydney remembers very well making a screen test for Judy on Stage One and that he describes on *The Harvey Girls* DVD release. One audition was on September 13; she signed the contract on September 27, and ratified by Superior Court on October 13, 1935.

Frank wrote to friends in Lancaster saying, "Babe got her seven years contract with MGM starting October 1 at $150 a week."[25]

The studio put her in an NBC evening variety program The Shell Chateau Show on October 26 and again on November 16. On the second Saturday night program with Wallace Berry substituting for Al Jolson as host, accompanied by the Victor Young orchestra, Judy sang, "Zing! Went the Strings of My Heart" for her father. She had just learned that he had been rushed to the hospital. Frank had suffered from continuing ear infections, and an abscess had developed which later ruptured, spreading infection spread to the brain and spinal cord.

Sadly, Frank Gumm died on November 17 and Judy felt lost. The one person who was always on her side was gone; she was now at the mercies of her mother and the studio. "Now," she thought bleakly, "there is no one on my side."[26]

Judy was thirteen years old and her life completely changed as she went into the MGM studio system. Did she want to go into the studio system or was she just on a very fast train driven by her mother with no stops along the way? Does any child at thirteen really know what is best for her? She spent the last seven years going back and forth from Lancaster to Los Angeles in a continual effort to be discovered. She learned to hate the unpleasant men who glared at her during the audition process, and she would remember their looks and pay back later those directors who shouted at her and theatre managers who treated her unkindly. The pattern was set for continual performances with Judy loving the audiences but hating the authoritarian figure of agent/manager.

Judy was beginning her movie career, but it had taken a lot of work and determination, particularly on the part of Ethel, to get her there. As Michael Apted explores in *7-UP* to understand a person, one has to look to the early years between birth and ages 5-7 years, because what a person is at seven years old is what they will be for the rest of their life.

One can see that in Judy's case there would be a life of continual performances, singing, dancing and acting. Also at times difficult situations when her health and strength was depleting. There were many house moves and little stability except in the context of the family.

After the career at MGM was over and Judy would attempt to keep her children with her when she was out on the road doing concerts and we see the same pattern of change and excitement similar to her life when she was a child.

PART THREE

MGM YEARS

1935-1950

Chapter 6

Early movies- *The Wizard of Oz* - Radio

Judy would often comment, "I was born at the age of 12 on the Metro-Goldwyn-Mayer lot. I missed the gentle maturing most girls have." She also said, "If you want fame, you have to pay for it. And I have. Even from my earliest days at MGM, when I was a child star with the great Mickey Rooney....There were good times, too. Mickey and I clung together like two on a lonely island. I guess that's when I learned to laugh at myself. It's the fun that gets you through the heartache and tears and misery." [1]

There will never be another Judy Garland and we might wonder why that should be. Judy arrived on our planet at a very special time. The era of vaudeville was ending, where Judy, or little Frances Gumm, obtained her first training, and developed her love of the stage and performing. For this reason, there will never be a time when a performer can evolve and become the person that Judy became. The training she had received with her family on stage in vaudeville was the stepping-stone to her second career at MGM.

Movie studios came into being at the turn of the century, taking the place of vaudeville for family entertainment, and their names are still with us: MGM, Paramount, Warner Bros, Twentieth Century Fox, RKO. Their form is different now; they are mainly distributors issuing movies made independently, but in the mid-1900s, the studios were nothing more than factories. There was a great demand for movies. The New York motion picture theatre owners realized they needed bigger and better movies to fill their theatres, so many of them became involved in the making of the movies themselves.[2]

Many of those early studios started with people who had originally worked in theatres either as managers or as song distributors, as Frank Gumm had been. Frank was a song distributor, movie operator, as it was called in those days, and ran his own theatre but had no interest in the making of movies himself.

The studios hired people to build sets, electricians, and carpenters who were glad to have regular and secure jobs. There were also positions for camera operators, technicians, writers, and musicians. Many of the actors, comedians, and singers came from vaudeville, and as this method of entertainment was failing, they were glad to have regular employment. In this arena, the producers and directors were the most powerful people. Most performers had five to seven year contracts that restricted them from working elsewhere. The actors got publicity, training and stardom, along with regular employment—a very heady attraction. But there were restrictions in their contracts regarding just what they could do on and off the screen. In effect, the studio owned them. The publicity department issued stories about the activities of their stars; what they wore, where they went, and their homes. Judy Garland at the age of 13, this must have been very confusing—reading stories about her life, which did not have any resemblance to what was actually happening in her life.

"When Dad died," she later said, "MGM took over as my father. In our house the word of Louis B. Mayer, who ran the studio, became the law. When Mother wanted to discipline me, all she had to say was, 'I'll tell Mr. Mayer.'" [3]

Later, as the years went by, when many performers wished to broaden their skills or work in different types of roles, they could not. They were under contract and not able to attempt other work on radio or by personal performances. Times have changed; the movie moguls do not have the power they did. Never again will there be a time when organizations such as MGM, Paramount, Warner Bros., Twentieth Century Fox, were as powerful as they were then.

Louis B. Mayer was born in Russia. His family immigrated to Canada and he subsequently entered the United States. In 1904 he purchased his first burlesque house cinema in Haverhill, Massachusetts. In 1907, he bought his first cinema and by 1913 he was distributing films to his chain of theatres. He moved to

Los Angeles in 1918 and started his own company to make movies. In his first five years in Hollywood, he produced many movies and released them through First National and Metro. The Metro Corporation had financial problems and in 1920 Loew

Incorporated, a growing chain of theatres throughout the United States and Canada, purchased it. Loew got the Metro studios and its stars in New York and Hollywood and its stars. Metro got the market they needed. Louis B. Mayer Productions evolved into Metro-Goldwyn Pictures. Initially the movies indicated "Louis B Mayer presents a Metro-Goldwyn picture," but it soon changed to "Metro-Goldwyn-Mayer presents."[4] Mayer's dream was to make the biggest and best movies. The MGM theme was that "there were more stars there than there are in heaven."[5] They spared no expense to bring the best talents in artists, such as writers, composers, and performers to work on their movies. The Technicolor of the MGM movies was brighter than other studios, the music was more memorable, and the stars larger than life. From 1924 until 1970 when the studio was auctioned off, 1700 movies were made at this studio. They had the greatest stars: Clark Gable, Greta Garbo, Joan Crawford, Jean Harlow,

Spencer Tracy, Rosalind Russell, Marlene Dietrich, Jeanette MacDonald, and Nelson Eddy—to name just a few.[6]

When Judy signed her contract with MGM, the studio had 22 sound stages on 180 acres, its own police and fire departments, and a hospital. Initially the studio did not know what to do with Judy, so they put her in a showcase short with Deanna Durban called *Every Sunday* (1936). The girls were both under contract, so this short was an opportunity to feature their different talents, Deanna singing classical and Judy singing swing. The studio chose not to renew the contract options for both girls, but Arthur Freed, who now had his own group and considerable power, went to Mayer and fought for the studio to keep Judy. Deanna went to Universal Studios and Joseph Pasternak made her an international star in the movie, *Three Smart Girls* (1936).

Judy's first assignment at MGM was to work under the guidance of Roger Edens, a musical director who had been present at her first audition and realized the child's enormous talent. He would turn out to be the most powerful influence on Judy musically—as later musician, arranger, performer and friend Kay Thompson would be on her style. Judy went to school in the morning and worked with Edens two

hours a day six days a week. He did not make her sing scales, but made her sing the special arrangements he made for her. He was to go on writing songs and special arrangements for her the rest of her life.

The first change Edens made was to find songs more suitable for a child of her age than the torch songs Ethel had prepared such as " Bill."

Judy's first movie was *Pigskin Parade* (1936) for Twentieth Century Fox-a college football comedy with Betty Grable, Tony

Martin and Jack Haley, produced by Darryl F. Zanuck. The term "teenager" had not really evolved in 1936; the studio heads did not really know where or how to use her. One can see Judy as she was then - young, fresh, and enthusiastic. Judy did not like the way she looked when she saw the movie, thinking that she appeared pudgy and unglamorous, but when she sang "The Texas Tornado" and "The Balboa," the screen came alive. The *New York Times* review said:

> Also in the newcomer category is Judy Garland, about whom the West Coast has been enthusing as a vocal find…She's cute, not too pretty, but a pleasant fetching personality, who certainly knows how to sell a pop.[7]

The comment that she was "not too pretty" must have hurt her, especially as she was sensitive that she was not the usual Hollywood beauty. "Who would you like to look like?" a friend asked her. Judy's reply was instantaneous. "Lana Turner. That's beauty."[8]

Irene Sharaff, costume designer at MGM once commented, "Mr. Mayer calling her 'my little hunchback!'" "Do you know what that did to a girl who was basically shy? A girl who was competing with the glamour pusses? It was torture."[9]

In the summer of 1936, Jackie Cooper appeared to be Judy's first boyfriend. He came out of a vaudeville family and both their mothers were friends. Later Judy him for Billy Halop, one of the Dead End Kids, but she and Jackie remained friends. At that time, Peter Lind Hayes was another friend. Ethel bought a bigger house at 842 N. Mariposa Avenue for Judy and Jimmie. Her elder sister Suzanne had married Lee Cahn and did not live with them.

RECORDING CAREER

Judy's recording career really took off when she signed a contract with Decca Records in 1936 and went on recording with them until 1947. Some of her early work was with Bob Crosby's band singing songs like, "Swing Mr. Charlie," and "Stompin' at the Savoy."

(There is a beautiful CD called A Portrait of Judy Garland and listening to it brings back so many memories of my childhood when Judy was on the radio daily during World War II. "Zing," "It's a Great Day for the Irish," "FDR Jones," "I'm Just Wild About Harry," "A Pretty Girl Milking Her Cow," being jolly, upbeat songs that were played constantly on the radio to keep our spirits up. It is not surprising then that Judy came to the London Palladium in 1951, soon after World War II, and she was welcomed with open arms. I particularly loved the softer songs such as, "I'm Always Chasing Rainbows," "Our Love Affair," "Embraceable You," "I'm Nobody's Baby," "Poor Little Rich Girl," "But Not for Me," and "Blues in the Night." Then there were the lovely songs from Meet Me in St. Louis and For Me and My Gal. I particularly enjoy "Love," the Lena Horne song from the movie, Thousands Cheer (1943). This was in the style that Judy used later during the concert years. The disc finished with Oscar Hammerstein's

"You'll Never Walk Alone" from Carousel. I do not often listen to Judy's recordings because her voice sings in my head always, so when I do sit down as I did that afternoon, it is a treat. Actually, I am not able to function when Judy sings; I just sit transfixed.)

Clark Gable was coming up to his thirty-sixth birthday on February 1, 1937, so the studio wanted a big party and encouraged performers to prepare something to perform. Judy went to Roger Edens and asked him to help with a song for her to sing. He wrote the introduction to "You Made Me Love You" and at the party, Judy sat next to him at the piano, singing to a photo of Clark Gable. This is one of the first "Judy events" that would go down in movie history.

When Judy had finished the song, everyone was enchanted with the emotion and charm of Judy's performance and Clark

Gable came over to hug and kiss Judy. She threw her arms around him, but she did not miss noticing how pleased Mr. Mayer looked at her performance. Mayer held his arms out to her, she ran to sit on his lap, and everyone cheered.

A few weeks later when the MGM national exhibitors came to town, Stage 25 became a nightclub, and once again, she got a tremendous ovation when she sang, "Dear Mr. Gable." Interestingly Judy was to say later that she really had a crush on Robert Donat and would have preferred to sing the song to him!

The studio decided to include Judy singing the song to Clark Gable's photograph in the movie, *Broadway Melody of 1938* (1937). This movie included Eleanor Powell, Robert Taylor, Sophie Tucker, Billie Barnes, George Murphy and Buddy Ebsen: many of whom would go on to work with Judy in later movies. Behind the scenes, she met Sid Luft briefly who was working for Eleanor Powell at the time.

In 1937, a 12-inch 78 rpm vinyl recording was released of "Dear Mr. Gable" with another in the same vein on the other side, "I'm Just an In-Between." This was my most precious record many years ago, emphasizing Judy's youth and vulnerability.

Judy was teamed with Mickey Rooney next. She had, of course, met him at various talent schools and enjoyed his sense of fun. Their first movie together was *Thoroughbreds Don't Cry* (1937). Judy was fifteen years old, and Robert Sinclair was in the cast. Rooney and Sinclair jockeys, Sophie Tucker ran a boarding house, and Judy played her niece. Judy got to show her humor in some scenes with the boys in the boarding house. "Got a Pair of New Shoes" is particularly joyous.

Mickey and Judy would go on to make ten movies together, and he continues to talk with enormous respect and love about Judy and her talent. In his 1966 memoir, *I.E. An Autobiography,* he comments about her timing, saying that it was like a chronometer. He admires the way she could deliver a comic line or say a poignant line without being schmaltzy. He also feels she could take an ordinary scene and make it memorable.[10]

Everybody Sing (1938). Allan Jones and Fanny Brice and Judy holds her own in the vaudeville numbers with Fanny Brice doing her Baby Snooks persona in the droll "Why, Because!" Other songs are the sweet "Down on Melody Farm," and in black face, "Swing Low, Sweet Chariot." In this movie, Judy's character has the same name, Judy, and her mother in the movie, Billy Burke, refers to her daughter, as "poor little ugly duckling." Again later in the movie, she says to both daughters, "You are looking pretty today, even Judy!" How strange that MGM to allow a script with such negative comments addressed to a child of sixteen, particularly a child who would become their greatest star!

In the same year, Judy (or Ethel) changed agents. Al Rosen  had been Judy's agent since her discovery in Lake Tahoe, but Ethel had dropped him earlier for Jesse Martin, who she felt had more connections in the industry. However, Mayer was suspicious of Martin after Martin tried to book Judy into the Loews rival Paramount Theatre in New York. Martin negotiated for Judy to perform at Loew's in New York as a part of a tour and got her $1,750 for this appearance instead of her usual $300 a week. Judy was very fond of Martin and thrilled with what he had obtained for her, but she told him "How can I live up to it? I won't be able to do it." Even then Judy was beginning to worry about her abilities to deserve a high salary.[11]

So in March 1938 Judy and Ethel went off on a two-month tour to promote this movie in Houston, Florida, Pittsburgh, Detroit, Chicago, Columbia Ohio, and Grand Rapids, Minnesota. Therefore, Judy did have opportunities to perform for audiences in the years she was at MGM. The performance at

Loew's State was a great success, and Judy headlined the bill. Roger Edens was with her, and she met Sammy Cahn and Saul Chaplin. Among the songs she sang were, "Bei Mir Bist Du Schon" Cahn and Chaplin had adapted it from its original Yiddish. "It was the most incredible arrangement of that song I had ever heard," said Chaplin, who returned again and again to hear it. "There was nothing like it. The way she did it was fantastic!"[12]

During this tour the press described Judy as being fourteen years old although she was nearly sixteen. Howard Strickling MGM resident doctor and protector of a star's imagine, produced a four-page picture spread, "Life Goes to a Party," about Judy. Interestingly, she says she does not want a film career, it was all an accident, and her main life would be in nursing. She talked of building a hospital for crippled children with gay walls and colorful decoration because she remembered her experiences in hospital as a child.[13]

Now you can put this down to Judy's rambling or something cooked up by the publicity department, but she would often come back to this theme. Later we will see that Judy became closely involved with the sick children at Peter Bent Brigham Hospital in Boston when she herself was sick.

Meanwhile, Mayer never forgave Jesse Martin, and he could be quite vindictive. He would later refuse to talk to him, so Ethel knew she had to find a new agent who had Mayer's approval. The agent Mayer suggested was his old crony, Frank Orsatti, so because of conflict of interest, Judy did not receive fair representation. Orsatti negotiated a salary of $500 a week for Judy and Ethel, while Mickey Rooney was getting $5,000 a week. However, what goes around comes around, and Ethel got her due: Orsatti told Mayer he wanted Ethel off the set and banned her from MGM. Still later on Judy's contract went to Leland Hayward and he negotiated better terms.

When Judy signed a new 7-year contract when she was eighteen, she received $2,000/week for three years, then $2,500/week for the next two years, and finally $3,000/week for the last two years. This was a high salary and she must have wondered whether she deserved these monetary rewards.

Listen Darling (1938) came next. This was an enchanting movie with Judy and Freddy Bartholomew playing the children of a widow, Mary Astor. Judy sings, "Zing! Went the Strings of

My Heart" to her film mother and one cannot help considering how many times Judy herself had sung it to Ethel at auditions, not to mention singing it on the radio the night her father died. In the movie, the children meet Walter Pidgeon and feel he is a much more suitable marriage partner for their mother than the older, boring man who their mother had been planning to marry for financial support. Judy has some hilarious scenes trying to get the two adults together. This early film gives the viewer the opportunity to see how fresh and enchanting Judy was at that age, and one can understand how she became so beloved in Hollywood. Roger Edens composed the arrangements for this movie, and the plaintive "Ten Pins in the Sky" brings out the yearning in Judy.

Later in 1938, Judy was back together with Mickey Rooney in the next movie, *Love Finds Andy Hardy*. Lana Turner and Anne Rutherford are the romantic interests for Mickey in this film. Judy's songs are the rousing "It Never Rains but What it Pours" "In Between," "Meet the Beat of My Heart" and "Bei Mir Bist Du Schoen!" The studio was determined to keep Judy as young as possible, and in the movie, Judge Hardy (Lewis Stone) refers to the young relative Betsey Booth (Judy), who is staying with a neighbor, as a twelve-year-old! Judy was sixteen years old then, so this must have been very humiliating for her to be referred to as a child. One sees her fresh, appealing spirit bursting out of this silly situation, and she manages to make it believable. The redeeming feature is watching Judy sing "In-Between" which Roger Edens composed for her.

RADIO WORK

Judy's first work on the radio started in October 1935, when she appeared on the *Shell Chateau Hour*. From January the next year until the following June, she was a regular on CBS's *Jack Oakie College Show*. From the age of fifteen years, she was working regularly, and the experience on the radio gave her confidence. She did not have to worry about what she looked like, she was valued for what she did well, and that was to sing.

Bob Hope loved to have Judy on his show because she had such quick wit and was able to joke around with him, along with her singing talents. She appeared with him many times- March 7 and May 9, 1939 and a weekly guest from September 9, 1939, until May 14, 1940. In December 1939, she appeared with him on Christmas Eve. Judy also appeared with others including Bing Crosby and Frank Sinatra.

The fan magazines had also discovered Judy and reported in *Modern Screen* November, 1939, that she was five feet two-and-a half inches tall and weighed one hundred and eighteen pounds. Well, the one hundred and eighteen pounds may have been correct, but Judy was only four feet and eleven inches. The magazine also reported that Judy loved to buy shoes and had seventy-three pairs at that time. The truth was, however, that she considered herself a natural born saver. Her dream was to own a house with a roomy, old-fashioned attic where she could store away the accumulation of her lifetime so that her great grandchildren could find the things in the years to come. It would have been marvelous if this happened, but it never did.[14]

ARTHUR FREED

Arthur Freed had been at MGM for years as a song writer and was responsible for bringing to the screen *The Wizard of Oz,* so without him Judy Garland's career might have been quite different. Freed started at MGM as a lyricist with "Singing in the Rain" and "I Cried for You" and other songs to his credit. In the early 1930s, he was involved with several movies including *Broadway Melody of 1936* and enjoyed watching the actual filming. Freed had the ability to recognize talent, and after hearing Roger Edens playing in 1934, offered him a contract. Edens had been working on Broadway as the pianist and arranger for Ethel Merman.

Freed had great ambition to produce musicals and finally gained the confidence of Mayer who told him to find a subject and go ahead. Freed had earlier recognized the talent of Judy and felt she could be the one to bring him to power and influence. Freed went to Frank Orsatti and told him to buy the rights for *The Wizard of Oz* from Sam Goldwyn.[15]

Although Mayer was giving Freed a chance, he assigned the more experienced Mervyn LeRoy as executive producer on the film; for insurance. LeRoy felt they should have a big name to star, so they tried to get Shirley Temple, but Twentieth Century Fox would not release her. This was just as well because Freed had sent Edens to check out Shirley's vocal abilities, and he reported that she had vocal limitations.[16]

Freed went to Harold Arlen and lyricist E. Y. Harburg and said he wanted a song to show yearning of a young girl and to be the bridge between Kansas and Oz. Harburg had always been involved with the political issues of the day, namely the Great Depression, and used his lyrics in *The Wizard of Oz* to inspire confidence in line with F. D. Roosevelt's new deal philosophy. He saw the Scarecrow as showing the longing for knowledge: "I would not be just a nuffin'/My head full of stuffin'" was his translation of "Let us have freedom from want." FDR's good Neighbor Policy was translated into the Tin Man's desire for a heart, and the Cowardly Lion embodied FDR himself: "The only thing we have to fear is fear itself."[17]

The movie had several directors: Norman Taurog, Richard Thorpe, George Cukor, Victor Fleming, and King Vidor. This happened because of conflicts with other projects, yet they each added something special to the movie. For an excellent look behind the scenes, see *The Wizard of Oz: an Illustrated Companion to the Timeless Movie Classic*, by John Fricke and Jonathan Shirshekan. [18]

The song "Over the Rainbow" was nearly cut after an early preview, but luckily Freed had it put back in the movie before release by threatening that he would leave the studio if the song was cut from the movie. Judy once wrote to Arlen about the song: "It is so symbolic of all my dreams and wishes that I'm sure that's why people sometimes get tears in their eyes when they hear it."

I must admit I missed Judy in the Wizard when I first saw it as a small child about seven years old. I was mainly attracted to the three little ballet dancers. When my granddaughter was about three years old, we enjoyed watching Wizard together, and many months later when The Harvey Girls movie was on television, she rushed in and said, 'That's the same lady who was in The Wizard of Oz!' How distinctive is Judy's voice!

Although this movie has placed Judy centrally in American culture now, at the time it must have been irksome to her once again to be strapped in a corset playing a twelve-year-old girl when she herself felt she was in love with a famous intellectual clarinetist.

Margaret Hamilton, who played the Wicked Witch, seemed to be Judy's main friend on the set, and saw the pills that she needed to help her get through the day. Therefore, we can see that by the time she was 17 years old she was on amphetamines, which were becoming fashionable in Hollywood then, or

Benzedrine, Dexedrine, and finally Phenobarbital. In addition, Judy was on a strict diet, and so began the chicken broth with the diet pills. Consequently, Judy needed sleeping pills to counteract the effects of the up drugs.

While Judy was making *The Wizard of Oz,* she formed a friendship with Artie Shaw, a man twelve years her senior. He was tall, dark, and handsome, a clarinetist who found fame in 1938 with the recording of "Begin the Beguine." He was an intellectual who studied Freud and Nietzsche. Judy met him in New York, and he came out to the Palomar Ball Room in Los Angeles on in February 1939, and collapsed on opening night. They rushed him to the hospital with complications from a strep-throat infection, which led to a blood disease called granulocytosis. Ethel and Judy visited him, and later Judy would go with Betty Asher, her publicist. Judy's big heart was always there to care for someone who was ill. This friendship went on for a while, much to Ethel's annoyance. Judy would often get Jackie Cooper to pick her up from home and take her to meet Artie Shaw. Artie Shaw did not think of her in a romantic way because as he was involved with Betty Grable, who was performing on Broadway, but Judy definitely had a crush on him.

The friendship with Artie Shaw ended after Phil Silvers took Shaw in February 1940, to the set of *Two Girls on Broadway* and introduced him to Lana Turner. That night Shaw and Turner went out together and fell madly in love, flew to Las Vegas, and got married. When Ethel called Shaw and yelled at him, he was surprised—thinking that Judy and he were only friends. The marriage to Turner would only last about three months, but it was another thing that made Judy feel she was not desirable.

Judy was very distressed over Shaw's marriage. Though devastated, she had to keep a recording date at the studio the next day. David Rose, the conductor, was kind and offered her a piece of his mother's chocolate cake in sympathy. So began their relationship; Rose was thirty-one years old, born in London, married but separated from Martha Raye, the comedienne.

Life must have been full of confusions; Judy portrayal on the screen was a child but knew she was a woman. In addition, she received directives that she was too fat and had to diet, but she still had to be the life and soul of the party on screen.

Although Judy's salary certainly purchased her Stone Canyon Road house, she wanted it to be her mother's house. The fan magazines of the day were full of stories of Judy decorating and enjoying the house and garden. At this time, Ethel began to see more of Will Gilmore, who was now a widower, and she would eventually marry him on her birthday, November 17, 1939, which happened to be the fourth anniversary of Frank Gumm's death--and this was a particularly painful time for Judy. Soon after the marriage, Ethel bought a car for Gilmore's elder son and a large Packard for herself. There began to be more family arguments about money, and Judy began to realize she was supporting the whole Gilmore clan!

By the end of 1939, Judy had completed a book of poems. She liked to think of herself as a writer and wanted to give up performing. Many of these poems are included in Anne Edwards' book, *Judy Garland*. This was the one of the attempts she made to get out of show business. However, so many people were making money off her that pressures were always on for her to keep working.[19]

Freed had been continuing with property acquisitions even while *Oz* was being made. He told Mayer about a Richard Rodgers and Lorenz Hart show, *Babes in Arms*, that he had seen on Broadway and persuaded Mayer to allow him to purchase the rights, which he felt would be an ideal vehicle for Judy and Mickey Rooney. He was a now a fully-fledged producer, and he moved out of the music department and into a small bungalow, at reduced salary but increased power. He hired Busby Berkeley as director. He would have a twenty-year career at MGM producing musicals. The movie plot of *Babes in Arms* (1939) concerns some ex-vaudevillians living in a small town on Long Island. Mickey plays a young showman who wants to put on a show. The film features a Judy and Mickey's big production marching number of

"God's Country," a minstrel show number with Judy singing "I'm Just Wild About Harry" and Judy and Mickey do impersonations of Franklin and Eleanor Roosevelt's fireside radio chats entitled, "My Day." The original Rodgers and Hart tune "Where and When" from the Broadway score remains in the film. Judy, on a bus, sings the wistful "I Cried for You" including new material by Edens. Other songs are "How About You," "After You've Gone," "I Like Opera, I Like Swing," "Figaro," "Broadway Rhythm," "Babes in Arms," "My Daddy Was a Minstrel Man" and "Oh! Susannah." *Babes in Arms* was one of the top ten grossing movies of 1939.

Judy received a Juvenile Oscar for her performance in *The Wizard of Oz* and *Babes in Arms* (1939). She put her hands and feet in cement at the Grauman's Chinese Theatre.

Babes finished on July 18, and Judy and Mickey Rooney went on a publicity tour. The *New York Daily News* reported on August 17, 1939, that 20,000 fans nearly mobbed the child stars when they arrived at New York's Grand Central Station from Washington DC. At Loew's Capital Theatre, they did seven shows a day, starting at 9:15 a.m. through 10:45 p.m. In between, they did broadcasts and luncheons. One of these broadcasts, on April 6, 1939, was on Bill Spier's CBS Radio Theatre 1 "Tune-Up" where she sang Kay Thompson's arrangement with Andre Kostelanetz, of the song, "F.D. Jones" with Kay's Rhythm Singers. Roger Edens had accompanied Judy on this tour and the three of them worked together for the first time and laughed a lot, and found they share the same birthday.[20] Edens and Thompson would continue working with Judy for the rest of her life.

At that time performers under the age of 18 years were not allow to work after 7:30 p.m. and the owner of the theatre was fined $25. Ethel had to sign special papers to allow Judy to continue. Ethel had been through this situation before, often taking one of the older sisters' birth certificates with her and insisting Judy was one of them.

Judy made some interesting comments to reporters then. She said that although she liked to sing, she would rather be a fine actress like Bette Davis. She also mentioned that she intended for a good part of her money go to build a hospital for crippled children, so here she is again talking of a hospital for children. This theme and desire to do something for sick children would come up repeatedly in her life.

Andy Hardy Meets Debutante followed in 1940 with Judy playing Betsey Booth again, trying to keep Mickey Rooney on the straight path. Among her beautiful songs was "I'm Nobody's Baby" and "Alone."

Judy once talked of the chaos of those days:

No wonder I was strange. Imagine whipping out of bed, dashing over to the doctor's office, lying down on a torn leather couch, telling my troubles to an old man who couldn't hear, who answered with an accent I couldn't understand and then dashing to Metro to make movie love to Mickey Rooney. They'd give us pep pills then they'd take us to the studio hospital and knock us cold with sleeping pills....after four hours they'd wake us up and give us the pep pills again. That's the way we got mixed up and that is the way we lost contact.[21]

Judy's recording at Decca of "Poor Little Rich Girl" summed up her life then, with words about life being a constant whirl and no time to stop and think.

Judy missed many of the activities of other girls in her age group and was disappointed she could not graduate as other high school students did. Ethel managed to get permission from the University High School that conducted the MGM courses; for Judy to participate in graduation with the regular students in June 1940. Ethel did not invite the press. They were very annoyed when they found out about it four years later.

Again, in 1940 Busby Berkeley was back in Judy's professional life, directing *Strike up the Band.* Berkeley was not originally a choreographer but a military drill instructor in World War I in France. We can see this influence in the dance formations he created with the dancers in his movies. He used to scream at Judy, "Eyes, eyes, I want to see your eyes! Open your eyes!" Once Hedda Hopper was on the set and witnessed Berkeley screaming at an agitated Judy. "She was close to hysteria," wrote Hopper. "I was ready to scream myself. But the order was repeated time and time again: 'Cut. Let's try it again, Judy. Come on, Judy! Move! Get the lead out'"[22]

This movie came from the Freed Unit with screenplay by John Monks, Jr., and Fred Findlehoffe, who would turn out to be a continuing friend to Judy. This was a powerful movie with lyrics and music by Roger Edens, George and Ira Gershwin and Arthur Freed, with the Paul Whiteman orchestra in the finale. Songs were "Our Love Affair," "La Conga," "Nobody," "Dear Gay Nineties," "Nell of New Rochelle," "Heaven Will Protect the Working Girl," "Father, Dear Father," "Drummer Boy" and the fabulous, "Strike Up the Band."

I have to admit that although I had seen the previous Judy movies, I did not really discover her until this movie. I remember coming out of the Embassy Theatre in North Harrow, England, and pointing to the advertising photograph outside the cinema and saying to my mother, "I want to see ALL this girl's movies." The scene in the library particularly captivated me. My mother told me that I had already seen this girl in The Wizard of Oz, *but I insisted that was a different girl because the girl in Oz had pigtails. My mother tried to tell me I was wrong, but as anyone knows when arguing with a small child--that is there is no changing their mind when they get something into their head.*

I recently reviewed all the Mickey/Judy movies and realized this was the first time Judy's sense of humor really came into play, so it was her humor which caught my attention.

There were romances. At the two evenings, multiple performers entertained us at the *Garland Carnegie Hall Celebration* produced by John Fricke and hosted by Lorna Luft in 1998; Robert Stack reminisced fondly about how Judy would drop her activities and devote herself to him when he came home on leave from World War II. Judy formed friendships with two unlikely highly intelligent and funny men, Oscar Levant and Johnny

Mercer. She met Mercer, who was thirty-one at the time, at a

party at Bob Hope's house and quickly became very close. Hope was to record with Judy but he suggested Judy record with Mercer. Mercer, a poet, went on to write, with Arlen, "That Old Black Magic" for Judy, which she later recorded for Decca. When I listen to this song, I guessed this was how he felt about Judy.

Lauren Bacall remembers seeing Judy with Johnny Mercer entertaining the troops at the Hollywood Canteen in New York in 1940. Johnny Mercer talks about how Judy was the inspiration for many of his songs in the book, *The Complete Lyrics of Johnny Mercer.* Johnny was married and the relationship would not last, but Judy enjoyed intelligent men, particularly those who were musicians.[23]

In 1940 came *Little Nellie Kelly*. Judy plays two roles with the same name. First, as a young woman in Ireland who marries Jerry Kelly (George Murphy). Her unreasonable father Michael Noonan (Charles Winninger) does not like her new husband. This was another Freed movie but a relief for Judy as Norman Taurog was the director. Judy was able to use the soft lovely

Irish accent she must have learned from her Irish Grandmother, Eva. In the movie, the family immigrates to the United States and the elder Nellie dies giving birth to her daughter Nellie. The photographs we see of little Nellie growing up are, of course, those of Baby Gumm. A nice touch! Judy sang "Singin' in the Rain" and as Young Nellie she bursts on the scene as a teenager, singing, "It's a Great Day for the Irish"—this is my main

childhood memory of this movie—in the New York St. Patrick's Day parade. Roger Edens also wrote and arranged a song that would remain with Judy all her life, "A Pretty Girl Milking Her Cow." Judy would often sing this as an encore at her concerts. Even when Judy was in her mid-forties and must have been tired, having already sung over 30 songs, she would transform herself into a teenager by singing it.

So the early years at MGM appear to be full of fun; she has a sparkling relationship with Mickey Rooney, who keeps her spirits up even with the brutal schedule. Judy makes twelve major films between the years of 1936 and 1940, along with her recording sessions and personal appearances. Judy is still living with her mother, and the uppers and downers are in play.

Chapter 7

Marriage to David Rose

Becoming a Young Lady

On June 15, 1941, there was a big party with 600 guests for Judy's nineteenth birthday and Judy announced her engagement to David Rose. This was David Rose's birthday, just five days after Judy's—another Gemini! All the Hollywood royalty came—including Joan Crawford, Ann Southern, James Stewart, George Murphy and Robert Sterling.

The plan was for Judy and David to marry later in the year after the completion of *Babes on Broadway*, but in July, Judy and Rose flew to Las Vegas and were married accompanied by Ethel

and Will Gilmore. Maybe Judy could not face the big wedding the studio was planning, or perhaps she was trying to follow Lana Turner's lead and romantically fly to Las Vegas to be married. The studio was not happy and Freed ordered Judy back to the studio. One can see that Judy was particularly lovely and glowing with happiness during the making of this movie. A month later Judy had the thrill of singing her own lyrics to David's score in a sketch, "Love's New Sweet Song," on CBS's Silver Theatre.

One of Judy's closest girlfriends at that time was Lana Turner. They had been together at the MGM schoolhouse and shared going out together in social groups when they were teenagers. Even Lana's short-lived marriage to Artie Shaw did not end their friendship. Tony Martin and Lana Turner were at the Ciro's celebration of the wedding of Judy and David and often socialized together. When Lana married, Stephen Crane, Judy, and David gave them an impromptu party.

Babes on Broadway's with Busby Berkeley directing took three months to finish and had many marvelous numbers include "How About You," "Hoe Down," "F.D Roosevelt Jones," "Waiting for Robert E Lee," "Chin up! Cheerio, Carry On!" and

a minstrel show. The story was by Fred Findlehoffe, who was to write many of the scripts at that time and was to remain a friend to Judy always. (In fact, he was her companion years later in New York when Judy met Sid Luft.) One can tell how Freddie felt about her when he wrote lines for Mickey to say: "You sing when you talk, sing when you walk, and your eyes are singing." (Observe the wig Judy wore, presumable to correct her uneven hairline. I wonder how humiliated she found this and perhaps this is why she wanted a similar scene included in the movie, *A Star is Born*.)

Christmas that year saw Mickey and Judy being broadcast on radio while greeting fans and wishing everyone a Merry Christmas on a Wagon along Hollywood Blvd.

The big production movie *Ziegfeld Girl* was also released in 1941.

James Stewart has top billing, but Judy comes next before Hedy Lamarr and Lana Turner. Judy has the charming "I'm Always Chasing Rainbows" to sing in the film, and both Judy and Lana Turner looked as if they were at their normal healthy weights for their age. Charles Winninger is with Judy again playing her vaudeville father trying to get back into the business. Here Judy was appears with two very beautiful women, and this must have added to her feelings that she was not adequate. Judy had the biggest dressing room, but Lana Turner takes the picture with her death scene at the end of the movie.

Judy and David took a lease and moved into Jean Harlow's mansion, where fan magazines reported Rose's hobby was railroads; he had 780 ft. of tracks all over the property.

Judy's last Andy Hardy movie was *Life Begins for Andy Hardy* in 1941. It was really a waste of Judy's talents playing Betsey Booth again and everyone referring to her as a child when she was a slim, glamorous 19 year old year. On November 17, 1941, Judy and Mickey did a show for Lux Theatre, "Merton of the Movies." It is on one of the DVDs. What a joy hearing Judy laugh while performing her corny lines! One can also find this and many other videos of Judy on The Judy Garland Experience.

The first year or so of marriage for Judy and David appeared to be happy because they were together entertaining the troops. Later in 1942, a movie short called "We Must Have Music" was released featuring movie clips and rehearsals from *Ziegfeld Girl* and *Babes on Broadway*.

At the end of 1941, Judy found that she was pregnant. The studio was furious and told Ethel that Judy must have an abortion. David Rose did not seem to be able to stand up against the Ethel and studio. He did not defend Judy, so the pregnancy was terminated. Judy would never forgive Ethel for this action, she was angry with Arthur Freed and disappointed in at the reaction of her husband.[1]

A similar occurrence seems to have happened to Veronica Lake about the same time. Perhaps we can imagine what went on in Judy's family from Veronica's documentation. We may be surprised that the studio would order an abortion, but at that time, the star was a commodity, and nothing must stand in the way of studio production. Veronica Lake talks about her experience in her book, *Veronica*.[2]

In February 1941, Veronica Lake, aged 19 years, found herself pregnant (Judy and Veronica were born the same year). Lake was married to John Detlie, an art director and set designer. Veronica's mother told her it was a selfish, stupid thing to do to get pregnant after all the work she had done to help her career. Veronica refused to listen and insisted she would go on with the pregnancy, and the movie studio planned *Sullivan's Travels*.[3] There were many telephone calls that day; Lake's mother was  blaming John for the pregnancy. One can imagine the similar exchange in Judy's world. Veronica had already started on her movie, and she had the support of director, Preston Sturges. Veronica was perhaps stronger emotionally than Judy and defied her mother. She was very angry at the reaction of her mother and husband and left the house for two days. When she returned the matter was not discussed with her husband, but the marriage was, in all senses, over. In the film *Sullivan's Travels*, Veronica was disguised as a Hobo, with the typical, baggy clothes doing more than just representing the character, but hiding Veronica's baby bump as well.

Today's young performers do not allow studios to determine when they have children. Lucille Ball changed things by incorporating the birth of her children into her television series. But in Judy's case everyone was against her. This was probably the event that caused the first rift between Judy and her mother—there would be further rifts—but this was the beginning. It was also the end of her marriage to David Rose, although they were not divorced until June 1945.

It was not only Judy who experienced Mayer's interference in their private lives. By all accounts, he interfered in the romance of Joan Crawford and Clark Gable.[4] Crawford was a bigger star than Gable during the making of the movie, *Possessed* when they asked to get married. Mayer told Crawford to give up Gable or he would fire and blackballed them from films. He suggested Gable go back to the lumberyard and she, Crawford, back to the laundry. Mayer also interfered in the love affair of Jeanette MacDonald and Nelson Eddy. Mayer tried to cut out Nelson's good scenes from the movie they were making, *Rose Marie.*[5]

Mayer also tried unsuccessfully to tell Esther Williams that she could not have any babies without his permission after her marriage to Ben Gage. She went ahead and gave birth to her son in August 1949.[6]

GENE KELLY

Judy looks very thin at the beginning of the movie *For Me and My Gal* (1942) after the loss of her baby, but nothing shows in her performance. The film was made under the Freed/Berkeley banner; for the first time Judy gets top billing above the title. Judy was teamed with Gene Kelly for his first musical

appearance. Judy and Gene had met in New York a year or so before when he was appearing in *Pal Joey,* on Broadway and at that time they spent many hours talking and enjoying each other's company after his performance, and planning to make a movie together sometime. Gene has documented how kind and helpful was to him during the making of this movie and their friendship would continue through the years. Judy as vaudevillian Joe Hayden sings many songs in the film, including "After You've Gone" and "How You Gonna Keep 'Em Down on the Farm?," and she and Gene as performer Harry Palmer have several duets, "When You Wore a Tulip," "For Me and My Gal," and "Ballin' the Jack." [7]

There were tensions on the set because George Murphy wanted the part of Harry Palmer and Mayer and Berkeley did not like Kelly but Freed and Judy supported Kelly. Judy told Freddie Findlehoffe that the script was corny, but he had said if she said the lines, people would believe them, and they did. Judy told fan club members in London in 1964 that this was one of her favorite movies, even though it was corny!

In the home life, her sister Jimmy's marriage to Bobby Sherwood had broken up, she got a job as a script girl at MGM,

and Judy saw more of her and was very attached to Jimmy's daughter Judalein. Suzanne and Jack Cathcart lived in Las Vegas and Ethel sold the Stone Canyon house. David Rose and Judy were still together in June 1942, when they attended a friend's wedding in Lancaster, but soon after Rose joined the army and they grew apart.

Gal finished in the middle of the year, and Judy went straight into *Presenting Lily Mars* (1943) directed by Norman Taurog and produced by Joe Pasternak. This movie was planned for Lana Turner, but they decided to lighten the script and bring more humor into it, so it became a vehicle for Judy.

Van Heflin plays the part of a Broadway writer/producer John Thornway and Judy is Lily Mars, the daughter of a neighbor of his mother in the old hometown. When Thornway visits his mother, Lily tries to get him to audition her and give her a part. There are some hilarious scenes with Lily coming down the Mars home staircase pretending to be an actress and later escaping from the Thornway backyard (after crashing a fancy party) by climbing over the wall. The original script called for Thornway to give Lily a spanking, as he threatened, after she sang, "Tom, Tom, the Piper's Son." Judy discussed this spanking with her mother, and they both decided it was demeaning and a bad example for men and women. Judy went to the studio and had the script rewritten. Other songs included in the film were "Ev'ry Little Movement," "When I look at You" and "Broadway Rhythm." When "Paging Mr. Greenback" number was considered not suitable, Kay Thompson jumped in and expanded the refined the ten-minute medley prepared by Roger Edens, Hugh Martin and Conrad Salinger, "Where's There's Music" for Judy to sing in the finale.[8]

TYRONE POWER

In October 1942, a new man came into Judy's life. Her marriage to Rose was over and she attended a party at Keenan Wynn's

house where she met Tyrone Power. Earlier that month he and his wife, Annabella, had viewed an early screening of *For Me and My Gal,* and Tyrone had been enchanted with Judy's performance, commenting to Annabella on how she had matured. Annabella was out of town at the time of the party where Judy and Tyrone met, and they fell madly in love and embarked upon a relationship which was to last for six months, until the following April.

Judy's friends tried to warn her about Tyrone's previous romances, but Judy was euphoric and they were seen arm in arm on the sets where she was filming, and at lunch at Café de Paris, the studio commissary on the Fox studio lot. Both studios were not happy about their relationship, but the Publicity Department covered up any romances that they did not feel were suitable for the public to know about, especially with both parties in this romance married to other people.

Judy, at 21 years old, was particularly beautiful, not too thin and not too plump; one sees how lovely she was at that time in the movie *Presenting Lily Mars* -perhaps being in love with Tyrone Power added to her glow.

Tyrone was not only handsome; he was also charming and cultured. Many actresses have commented on his appearance. Rosalind Russell, who was with Power and Annabella in the movie *Suez* (1938) when they all met, commented once that when Tyrone entered a room, it was like a light turning on.[9] Russell and Power were beautiful in this movie, their scenes exquisite and moving. Annabella, in contrast, was less attractive but had an assertive manner, and she managed to marry Power the next year. This was her third marriage and she was seven years older than Power.

Mainly his mother Palia had brought up Power, with sister, Anne. His English actor father was away most of the time. At the time Judy met Tyrone, he was living with his mother, wife and sister, who was staying with them awaiting the birth of a child while her husband was away in the military. Significant women surrounded him in his life—wife, mother, sister, and clearly, he was not in charge of that household!

Much of the documentation about the Power/Garland romance is in Fred Lawrence Guiles' book about Tyrone Power, *The Last Idol*. A New York millionaire, J. Watson Webb, Jr. came to Hollywood fascinated by the movies and became an editor at Fox Studio where he met Power and became good friends. He was often at the house and was included in their family and social life. Watson, being his confidant, was the one that Tyrone turned to help him look after Judy while he was dealing with his new life in the service.

Power was to write many letters to Webb concerning his relationship with Judy. Tyrone asked Watson to look after Judy when he started his military training in Camp Pendleton in San Diego, the day after New Year's Day. Judy had begged Tyrone to get a divorce in January, but he hesitated because of Annabella's worries about her family in Europe. In the next few weeks, Tyrone felt he should go home on weekends, but his home life was uncomfortable because Tyrone had always told his wife about his extramarital affairs, but in Judy's case, he was evasive.

The announcement of Judy's official separation from David Rose came on February 2, 1943.

In late March, Tyrone admitted to Annabella that he was in love with someone else. She was aware that Judy was involved, but was not receptive to any request for a divorce. Tyrone received a call back to the army, and this ended any further discussions. He spent all the time he could with Judy in March and promised to talk to Annabella, without success.

Then, Power was called to officer training school in Virginia and left the first week of April. He wrote to Watson saying how he wished he were with Judy and how much he loved her. A week later he wrote commenting on the child that was expected.[10]

There are photos taken of Watson escorting Judy to a party by Decca Records honoring Leonard Bernstein in early April, so this confirms their friendship. Soon after, though, Judy gave up on their romance, feeling that Annabella had an iron will and would never give Tyrone a divorce and so became disheartened and disillusioned with the whole situation. Friends embraced her and the writer-director, Joseph Mankiewicz, began organizing her life. There were rumors of an overnight abortion in Mexico, and Judy continued with *Girl Crazy*. When Power found out, he knew it was over, he stated that he would have got a divorce had he known Judy was pregnant and that he loved Judy very much. None of this makes much sense; their romance was not to be. However, Tyrone continued to write to Watson about how sad he felt about losing Judy.

Most books about Judy refer to the Power affair as being a minor event in her life. However, Judy herself believed it was a major event, and said later "it was no small affair."[11] The affair lasted from October 1942 until the following April 1943, and Power was still writing sadly to Watson in July.

Girl Crazy (1943) was another Freed production (and by now we can see the driving side of Freed) with Norman Taurog directing. The big production number "I Got Rhythm," directed by Busby Berkeley, was filmed first. Berkeley's demanding style caused Judy to collapse that day on set. Charles Walters was brought in to direct the rest of the movie with a more gentle manner with the musical numbers "I'm Bidin' My Time," "But Not for Me," "Embraceable You," and "Could You Use Me?" with Mickey Rooney.

At this point Joseph Mankiewicz was the man in her life, consoling her after the end of the Tyrone Power love affair. He was a talented writer who had won several Oscars, but had a huge drawback; he had a wife who was in a mental hospital, making divorce impossible. Anne Baxter talks about Mankiewicz in her book, *Intermission*, and admits she had a crush on him while they were making *All About Eve*, even though she was happily married to John Hodiack at the time. She commented that all the ladies on the set enjoyed his company.[12]

There is an audiotape of a Joseph Mankiewicz and Dore Schary of an informal production for Judy's twenty-first birthday party in 1943 called, *The Life of Judy Garland*. Danny Kaye, Keenan and Evie Wynn, and Van Johnson played various parts. Danny played the 2 ½ year- old Judy belting out "Jingle Bells." (Judy had met Danny in New York when he was appearing in *Lady in the Dark* and introduced him to friends when he came to Hollywood. They were great friends; he appeared at the Palladium in London in 1951 just after Judy.)

Mankiewicz talked with Gary Carey in 1972 about Judy.

[A]t the age of three you're shoved in the spotlight to sing 'Jingle Bells.' And from that moment on, you're told and told and told by everyone--audiences that cheer you in that spotlight when you sing, to a draconian mother who drills the unshakable conviction into you …that only in that spotlight, singing as loud as you can… were you even acceptable to society, much less attractive in any way at all-- how the hell can you possibly, for the rest of your life, know who you really are? … [13]

Mankiewicz felt Judy was in a dream world and felt she should see a therapist and thus began her visit to psychologists.

Her sister Jimmie disagreed and she felt there was nothing wrong with Judy's elaborate story telling. Jimmie insisted that Judy just embellished funny stories to entertain people and that if this was lying, then all comics are liars.[14]

Mankiewicz talked more with David Shipman in 1982 about the situation when he left MGM.

He had persuaded Judy to go to a therapist and her mother found out. Mayer called him in:

He was *choleric* as I walked in….Mrs. Gumm was there screaming, and Eddie Mannix, the wonderful Irish manager sitting in a corner. And Mayer yelled, how dare I interfere in the life of Judy—a mother's love was all she needed. And I said, "A mother's love my ass." The mother said, "I know what to do with my daughter"—and it got into one of those screaming fights. I was so aghast that I finally said, "Look, Mr. Mayer, the studio is obviously not big enough for both of us. One of us has to go." At that Eddie Mannix fell off his chair and I was at Fox within a week.[15]

Thousands Cheer (1943) came next and there was only one song for Judy at the end of the film. Roger Edens wrote the song "The Joint is Really Jumping Down at Carnegie Hall" for Judy to sing with Jose Iturbi, the classical concert pianist. Mickey Rooney introduces, "a young lady and can she sing a song: Judy Garland." Judy enters the stage slowly from behind Jose, who is playing classical music, and she looks disapprovingly at him. She wears a simple cream or pale pink dress, brown knit vest, and no jewelry, which is what I felt she would look like off-screen. She watches, Jose, looks bored, and starts to sing.

Judy initially did not want to make the movie *Meet Me in St. Louis* (1944) because Joseph Mankiewicz told her she was too old at 21 to play an 18 year old, but Arthur Freed persuaded her to make it.[16] The role

of Esther Smith became one of Judy's favorite pictures and brought director, Vincente Minnelli into her life. When filming began, Judy was uncomfortable with the Minnelli style of directing, but later understood what he was trying to create. Several songs from the film she continued to sing for the rest of her life, particularly "The Boy Next Door," "The Trolley Song," "Have Yourself a Merry Little Christmas," along with "Meet Me in St. Louis," "Skip to My Lou," "Under the Bamboo Tree," and "Over the Bannister." Freddie Findlehoffe, who understood and cared deeply for Judy, was the writer on this movie.

This is the first time veteran make-up artist Dottie Ponedel worked with Garland and developed the new Judy look. She was to remain with Judy through the rest of her MGM years under exclusive contract, and worked for Garland after MGM released her in 1950 at performance engagements such as the London Palladium in 1951. Ponedel was stricken with MS in the early 1950s and stopped active work at that time. Judy and Vincente Minnelli became romantically involved during the making of the movie, but they drifted apart when it was finished, and she went back to Mankiewicz.

Early in July 1944, Judy rehearsed and filmed "Madame Crematante" for the movie, *Ziegfeld Follies,* which was released in early 1946. In this movie, Judy displays a delightful flair for satire

as The Star in her grand number with eleven leading men, "A Great Lady Has an Interview," about the invention of the safety pin. Here we can really see the influence of the talented Kay Thompson working magic with a part that was originally planned, but turned down by Greer Garson.[17] In my opinion, no one else could have done the role justice except for Judy.

Judy went on to record one of the songs Lena Horne sings in *Follies,* "Love" and "Liza" (cut out of final). I was always interested in Kay Thompson and the influence she had on Judy's singing style. One does not see much of her in movies, but she is in *Funny Face* and even sings with a lot of gusto or pizzazz in a style that Judy utilized later on. It was nice to see Liza paying tribute to Kay in the second act of her show *Liza at the Palace*

December 2008. She was Kay's godchild; Kay lived with Liza in the last few years of her life. There is an excellent book written by Sam Irwin, *Kay Thompson,* an absolutely "must read" for anyone interested in what happened behind the scenes at MGM during those musical years.[18]

The Clock (1945) was a non-singing role for Judy. The movie started with Fred Zimmerman directing, but something was wrong and it was shelved. Judy definitely wanted to make the film, but she wanted Minnelli to direct, so she went straight to Louis B. Mayer and asked. Minnelli looked at the work which had been filmed and decided to re-do it, emphasizing the city of New York as an important feature of the film. Although the movie was made in Hollywood, Minnelli used stock footage of New York and shot the film using special techniques to help disguise the fact that they did no actually film in New York. *The Clock* finished filming in November 1944. After finishing the movie, Minnelli took Judy to New York; she met his friends, and they appeared to be in love.

Judy wanted to do movies that were more serious in nature, but MGM insisted on pushing her into musicals. Ginger Rogers was able to break away from the flossy material of musicals and in 1944 appeared in the sensitive *I'll be Seeing You* with Joseph Cotton, about a woman out on leave from a prison sentence.

So although she requested more serious roles, MGM kept Judy making musicals. It took six months to make *The Harvey Girls*, starting in January 1945 and finishing in June of that year. George Sidney was directing. Johnny Mercer and Harry Warren got an academy awards in 1947 for the song "The Atchison, Topeka, and the Santa Fe." The movie cost $2,524,315 to make and grossed $5,175,000, so Judy was now a money-making machine.[19]

Chapter 8

Entertaining the Troops

Visiting Veterans' and Children's Hospitals

I feel a certain aspect of Judy's life has not been explored, namely her work for service members during World War II and later at veterans' hospitals all over the country. In addition, her caring and support for sick children in hospital and those who were handicapped has also been neglected.

ENTERTAINING SERVICEMEN

Judy was one of the first entertainers to go out and perform for the soldiers. She was a member of the Hollywood Victory Committee. She already had a long history of public service, including participating in benefits and broadcasts for British and Greek War Relief under the guidance of Eleanor Roosevelt. Before America became involved in the war, she had also performed at a Chinese New Moon Festival. She was the only west coast artist at the studio 8 a.m. one morning for a radio broadcast to Britain in 1939. JSP Records from England has just released some old recordings of Judy under the title of *Lost Tracks*. The second CD contains

many of the recordings Judy did for Britain, such as *Bundles for Britain,* recorded on January 1, 1941, featuring "Auld Lang Syne" with special lyrics "for Englishmen." Another broadcast on April 27, 1941: "Chin up, Cheerio, Carry On," written by Harburg and Lane. [1]

On December 3, 1941, the Japanese attacked Pearl Harbor. Judy and her first husband David Rose were out at Ford Ord in Monterey, California on December 7, putting on a show for the troops. Judy was due to make an appearance on *The Charlie McCarthy Show* sponsored by Chase and Sanborn that same evening, featuring Edgar Bergen and his wooden pals, and Abbott and Costello in addition to Judy. Judy sang "Zing!" and found herself among the first entertainers to perform for troops in a state of war. There were many interruptions to the NBC show with frequent news bulletins. On Sunday, December 14, Judy received the honorary title of Corporal. Judy was on the cover of the newsletter for the First Medical Regiment at Fort Ord, California, *"Esprit de Corps"* receiving her stripes and citation. A few words from the article follow:

JUDY GARLAND JOINS REGIMENT -- STAR MADE
HONORARY CORPORAL IN H COMPANY

She was dressed in an attractive black-and-white outfit....Major Martin had Judy line up with a squad of men from Company H, and First Sergeant Marshall Hummel pinned corporal's stripes on each sleeve of Miss Garland's sweater. A corporal's warrant was then presented while a pair of identification tags were placed around her neck.[2]

In January 1942, Judy and David Rose went off on a three- week tour of training camps, entertaining the troops around the country by playing four shows a day.[3]

Judy also sang for the troops at Baer Field Army Air Base in Fort Wayne, Indiana, now Fort Wayne International Airport, and she ate in the mess hall with the enlisted men.

These stories show how Judy cared for the servicemen during the war years and later for those wounded in military hospitals. She continued to sing for the military hospitals for the rest of her life, without any publicity, so it is hard to find evidence; however, the following are some such performances that I found.

First, there was a nice write up in the *Boston Record American* on Sept. 1, 1967, pages 12-13, when Judy visited the VA Hospital there.

Mist was forming in her big brown eyes. Mike Pallamary saw it as she took his hand. "Judy, if there were more people like you to come back to, we wouldn't mind fighting for 30 years." And with that, Mike reached across his hospital bed, took a bouquet of flowers from a table and handed them to JG. "Thanks for stopping by," Mike said. And there was a mist in his eyes. It's contagious—

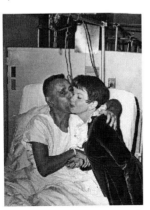

that mist. It moved from ward to ward at the VA hospital on South Huntington Ave., following the 90 lb. wisp of a songstress. For an hour and a half last night, Judy moved through the hospital, clinging to hands, whispering good wishes, singing a few verses of "Over the Rainbow," and ending with a brief concert in the motion picture room of the hospital. Mike Pallamary of Jamaica Plain, a naval veteran who shattered a hip during WWII, had called Thursday to see if Judy could stop by the hospital before she left Boston. "And just like that," Mike said, "she said she'd be over the day after her concert." It was sort of a "thank you" from Judy to the veterans and the people of Boston—before she went to the hospital...

One of the officials asked her if she would like to sing for them. "I think we'd be happy to," she said, turning to Cole who accompanies her on the piano. At first there were only a couple of dozen men in the theatre but after the sound of her voice filtered into the halls, the number swelled to more than fifty. She sang, "Just in Time," "Rainbow," Then a duet with Cole, "Bye Bye Blackbird." An official sadly commented, "You know, she's the first entertainer to visit this hospital since Jimmy Durante was here … 8 years ago."

As she was leaving Mike's ward, one of the patients yelled at her, "I just saw a re-run of *A Star!*" Judy tilted her head and yelled back, "Oh, it's so sad! I cried at that myself." Further, down the hall, Stanley Laben of Melrose cried out, "Oh Judy, how do you stay looking so young?" With that, Judy hesitated, and with a twinkle in those misty brown eyes replied, "clean living, I suppose."[4]

Judy also went to Bethesda Naval Hospital on September 10, 1967. Dick Wotten of the *Cleveland Press* reported on September 19 (18):

Sunday she was at the Great Lakes Naval Hospital in Chicago talking to Vietnam vets. She tried to visit every hospital in every town on the tour "Those young men make me feel proud," she said. "They have such dignity and humor…you can't feel sorry for them because they don't feel sorry for themselves….they have no self-pity or cynicism….you really come away feeling inspired."[5]

On May 17, 1968, she was at the Crippled and Paraplegic Chelsea Naval Hospital in Boston. She stopped to autograph a cast on the leg of a Marine Lance Corporal. She went from ward to ward singing and conversing with injured sailors and marines.

SICK and HANDICAPPED CHILDREN

The sweet and loving nature of Judy came out in her caring for sick children. *Modern Screen* in October 1940, ran a piece about the mother of a sick child in the hospital writing to Judy asking for an autographed photograph of her as Dorothy. Instead of sending it, Judy went to the hospital with the photograph—so the child had Judy/Dorothy standing next to her bed! In another early fan magazine, she talked of opening a hospital for sick children.

During a stay at Peter Bent Brigham Hospital in 1949, Judy had to go over to the children's hospital next door to have an electroencephalogram to rule out a tumor. It was there that she became involved with handicapped children and grew to love them. This occurrence may have led to her wanting to work on the movie, *A Child is Waiting* (1963).

Tom Green has not written much about his two years with Judy, except for the following in 1965:

Twenty Years ago: The Legend: An Intimate Bio of JG Sunday August 18 Cardinal Kennedy Memorial Hospital

Judy was all anxious and ready to depart before noon. We arrived at the outdoor affair, held at an out-of-season racetrack, early, which must have shocked a few folks who had heard that Judy Garland never showed up on time for anything, but, of course, her appearance hadn't been publicized anyway because no one had been really certain she would show up anyway. There were hundreds of people awaiting the arrival of the Cardinal, including fifty crippled and retarded children in wheelchairs, on crutches and in braces or in the arms of nurses and nuns. The good Cardinal finally made his appearance, considerably late, and after an extremely short spurt of rhetoric about the need for funds to support his charity, he granted his co-stars on the stage a moment's audience, by-passed the children and disappeared into his car….it was left to the only remaining celebrity to do something. Judy burst into a rendition of "Rainbow" that sounded as though God had just blessed her. The audience hurrahed, the children's faces lit up at the sound of a song coming from the little lady they knew as Dorothy of Oz and the money flowed. But Judy was not satisfied to leave it at that. She scrambled down from the stage into the crowd, and kept everyone riveted in their chairs while she went to each and every retarded or crippled boy and girl and chatted, hugged, kissed or held their hands, spreading so much love and happiness and hope, it was probably worth a year of therapy to every child there. What Judy did for those children that afternoon, far more than she had been asked or expected to do, was a simple manifestation of a woman's instinct and perfect proof of her feelings towards children. She always did her best to care for her own three with as much love, affection and understanding as she showered on those assembled in the heat of that Boston afternoon.[6]

When Judy was in London in 1962 to make *I Could Go On Singing* she spoke of the movie *A Child is Waiting* which she had completed earlier that year. She mentioned she had always taken a personal interest in such children and had found that contact with them is very rewarding as they give their affection unquestioningly and completely. She also said that the spastics and mongoloid in the picture proved to be much pleasanter and easier to work with than the so-called "normal" children with their pushing mothers.[7]

Chapter 9

Marriage to Vincente Minnelli

Back to Hollywood and the Work Grind

As soon as the movie *The Harvey Girls* (1946) was finished, Vincente Minnelli and Judy were married on June 15, 1945, and left for New York on their honeymoon. Judy was very happy there, seeing shows and expressing a desire to remain there. In

July, she recorded "You'll Never Walk Alone" and "Smiling Through," two beautiful ballads. Her desire grew, culminating in her wanting to perform on Broadway. She had worked for eleven years at MGM and wanted to do something different. She told anyone who would listen:

> I'm not going to re-sign with the studio when my contracts expires. Oh, they're been wonderful to me at MGM, but I want to go on the stage. I was in vaudeville so many years when I was Frances Gumm, and I miss the sound of applause. If I could get a play on the order of "Lady in the Dark," a drama or a comedy with music, I would be terribly happy.[1]

One wonders whether this was why Mayer was so enthusiastic about the Vincente/Judy marriage, knowing that this would keep Judy at MGM.

A move to New York was not to be; she had married Minnelli, and he had a successful career in New York, son of circus performers, he was a sketch artist, photographer, designed sets for Broadway musicals; now his future career would be in Hollywood.[2] Also, she was pregnant, so back to Hollywood she went and to Minnelli's Evanview house. But as we will see later most of the future movies Judy did at MGM were done with reluctance because her heart was not really in them, even with the marvelous performances she gave.

Judy had told Minnelli earlier about the pills she needed to get her through the day when filming, but after she realized she might be pregnant, she threw them in the river.[3]

The fan magazines were full of the Judy/Vincente love story and gave the impressions that they were very much in love, presenting a oneness and unity of purpose that was reassuring.[4]

Judy had a cameo role as Ziegfeld star, Marilyn Miller in the movie *Till the Clouds Roll By* (1946) when she was pregnant with daughter, Liza. Judy's interpretation of "Look for the Silver Lining" is one of the most beautiful ever heard. "Who?" was a magnificent full production number done while Judy was three months pregnant with Liza. No wonder her daughter wanted to be a dancer! Minnelli directed these two numbers, as well as "Sonny."

Daughter Liza was born in the following March 1946. Kay Thompson and her husband, Bill Spier, were her godparents. Kay Thompson was a good friend to Judy, remaining in both Judy's and

then Liza's lives (and living with Liza for many years) until her death in July 1998.

After the birth of Liza, Judy took eight months off from work before *The Pirate* went into production in late 1948. In November of that year, just before beginning the movie, Judy reluctantly signed a new five-year contract for $5,619.23 a week making no more than two films a year. This contract had fearsome penalties for illness.[5] This was obviously a mistake, as we shall see later, but no one supported her desire not to sign the contract. As we saw in a previous chapter, if Judy was forced to appear and perform when she did not want to, there would be trouble; this goes back to the resentments she felt at the age seven years old when she had to perform for unresponsive agents and managers.

The location of *The Pirate* was in the Caribbean in the 1830s with a Cole Porter score. Judy played Manuela, who was in love with Macoco, the pirate played by Gene Kelly. Freed said that this movie was twenty years ahead of its time, so it wasn't as accepted as it should have been. I loved it, though, and it has always been one of my favorites even though the critics found fault with it.

Our family had the tradition of going to the movies at 6 p.m., as soon as my mother left work. This came from the wartime years when one would want to get home before dark and the bombing raids started. The main feature usually started at 7:30 p.m. with a "B" movie showing first. Consequently, when we arrived at 6 p.m., we always arrived in the middle of the main feature already underway. As this cinema also showed dramatic Warner Bros. films, I used to wonder as a child how the main characters got themselves into such dreadful situations. That evening we arrived just at the point in the movie where Judy sings "Mack the Black," and I was as mesmerized by her as she was by Macoco. When the film came around to this number, my mother got up and started out of the cinema. This was the first time I defied her; I insisted we stay until I could see the number through a second time. I feel this number evokes something of the magic that Judy would later bring to her live theatre shows. I had the 78-rpm record of "Mack the Black" with "Be a Clown" on the backside, and I wore the record out so that it was impossible to play; the needle literally would not go over the surface.

Douglas McVay, the critic, writes about "Mack the Black":

Yet beyond all these numbers I treasure the closing, tumultuous seconds of "Mack the Black" in *The Pirate*, where she sweeps to a visual-vocal climax with a mesmerism that must be seen and heard to be believed, before freezing into entranced and entrancing, immobile exhaustion, and being dragged by Kelly in intricately twisting tracking-shot up on to the stage to face the wildly applauding crowd... [6]

The studio blamed Judy for any delays in the film's production. But as we know now any of the problems on the movie set were not her fault. How frustrated she must have been when two of her big numbers, including the expressive

"Voodoo" with Gene Kelly, had to be reshot? The whole movie was restructured because Mayer considered "Voodoo" too sexy. The first version of "Mack the Black" was originally recorded (and filmed) for the beginning of the film, but it was destroyed and the new version inserted into the middle of the film. One can hear the original on the CD of the *Motion Picture Soundtrack Anthology* with vocal arrangement by Kay Thompson.[7]

One sees her comic genius in the scene on the waterfront when Manuela meets Macoco, a circus entertainer, and she loses her wide-brimmed hat and a flirting skirmish ensues. Later one must not miss Judy saying, "He asked for MEEEEE!" when Macoco orders her to be given to him. Gene Kelly had a big voodoo dance and because of the time spent by Minnelli and Kelly on the rehearsals and filming, Judy began to feel that they forgotten about her.

During the end of the filming Judy found Vincente involved with another person. Judy tried to cut her wrists instead of attacking the couple.

Judy was ill, so after the film was finished, she went to Las Campanas in Compton, a nursing home and then on to The Riggs Foundation in Massachusetts. It was obvious to those who cared for Judy that the pressures of work were causing her health to fail, but MGM had money invested in her and had purchased the right to Irving Berlin *Annie Get Your Gun* for her, which she found hard to refuse. They could not start on making this movie because the show was still on Broadway.

Not surprisingly, Judy did not want Minnelli directing her next movie, and she asked Mayer if Charles Walters could be the director.

Initially Twentieth Century Fox had contacted Berlin, but that studio would not pay Berlin's price for *Easter Parade*, (1948). I suppose this fact absolutely explains concisely just, why the MGM musicals were and still are the best in the world — they spared no expense to get the best in any field. MGM gave Berlin $650,000 for *Annie Get Your Gun* [8] and $500,000 for *Easter Parade*,[9] and even persuaded him to write seven new

songs. Freed was to say later, "The only reason Irving Berlin let me buy the picture was because he wanted to do a picture with Judy." Berlin gave consulted on the movie. There is a story that Berlin once suggested to Judy how she should sing a song, and she replied, "You write them, Buster, and I sing them!" Berlin was very amused and accepted Judy's judgment.[10] The new songs were "It Only Happens When I Dance with You," "Better Luck Next Time," "Drum Crazy," "Stepping Out with My Baby," "A Couple of Swells," "A Fella with an

Umbrella," and "Happy Easter." Another new one, "Mr. Monotony," was filmed but not used in the final film. It later showed up at fan club meetings and was included in MGM's "That's Entertainment III."

Initially, Gene Kelly was to be Judy's partner in this movie, and in fact, Judy and Gene had planned the Tramp outfits to be used in a "Couple of Swells". *When I watch the Tramp number in the movie and on the many occasions when she did it on stage and TV shows, I think about Gene and wonder what it would have been like if he had been with her instead of Fred Astaire. However, I suspect, as with all her partners, we would have still only been looking at her.* Judy was understandably disappointed when Gene had to drop out of the film when he broke his ankle playing softball, and she was slightly apprehensive about having to dance with Astaire.[11] Judy had top billing over Astaire in the *Easter Parade*. But work on this movie was a strain for Judy.

In the *Time* magazine issue of March 7, 2005, Richard Corliss writes about the new DVD of *Easter Parade*, saying that "Better Luck Next Time" and a few other scenes did seem slightly at odds with the rest of the gaiety going on. Corliss sums it up beautifully in his review of the DVD *Easter Parade* in *Entertainment magazine*:

> ….[B]ut even at 25, in this genial 1948 Irving Berlin songfest with Fred Astaire there was an eeriness to her charisma. Garland is visibly depleted, her voice often reedy, her teen sweetness now a mask. And then, by an act of sternest will, she summons the old fun, as in the numbers "A Couple of Swells" and "I Love a Piano". The innocent girl from *The Wizard of Oz* is reborn, through her pain, as a depression-defying diva.

Even so, the movie is delightful, with Judy showing her funny side when she can't remember her left foot from her right and when she first meets Don (Fred Astaire). Judy is also a pure joy in their first classic ballroom number. Hannah (Judy) falls in love with Don, who has never really noticed her, and Hannah seeks consolation from Peter Lawford, whom she had met earlier in the rain and sang, "A Fella with an Umbrella." Apart from many marvelous Berlin songs—"A Couple of Swells," "Ragtime Violin," "Snooky Ookums," "When the Midnight Choo Choo Leaves for Alabam'," "It Only Happens When I Dance with

You"—this movie really shows Judy's humorous side, and these moments are irreplaceable. One has to admit that at other times the frail state of Judy's health is noticeable to those of us who really cared about her, and consequently there is a certain amount of pain in watching the movie. I think that it only goes to prove the point that Judy never let her problems interfere with her work; on the surface, her performance is pure perfection. Those of us who knew Judy well, if only from the screen, realized that something was wrong.

Now the management at MGM decided they had a winning combination of Fred and Judy, and regardless of how Judy felt, they were going to go ahead with another blockbuster. At this time Judy's drug addiction was common knowledge. A Los Angeles police officer informed Harry Anslinger, who was a retired commissioner of narcotics, about what he perceived was the drug problem of Judy. It was arranged for Judy to meet Harry Anslinger, and she told him she was exhausted from a demanding schedule of movie-making. This was conveyed to a reporter from the *Chicago Sun-Times*.[12]

Anslinger advised Judy to end her relationship with the physician who was supplying her drugs, but she said she needed him. Anslinger then spoke to a high official at MGM and told him that if they wanted Judy to be productive in the future, they needed to give her time to rest, but the reply was that it wasn't possible; they had fourteen million dollars tried up in her; she was the biggest star the studio had at that time. When Anslinger asked what would happen if Judy took too many pills one day, the answer was a shrug, and he was told they would have to take a chance. He countered with the question: What would happen if she had a breakdown and production stopped? Again, they did not seem to care about Judy. This did happen at the beginning of the *Barkleys of Broadway,* and they brought Ginger Rogers out of

retirement.[13] Anslinger published his thoughts on the drug business in his book, *The Murderers--The Story of the Narcotics Gangs,* and in order to protect Judy he referred to her as "one of our loveliest screen stars."[14]

There was a shake-up going on at MGM. Nick Schenck insisted that Mayer take on an assistant and Dore Schary came on board July 1, 1948. Mayer was left in charge of the musicals. *Easter Parade* made $3 million and Judy was Metro's prime asset.

Judy had moved in with her agent, Carlton Aslop, and his wife, Sylvia. Judy was on suspension, but Alsop negotiated $50,000 for two numbers in the movie *Words and Music* made in 1948. One day Judy was late on the set; Mickey Rooney said, "Pal, if she isn't here, there's a damn good reason for it. And when she shows—and she'll show, believe me— she'll jump right in and be the best frigging thing in the picture!" At 3 p.m., Judy showed and proved Mickey correct. Sylvia was feeding her well, and we can see the difference in her weight and length of hair between "I Wish I Were in Love Again" and "Johnny One Note" filmed some weeks apart.

Just recently, I found an extract from *Modern Screen Magazine,* May 1949, in which Ethel Gumm (or Garland, as she was calling herself then) defended herself and the way Judy was reared. It was a very strange article, full of misinformation that is quite fascinating in itself. She insists Judy went to a regular high school. This was not correct; everyone knew that Judy attended the MGM school and worked all day filming. Ethel denies that Judy was not

strong, although we know from records that Judy spent time in hospitals repeatedly for acidosis. She ends the article saying, "I know that Judy is completely happy." I can only assume that it was common knowledge around town about how ill Judy was, and some of the blame lay on Ethel.

In the Good Old Summertime, made in 1949, was a delightful movie. Judy recorded four of the seven songs in one session. "Meet Me Tonight in Dreamtime," "Put Your Arms

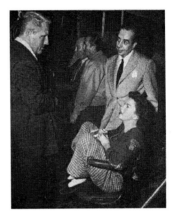

Around Me," "Play That Barbershop Chord," "I Don't Care," and "Merry Christmas." Judy showed off her comic talents again in the first scene when her skirt is torn, as she would in an early scene with Gene Kelly in *The Pirate* when her hat is ruined. During filming, Judy visited her friend, Spencer Tracy on the set of *Father of the Bride.* Van Johnson was to say later, "We made her feel wanted and needed. We joked with her and kept her happy." Joe Pasternak, who had a rose sent to her dressing room every day, said of Judy,

> But, in my view, a great artist is entitled to a lot more latitude than, let us say, a producer. The quality that makes her great makes her feel more deeply... All of us felt—and you don't often feel this way in Hollywood—that we would accommodate ourselves gladly to work with Judy...Those of us who worked with her knew her magical genius and respected it...For myself, I am lucky to have had the privilege of working with her." [15]

94

It is a pity others at MGM did not have the same respect for her.

MGM bought *Annie Get Your Gun,* and we all looked forward to seeing it. The production started off badly: Frank Morgan got sick, Howard Keel broke a leg, and the pressure was on Judy to begin shooting. She pre-recorded eight songs between March 25 and April 1, 1949, but with Busby Berkeley as the director, the stress was too much for her and she was replace with Betty Hutton as Annie Oakley. An illegal LP release of Judy's pre-recording was much loved by all the fans. How we wished we could have seen Judy in the role! Eventually, Berkeley was removed from the film and Charles (Chuck) Walters brought in, but by then Judy told him she did not have the energy or nerve to continue. "It's too late, Chuck," Judy sadly replied. "I haven't got the energy or the nerve anymore." Nor had she, "I couldn't learn anything," she recalled. "I couldn't retain anything. I was just up there making strange noises. Here I was, in the middle of a million-dollar property, with a million-dollar wardrobe, with a million eyes on me, and I was in a complete daze. I knew it, and everyone around me knew it. But I desperately tried to go on. I knew that if I didn't finish this one, it was the finish of me. So I kept on."[16]

In an effort to get her out of her depression, a new doctor, Fred Polirs, persuaded her to undergo shock treatment—six in all. This was their brightest star and they gave her shock treatment! Lorna Smith told me that Judy talked about this treatment in 1969 while Lorna was Judy's dresser at the *Talk of the Town.* [17]

Marc Rabwin had recommended Polirs who remained Judy's her doctor for many years.

Here we have a formula for disaster: Judy having to sing and dance for someone who used to scream at her, "Open your eyes, I want to see your eyes!" No wonder she reverted to her seven-year-old self and was unable to perform. She tried and tried but finally collapsed. No one cared. Therefore, they threw her out and got someone else in, as they told Anslinger a few years earlier.

Later Betty Hutton talked about the situation on the set in an interview with USA Today on June 19, 2000. The film was the top-grossing musical up to that time and a triumph for Hutton. Looking back on the movie fifty years later, however, Hutton's feelings for *Annie* have soured. She had snagged the role she wanted more than any other, but she says the cast and crew were angry that she had replaced Garland and treated her so coldly it destroyed the joy she felt in performing.

> "Me and Judy both died that day [when she replaced Garland]. We talked a lot when that *Annie* thing was over. We became very good friends....There's never been a talent like Judy Garland, and there will never be another one."[18]

These comments are in contrast to the ones issued from the studio to the effect that the cast and crew were angry with Judy and glad to have Betty in the role.

Judy talked about Louis B. Mayer to James Goode:

> He had moments of kindness and he followed them. I had just been thrown out of Metro, after 16 years. I was ill and I didn't have any money to go into a hospital. I went to L.B. Mayer and asked him if the studio would lend me some money. Mayer hadn't wanted to throw me out and he called Nick Schenck (chairman of the board) in New York while I was in the office and asked if they could loan me some money. Schenck told him that they were not running a charity institution. Mayer hung up and said something strange and somewhat marvelous: 'If they'll do this to you, they'll do this to me, too,' and they did, as you know. He lent me the money himself and I paid him back. [19]

Carlton Alsop took Judy to Peter Bent Brigham Hospital in Boston on May 29, 1949. It was a regular hospital, not a mental hospital. The hospital diagnosed her as suffering from malnutrition. Mayer paid expenses for Alsop. Sylvia was playing summer stock in the area. In three to four weeks, Judy was off all medicines and eating three meals a day and sleeping with lights out at 9 pm. She was free to come and go and attended baseball games. After a month, Judy moved to the Ritz Carlton Hotel and went in to see Dr. Rose at 2 p.m. each day. Sinatra sent a record player, jacket, and flowers and offered to fly out when she could have visitors. Liza came out with her nurse to visit Judy on her twenty-seventh birthday, and they went out to Cape Cod for a few days.

One of the tests was an electroencephalogram to rule out a tumor, and Judy had to go over to the children's hospital next door. Judy often talked about her visits to this hospital and how talking and singing to the children helped to get her well. Some of the children were classified as retarded or brain damaged. She particularly loved to tell the story of the little girl who had not talked while in hospital and finally on Judy's last day, called out to her.

At the end of August she returned to California. *In the Good Old Summertime* had done well, so of course, the studio wanted to put Judy back to work

Judy's last movie with MGM was *Summer Stock* (1950). Songs were "Happy Harvest," "If You Feel Like Singing, Sing," and "Friendly Star." Friends surrounded Judy, but this did not help her insecurities. Judy took a break from filming and visited her friend, Spencer Tracy on the set of Father of the Bride.

Actually, Judy asked to be relieved from the movie because she was 15 pounds overweight and didn't feel well, but Dore Schary insisted that Mayer get the movie done. Charles Walter directed and the cast included Gene Kelly and Judy's old friend Phil Silvers. Dottie Ponedel continued as Judy's make-up artist. The movie dragged on and Gene Kelly talked in the book, *Gene Kelly*, "Every time one of the kids left," Gene said, "we'd have a farewell party. Judy was always invited, and she always came. And not only did she come, but the same woman who the day before was incapable of uttering a sound, would sing her heart out. We had about nine or ten parties during *Summer Stock*; each time Judy was the star turn. She'd perform for hours and the kids just loved and adored her. Everybody did. As long as the cameras weren't turning she was fine." [20]

This goes to prove that Judy was quite capable of singing, and she was happy with her friends around her, but she could not work for the authority people when ordered to do so. She had no choice, the damage, done to her by her mother in Lancaster, came to the fore and she was incapable of performing. This confirms the thesis of the Apted study, which proves the Jesuit saying, *"Give me a child until he is seven, and I will show you the man."* The memories of the times she was forced to perform in front of unresponsive agents and managers came back to her, and she was physically unable to perform. These stresses on her body made her emotionally unstable and physically ill. Kelly says there were times she could scarcely stand; he and Chuck Walters had to support her. On one particularly good day, though, they filmed "The Portland Fancy" dance routine and we see the old Judy.

After the main movie was finished, Judy went away for a time and came back considerably lighter. Her final number at MGM was "Get Happy." Saul Chaplin sang the song to her three times, and after a few days, she came back to the studio and just looked at the words because she did not read music. By the third take, it was perfect. For filming Judy wore the outfit which had been created for "Mr. Monotony," in the *Easter Parade* but not included in the movie: the fedora, tux jacket and ascot. These publicity photographs from this movie are some of the classics in the Judy collections. Judy went up to Carmel for a rest as her doctor had recommended at least eight months off work.

However, the fates were against Judy. June Allyson became pregnant just as she was to start filming *Royal Wedding* (eventually released in 1951) with Astaire, and the studio asked Judy to come back. Unfortunately, she accepted. On May 23 she was back in Culver City. Things did not go well. By June 16, the studio informed Judy that she was under suspension again, and there was another half-hearted scratch on the throat. Judy could not perform, so they replaced her with Jane Powell. (Jane and Judy talked about this on episode 10 during one of Judy's 1963-64 CBS television series). This was exactly the way Mayer told Harry Anslinger, Commissioner of Narcotics that the studio would deal with Judy's inability to perform. She was just a piece of machinery that malfunctioned.

Some people realized what had happened to Judy. In June, 1950, *Daily Variety* ran a leading article written by its editor, Arthur Unger:

> …the people employed in films are human beings. And to single them out for the purpose of printing some juicy gossip or scandal about them seems to be the prime motivation behind the success of some columnists…. the studio to wake up and stop feeding the dirt mongers with insidious gossip; …they shouldn't try to get even with a star with whom they are peeved by giving the dirt mongers a lad to blast stars like Judy.[21]

The studio wanted the viewing audience to think Judy was incapable of performing. They believed they were justified in firing her, and pressure was on Bing Crosby not to have Judy on his radio show. However, Bing and Judy were good friends, so he ignored this pressure, and we can hear how well she sounded a few weeks after the mess at MGM when she had been able to rest. On February 7, Bing Crosby had Judy as a guest for four programs, and in March they sang, "How Could You Believe Me When I Said I Loved You When You Know I've Been a Liar All My Life?" from the *Barkleys of Broadway*, the movie Judy could not make. She also appeared on the Bob Hope show January 30, 1951, a couple of months before she left for England.

Tony Curtis talks of Judy with great sensitivity:

> Judy was a woman of infinite grace; a woman and a child at the same time. I don't think she really had a childhood. She got into show business with her family, the Gumm Sisters, and was on the road from the time she was a little girl, then ended up at MGM at the age of thirteen. She was under constant stress. She was never really happy in her marriages or as a person. She was only happy when she worked—when she sang and danced. In 1951 I met her again with Janet Leigh, who was a good friend of hers, and we went to a party where I couldn't take my eyes off her. She was so gracious and kind to everybody around her. Yet I always felt a sadness in her, something unreconciled and never as fulfilling as it should have been for her. [22]

The ending to this segment should be the words of E. Y. Harburg who saw Judy perform before MGM discovered her, saw a yearning in her, and watched what happened through the years. He wrote "Over the Rainbow" and spent many years in Hollywood then left disenchanted in 1943 to return to Broadway. He said:

> There never was a real world for Judy Garland. It was a phony world right from the word go when her father got her into vaudeville at the age of 4 [actually two years and a half] to sing "Jingle Bells." From then on this kid was exploited because she had a personality, a little voice, and a talent for the stage. She had no childhood; and then at the age of 14 she had a bang-up voice. Her voice, I think, was the greatest in the first part of our century. She went right through the bone and flesh into the heart.
>
> But what happens to a child of that kind? Immediately she's not a child but a commodity who gets a job in pictures.

And what do they do? The *Wizard of Oz* comes out a great big hit and Judy is a star so they think they must capitalize on her. One picture after another, three or four a year. And do you know what it is to make a picture? People think it's a romp but I don't think there is anything more traumatic to the nervous system. You get up at five every morning not having had a chance to sleep because there were studio parties the night before. Then there is the taking and retaking and constantly turning on emotions that are not yours. Your whole life is an emotional lie and an emotional drain. And when you are a child there is no play, no contact. You are aware of one thing all the time: applause, admiration, narcissism, how you look. How can you do that year after year and still be a child? And the worst damn thing of all is that your studio is exploiting you to the hilt while you're still good, but expecting you to fall. It's a tightrope.

Then we look at Judy Garland and we say, 'Oh, she's taken to drink. She's taken to drugs.' For God's sake, is there no humanity? The sheer cruelty of people, when you read the reports that she was booed when she came on the stage. That kid couldn't see straight. She couldn't stand on her feet. Her nervous system was shot. You were talking to a crippled person crippled by the studios, by exploitation – who never had one moment of naturalism since she was 4 years old.

Judy Garland's life was an elongated rack. I, who am only a writer who doesn't have to appear, feel this excitement, this tension, the working on a scene, the getting it, the not getting it.… It wraps me up at night so that the lyrics so racing through my head. So, like Judy did, you take one pill and at the end of a night it isn't working, so you take two, and then three. Then you mix them, and before you know where you are your nervous system is ruined.[23]

Judy was divorced from Minnelli; she kept Evanview House and Beach House. She sailed on the *Il de France* for England with companions and colleagues Myrtle Tully as secretary, Dottie Ponedel as make-up artists, and Buddy Pepper as accompanist.

PART FOUR

THE CONCERT YEARS

1951- 1955

Chapter 10

Judy comes to the London Palladium

Her love affair with Britain begins

How can I begin to talk about the Palladium and Judy? The impact of Judy upon London and the corresponding equally important impact of London upon Judy was a theatrical happening of major importance. Those who were there on opening night will never forget it. Next to singing "Jingle Bells" when she was two and a half years old and the birth of her three children, this was probably the next most significant happening in her life. [1]

We all have moments in life that define who we are; mine was in a youth hostel in Belgium in my early 20s surrounded by students of every nationality; I was completely at home and fascinated. I wanted to give up my job and wander off around the world talking to people. I did not realize at then that I am an anthropologist! Sadly, it took me many years and much study before I finally understood who I was. Judy knew when she return to the concert stage that this is where she was "home" and this was where she always had wanted to be. She was back on stage in an atmosphere similar to her father's theatres, and she was singing for people who loved her.

Judy's fifteen-year movie career MGM was over, but her stage career was not. Her talent and joy of singing and performing sent her across the Atlantic to the Palladium in London and her love affair with Great Britain. It was April, 1951, and Judy sailed into Southampton on the ship *Ile de France* on a bright spring day. Crowds cheered her, the ship's siren Morse-coded J_U_D_Y, and somebody handed her flowers. Judy said, "They told me that

people had a warm feeling for me in England, but I never thought it would be anything like this." Banners were out and many fans went to the dockside to greet her. Judy and her songs had helped the British people through the WWII years 1939-1945. Her movies, particularly those with inspirational themes including, *Strike up the Band,* and *Me and My Gal,* gave us hope. We heard Judy's voice on the radio continually during these years. Her bright, fresh, vital voice came through the sound waves and gave us joy - songs, such as "F.D. Roosevelt Jones" and "Great Day for the Irish," were constantly on our lips. In fact, I remember Judy's voice in my head even before I discovered her on the screen.

Europe had gone through a long and miserable war and life had been full of worry and anxiety. Life was still not back to

normal, there were food and clothing shortages, and bomb damage remained as a reminder. We in England had enjoyed the movies from Hollywood, particularly the musicals, with their swing music and vitality of the singers from the States. Among them, of course, was Judy. We were desperate for entertainment.

There had been a series of American stars appearing at the Palladium in 1950 and 51: Lena Horne, Frankie Lane, and

Mickey Rooney. Hoagy Carmichael preceded Judy, and as was the custom then, Hoagy introduced Judy on his last performance. The Palladium posters called her "Hollywood's Singing Sweetheart." Judy was nervous about this big career change even though she had with her secretary Myrtle Tully, pianist Buddy Pepper, make-up artist Dottie Ponedel, and the new man in her life, Sid Luft. Judy need not have feared the Londoners; they welcomed her warmly. The date was April 9, 1951.

There were two shows a night—6:30 and 8:30 p.m. On the first opening night, at 6:30 p.m., Judy wore a flared glittery lemon-yellow organza dress. I remember the words of John Barber:

> Bigger still for wearing yellow, with spangles, and with diamond ice at ears, throat and waist, and wrist—an ensemble that cheerfully upholds her reputation as the worst-dressed woman on the screen. I thought black would look better till I saw the black gown she chose for the second house.[2]

Judy started with special material by Roger Edens, "Here I Am," then a melody of "The Boy Next Door," "Embraceable You," and "Lime House Blues". Judy talked later about how

nervous she had been, how her knees locked and she could not move so she ended up falling over after jangling herself up with the microphone wires. She sat down in surprise, realized the ridiculousness of her predicament, and burst into laughter. The audience joined her. Her friends in that first night audience, like Noël Coward, stood up and cheered her on. Buddy Pepper, her pianist, helped her up. She went on with the show more relaxed. She did something which she would often do: kick off her shoes!

Judy would comment later that, "That's probably one of the most graceless exits."[3]

The newspapers were full of news about Judy; I read and re-read them repeatedly, and they became etched on my memory. *The Daily Telegraph* said, "It was not only with her voice but with her whole personality that she filled the theatre... Miss Garland's charm is in complete absence of affectation. She presented herself with no particular preparation and no preamble, and just did what she must have been born to do —sing...Not only is she in perfect control of her voice but she is a natural interpreter as well, seeming to feel—and able to transmit emotions she sing about. " [4]

I remember particularly Beverley Baxter's on the day after the opening.

> This sturdy young woman bowed and smiled as the cheering went on, but there were no tears, no trembling of the lips or wobbling of the chin. She was a trouper who had come to give a performance. She possesses a real voice, a voice which even has beauty in its softer moments and her face is expressive because she plays no tricks...The truth is that Miss Garland is now better than her material. This quality of vibrant sincerity opens up possibilities which probably she, herself has failed to realize. She can command pathos without being maudlin. She is above the wailing nonsense of the crooner who could not sleep a wink last night and all that sort of drivel. In fact, she is an artist. We saw a brave woman on Monday, but more than that we saw a woman who has emerged from the shadows and finds that the public likes her as she is, even more than what she was.[5]

Judy's friends were loyal; they loved her and would do anything to help her. Kay Thompson was there standing in the wings. Always in Judy's shows, one song would stand out for me. In the 1951 Palladium, the song was "Rock-a-bye Your Baby with a Dixie Melody". Before she left the States, Judy had shown her material to ex-husband Vincente

Minnelli and he had suggested this song.

It had been my life's ambition, at nineteen years old, to see Judy in person and the evening April 12 finally arrived. It really did not matter to me whether she spoke or sung; she could have  just stood there and I would have been content. Judy came out from stage right (the left side of the state her usual entrance); I was transfixed. Maybe I did not even clap or breathe for a few minutes. I sat there stunned. Of course, I eventually came alive and every minute of her performance was impressed in my brain. I would go on to see four more of Judy's shows during this run and each one was different. Judy performed on a different wavelength every evening; some nights the happy songs were ecstatic and the sad songs just quiet. Another evening the sad songs would absolutely break your heart and the happy songs were simply fine. I always felt that Judy could be compared to an artist like Monet. He painted  the same cathedral many times, but each painting was different. Every time Judy sang a song she brought a different interpretation to it. Later her conductors would make the same remarks about her talents.

Judy handed the Palladium stage to Danny Kaye and went on a two-week holiday to Europe. She bought clothes from Dior and Balmain in Paris. She went on to do shows in Glasgow and Edinburgh in May.

She was the first big American star to tour Scotland and Ireland. She told the audience in Edinburgh On May 28 that her grandfather's name was Milne, he was originally from Aberdeen and her grandmother was from Ireland. She told audiences that she and her sisters danced a fling with their grandfather with the house full of music. She also sang "Flower of Scotland" for them and, of course, completely captivated audiences everywhere. Many stories from this tour show Judy's accessibility and lack of ego. Many hundreds of "poverty row" youngsters waited all day at the stage entrance for her, not really know who she was because they had never seen her on the screen. One matinee she bought seats for all of them and treated them to an ice cream and cake party on stage afterwards. On closing night a five-year-old handed her a small nosegay of flowers.[6]

Judy had a marvelous time in Ireland in July, singing all her Irish songs: "Danny Boy," "Wearing of the Green," "Nellie Kelly," "It's a Great Day for the Irish," and "A Pretty Girl Milking her Cow." She was completely at home, and she and Sid felt as if they actually had a vacation.

Then there were weeks in Manchester and Liverpool. In June Judy returned to London for a midnight benefit for Sid Fields. Everyone one in London was there, including Danny Kaye, Sir Lawrence Olivier, and Sir Richard Attenborough. Three and a half hours into the show it was time for Judy to perform and the following words from Lord Attenborough sums up the evening perfectly, recorded by Gary Horrocks, in the Rainbow Review Issue 29/30:

> The first time I ever went on stage with Judy was in 1951 at the Sid Field Benefit. I think probably it carried with it the greatest galaxy of world stars perhaps that has ever appeared at the London Palladium. It was to honour Sid who we all adored. And that was the occasion when I first met Judy . I did try to summarise what I felt when I wrote this review. "In the small hours of a June day, back in '51 the waif like figure of Judy Garland stood in the centre of the London Palladium stage. She lifted her head with the curious little movement that is hers alone – half shy, half defiant, yet with artless humility, and began to sing Rockabye Your Baby With A Dixie Melody. To those of us listening on the stage and in the auditorium it was a moment never to be forgotten. We were all there that night to pay homage to a great comedian. When Judy began to sing, she released a wave of emotion. It wasn't just the song; nor was it

the way she sang it. It was nothing to do with pathos, or with memories – it was just magic. The lonely little figure, down by the footlights, made us all cry in the same way that Sid had always made us cry. Working from the same chemistry, she conjured up for us those rare and indefinable secrets that Sid had always shared in the same way with his audience. And I was reminded of this when I played a record called quite simply *Miss Show Business.*" She does make you cry, and she did make you cry, and you can't really talk about her without becoming emotional.[7]

The last stop was a week in Birmingham in July, and then Judy took Liza to the French Riviera for a week. Lorna Smith was present on this occasion and made the following comments in her book:

Initially the audience was more reserved than the Londoners, but by the intermission they were cheering and by the end of the second half, the audience rose to its feet and were standing in the aisles…she said she had no more songs except a slow one and they insisted she go ahead with "You'll Never walk Alone." The audience joined in picking up a passage usually sung by the choir. Finally, she had to repeat something she had done earlier, "The Trolley Song." A man commented afterwards that he had never seen anyone work so hard.[8]

These four months in Great Britain gave Judy a new lease on life and cemented her relationship with the people. Many times through the years, she would say she was home when coming back to England. She spent her last few months in London before she left us for the last time from her home in Cadogan Mews.

Chapter 11

The Luft Dynasty

Between London Palladium 1951
And Dominion 1957

The Palace, New York 1952, Luft Dynasty, A Star is Born, Capitol Records, Friends and Relatives.

Between Judy's visits to London in 1951 and 1957 she had been

PALACE TWO-A-DAY

RKO PALACE THEATRE

busy: in-between giving birth to daughter Lorna (in 1952) and son (in 1955), she worked steadily. The success of her British concerts (she performed all over England, Scotland and Ireland—the first American artist of any standing to do so) led Sid Luft to want to recreate this success and excitement in New York. He wanted to find a theatre similar to the Palladium. As he walked down Broadway one day, he noticed the Palace, which was being used as a cinema. In the old days of vaudeville, every act wanted to be booked into the Palace. Luft contacted the owners and negotiated for Judy to return to the Palace. Roger Edens agreed to write special material for her. On opening night, there was so much excitement in town that streets near the theatre were closed to accommodate the crowds. Judy was back on top! Everyone who was anyone in New York was there. Judy opened on October 16, 1951 and completed the 19-week extended run on February 24, 1952, for a total of 184 performances.

Jan Glazier, wife of Richard Glazier the pianist and entertainer, currently hosts a Judy Garland Family Group, of which I am a member, and in April of 2011, she arranged a get-together in New York to coincide with the 50th Anniversary of Judy's Carnegie Hall performance.

Our group was able to tour Carnegie Hall and the Palace Theatre— both venues where Judy

played to sold-out crowds. At the Palace, many in the group stood (Heather Siebert) and even sat on the edge of the stage where Judy had sung her "Over the Rainbow." Albert Poland (mentioned later in this chapter) was kind enough to arrange for us to meet Philip J. Smith, Chairman of the Shubert Organization and Foundation. Smith talked to us about the days in 1951-1952 when he worked with Judy at the Palace. At that time, he was the

General Manager of the theatre and had worked his way up from usher. He said that Judy was very friendly and "democratic" with everyone, and when she decided to have a party, she invited everyone from the ushers up to the general manager. At the Christmas party everyone received a present from Judy, each of which was personal and suitable to the individual person, like a sweater, for example. The words Smith used several times to describe Judy were "a sweetheart," "friendly" and "warm." I had often wanted to be inside the Palace to see the theatre where Judy spent so much time, and finally I was able to do so. I was surprised to observe that it seemed smaller than the Palladium in London.

During our time together on this occasion, there was a suggestion that a book should be written about Judy's fans. Gordon Stevens suggested Coyne Steven Sanders should write it, but he passed the project to me. So I am including some stories and photographs and perhaps someone else will pick the project up and finish it. These times when we are all together celebrating Judy's magic

are joyous time. In-between functions which Jan Glazier has organized, we have meals and socialize. Gordon Stevens came down from Canada, Gary Horrocks, Justin Sturge joined us from England, and Crystal Kalyana Crawford and Rose Stephens came from Australia to join the New York based friends of Judy, Mickie Esemplare, Daniel Berghaus, Elizabeth Rublein, Juliana Hanford, Heather Siebert, Bill Seibel, Stephen

Paley, Martha Wade Steketee and visit famed spots such as Sardi's.

On March 30, 1952, Judy received a special Antoinette (Tony) Award for her "Important contribution to the revival of vaudeville."

Judy and Sid's divorces from their previous partners were finalized at the end of March. In addition, it was during the 19-week Palace run that Judy met Dirk Bogarde for the first time. He was in New York with Kate (Kay Kendall, British actress) and she was dragging him reluctantly around to social activities. It was New Year's Eve and Dirk did not want to go out, but Kate insisted he had to attend "the best party in town" at the Gilbert Millers, so he went. Suddenly Kate came up to him and said there is someone in the next room who wanted to meet him.

> And there she was. Sitting in a bit of a lump in the corner, dressed in pink, hair very short, plump, jolly, and laughing a great deal at something that Rubinstein was saying to her. She had a thin jade bracelet on one wrist, pearl ear-rings…the wide, brown, laughing eyes I knew so well. Kate introduced us and I kissed her quite simply on the lips. I said, 'Oh…I love you!' and she laughed her extraordinary chuckling laugh and said, 'Oh no! I love you!' and I burned a hole right through the bodice of her dress with the tip of my cigarette. Judy Garland. She gave a little scream, and then we laughed, and she pulled me down beside her and made me sit there on the floor and I stayed there, on and off, for almost ten years. Almost..[1]

Judy insisted that Dirk come to see her show at the Palace show the night before he returned to England. On arrival, he was astounded to find the theatre almost empty and appalled at the first half with vaudeville acts like Hungarian dancers. After the interval, the theatre filled and out came Judy. Afterwards, Judy and Dirk sat on the steps outside her dressing room while he assured her that she was great. "Was I good? Did you like me? Did you really? As good as that! You're kidding? What's the matter with the dogs and the Hungarians?" He assured her she didn't need any opening acts, and I think this was the seed that was planted in her head when later she did the two concerts at the Palladium in August and September 1960 and later Carnegie Hall. [2]

After the Palace run, Sid and Judy spent two weeks vacationing in Palm Beach. Their companions were the Duke and Duchess of Windsor, whom they had met during Judy's run at the Palace. In 1997, Luft commented on this vacation when talking to fans at the Grand Rapids celebration. Judy had been thrilled to know that the Duke knew all of her songs, but this was not surprising to me because everyone in wartime England heard Judy singing regularly on the radio from the mid-1930's onwards.

Judy and Sid went back to Los Angeles and Judy opened a four-week engagement at the Los Angeles Philharmonic Auditorium on April 21. The opening was a great success. Everyone in Hollywood was there, and afterwards there was a big party at Romanoff's. Somewhere along this time, Judy recorded three Bing Crosby shows which aired in late May and June. Judy was riding on a big wave of success and ready to tackle Hollywood again. That month she recorded four songs for Columbia: "Send My Baby Back to Me," "Without a Memory," "Go Home Joe," and "Heartbroken."

Then Judy went to San Francisco for a four-week stint at the

Curran Theatre beginning on May 26. Two personal things happened during this period. Ethel Gumm unsuccessfully tried to make contact with Judy and Judy and Sid had a quiet wedding at Bob Law's large ranch in Hollister, ninety miles southeast of San Francisco. (Bob Law was the brother of Ted Law, Sid's racing partner and millionaire oil drilling friend.) The newly married couple returned to Los Angeles and rented a house on North Maple Drive, Beverly Hills—a fashionable street where Louella Parsons and Hedda Hopper lived.

Judy had done a radio production of *Star* with Walter Pidgeon in December 1942. She wanted to make the movie at MGM, but the studio preferred to keep her in flossy musicals. Now that her production company had control, Moss Hart would adapt the 1937 version of the script and Harold Arlen and Ira Gershwin would write the songs. But Judy was pregnant and the movie would wait until daughter Lorna was born in November.

Sid, Judy, and family went to New York over Christmas for a break. Judy's mother, Ethel died of a heart attack on January 5, 1953, in the parking lot of the Douglas aircraft factory where she worked. Judy and family flew back although Judy was afraid of flying. Jimmy, her husband, Johnny, and daughter, Judalein, flew in from Dallas. Suzy and Jack Cathcart were living in Los Angeles.

JUDY'S SISTERS

Judy's two elder sisters appeared to have a good relationship with their mother, and one cannot help but wonder about the reasons for Judy's anger against her mother. Was it those many trips from Lancaster into Los Angeles for auditions- or the abortion Ethel insisted Judy have when married to David Rose? Perhaps the final straw was when Ethel sued for maintenance. The case was dismissed when Judy pointed out that her mother had a good career as a pianist, accompanist, and theatre manager. She had records to show her mother had been paid when she was Judy's manager.

The sisters—all the changes of names, always fascinated me. Did that happen in other families? Why were they trying to change themselves, reinvent themselves or change history? Was there something about their 'crazy moving around show business life' that left them continually searching for something? We have to look at the lives of the sisters.

The eldest, Mary Jane, sometimes called Janey and eventually Suzanne, fell in love with a sax player, Lee Cahn, and married him in 1935, at the time Judy's discovery in Lake Tahoe. The marriage lasted until 1939 when she met and married Jack Cathcart, a trumpeter, whose band played for Judy for many years. The couple lived in Las Vegas for a few years and eventually Cathcart left Suzanne, who committed suicide in 1964 while Judy was recovering from illness in Hong Kong. She had no children.

Dorothy Virginia (Jimmie), the middle sister, married Bobby Sherwood, and they had a daughter, Judalein, who died in the 1980s. Jimmie seems to have been closer to Judy because they often lived in the same home with Ethel, and Judy adored her niece. Later, when the marriage broke up, she worked as a script girl for four years while Judy was making films at MGM. In 1949 Jimmie met and married Johnny Thompson, a graduate of the Julliard School of Music, and an arranger for Benny Goodman. He had moved to Hollywood in the mid-1940s and arranged for Harry James, as well as Judy. In the mid-1950s, they moved to New York where he arranged for Tommy Dorsey. They finally moved to his home town of Dallas, Texas, where he produced television and radio commercials, and later worked for the post office. Jimmie seemed to have the most settled life of the sisters, or so she tried to tell us. Interestingly, she gave many interviews concerning her sister Judy's life, unfailingly pointing out how difficult her sister was, and defending their mother. Later in life, she gave many interviews portraying herself as marrying a mail carrier and living quietly in Dallas. However, her husband was a musician, and they moved around while he was arranging for big bands, so again we have history re-written.

Life went on and in the summer or fall of 1953, Sid purchased a nineteen-room Tudor mansion on Mapleton Drive where they would live until 1960. In Grand Rapids in 1997, Joey told us it was a beautiful three-story house, and he loved living there. Because of an option in the contract with Warners, Sid was able to buy the set furnishing from *A Star is Born* at 20% of wholesale and so we can imagine the Mapleton house with furniture from Norman Maine's Malibu Beach House—the sofas, chairs and paintings.

JUDY'S FRIENDS

Judy had many close women friends during this time in Los Angeles; she was able to renew her friendships with many of them. In 1953, Judy was living next door to Lana Turner. Their kitchens overlooked each other. Cheryl Crane, Lana's daughter, writes about that time in her books.[3] Lana and Judy had been together at Metro and had many of the same friends and lovers: Artie Shaw, Robert Taylor, and Tyrone Power. Judy and Lana attended the MGM School together and went out socially with Mickey Rooney, Anne Rutherford, Virginia Grey, and Bonita Granville. MGM monitored fan letters in a nine-month period in 1944, and both Lana and Judy had 200,000 fan mail letters ahead of the rest of the actors in the studio.[4]

Liza and Cheryl became great friends—Liza was seven years old and two years younger than Cheryl was. Cheryl said that Liza knew all her mother's stage routines and would stand on the roof of the garage and belt out numbers using a pinecone for a microphone. Cheryl would sit at Judy's feet and listen when Lana and Judy were chatting. Judy was not like the usual movie star in fancy clothes with lots of make-up, she usually wore flats, black toreador pants, and a short ponytail. Judy was always full of laughter and easy-going and allowed Liza to ride her bike on Mapleton Drive wearing sneakers and blue jeans. Liza loved the glamour of Lana, and the girls decided to swap mothers.

Crane writes that the mothers decided to humor them and set out rules. The exchange did not last long because her first request of Judy was to ride her bike on Mapleton. "Sorry," said Judy, smiling sadly, "'No."[5]

Crane also mentions that Judy's mother was definitely a stage mother and appeared not to stop the uppers and downers that the studio provided to Judy, and she felt her grandmother would not have allowed this to happen to her mother.[6]

Another of Judy's friends was Lauren Bacall (called Betty) who lived two doors down on Mapleton Drive. Their children were of similar ages, and Lorna played with Betty's son, Stephen, and shared many family activities. Judy had become friends with

Humphrey Bogart way back in her early MGM years when she was married to Vincente Minnelli and in a social group that included Dorothy Parker, Ira Gershwin, Oscar Levant, Groucho Marx, Lena Horne, and John Huston. Both Lana Turner and Judy worked in a campaign organized by Bogart to help re-elect Roosevelt in November 1944 with Judy singing the fund-raising tune "The Song of the Checkbooks."[7] Judy had a long friendship with Bogart, who was not one to suffer fools gladly.

Other girl friends from the years at MGM who remained close with Judy were June Allyson, Kay Thompson, Dottie Ponedel, Lucille Ball, and Debbie Reynolds. June was a friend from way back in *Girl Crazy* times. Judy would often pick her up in those days and take her into the studio in her limo. Judy warned June, "Don't let Papa Mayer send you out to entertain at birthday parties. They'll treat you like hired help."[8] Judy also talked of her mother dragging her around the country to put in stage appearances as Baby Frances, while her father stayed home running a small movie house.[9] Judy felt that she was living the life her mother had wanted for herself.[10] Judy and June were friends all through the MGM years, when they both lived in Holmby Hills, through Judy's CBS television series and Judy's last days in England. She joined Judy at nights when Sid was out, the way Debbie Reynolds would do later.

Allyson said:

> Judy Garland was always the center of attention at any party she gave or attended and I would always be found walking around in her shadow, even at my own parties. When she would sing, I would sit on the floor near her and just worship her. I was a worshiper of talent. But in the case of Judy, I would bask in her warmth, her sincerity, her generosity. Whatever she did, at that moment, she gave herself to it completely.[11]

Dottie Ponedel was another great friend. She came out to Los Angeles from Chicago in the early 1920s, and initially she did extra work and dancing roles in silent movies but quickly moved into the career which was her real calling, making people beautiful. She made up all of the big stars of the 1930s, like Marlene Dietrich, May West, and Joan Blondell. Dottie was asked to do make up for Judy in *Meet Me in St. Louis*. They became great friends, and she was Judy's make-up artist in all her movies at MGM. Dottie accompanied Judy to London in 1951

for her Palladium appearance. Soon after returning home Dottie came down with multiple sclerosis. Her working days were over, but not her friendship with Judy.[12] Dottie's niece, Meredith Ponedel, went to live with her aunt when she was about 3 years ago and tells delicious stories of Judy's visits to Dot and their chatting and laughing in the kitchen of Dot's house. I hope that one day Meredith will get her book written about her aunt and everyone can enjoy her stories.

One of Judy's most consistent and longtime friends was Kay Thompson. Judy met her while working on a radio program in New York when Judy was 16 years old. Kay was known for startling vocal arrangements. Sam Irwin writes in his book, *Kay Thompson*:

> She loved to take a song, do the first verse straight, then reinvent it, changing the tempo, adding lyrics, and improvising, improbable flourishes that spiraled into the wild blue yonder. Her groundbreaking swing arrangements oozed Thompsonian gusto at every fast-and-furious turn. Now everyone appreciated her tampering, however. To the ears of übercolmnist Walter Winchell, she crossed the line by reinventing Hoagy Carmichael's "Stardust." Appalled that Key had "messed around with it on the air," Winchell chastised her for being "sacrilegious." Winchell did not forgive and forget, either. In 1937, he declared, "Kay Thompson simply spoils hits by re-writing them." [13]

By 1942, Thompson was in Hollywood and managed to get herself hired to work as a music arranger and voice coach for the finale of *Presenting Lily Mars*, referred to in an earlier chapter. She worked on many different movies and helped countless stars improve their performances, among them: Lena Horne, Van Johnson, Hazel Scott, Dick Powell, June Allyson, Lucille Ball, Frank Sinatra, Gloria De Haven, Ava Gardner and Margaret O'Brien.[14]

Although she worked on many movies, her prime interest was helping Judy. They became firm friends and enjoyed many social activities. Thompson and her husband, Bill Spier were godparents to daughter, Liza.[15] Thompson was present at many Judy's recording sessions and concerts guiding and helping her.

After the death of Judy in 1969 Thompson returned to New York from Rome, where she had been living, and stayed close to goddaughter Liza, supporting and encouraging her career, for the rest of her life, fulfilling the unspoken requirements of a godparent—to fill the role of parents when that parent is unable to do so.

Women's friendships are very important and digging back into my Anthropology background, we must look at these relationships. The most important thing to remember is that "99% of the time man, as a species, has been on earth, it was as a hunter and gatherer" told to me by the great Physical Anthropologist, Dr. Robert Jurmain at San Jose State University one day back in the 1980s. This profound statement opened my eyes to understanding of man, as a species. If we look at the lives of people then, we see they lived in groups with no more than 30-100, and they spent their lives following different herds of animals, from which they gained their subsistence. They would move when their herd moved, consequently enforced infantile restrictions applied. The families lived in caves, or shelters made of rocks, branches and animal skins. After about 8,000-12,000 years ago, settlements began to appear, mainly in the Middle East, and the groups could manage more than one child less than 5 years of age and populations increased. The men were the hunters and they would go off to look for an animal protein for the family–often they were gone for eight days or more. We see these male roles being played out today in the fishing and hunting men enjoy and participation at sports events. The women were the gatherers looking for fruit and seeds to sustain the family until the men returned. They tended the family site, looking after each other and the small number of children. The bonds formed then are the basis for women's relationships now.

The women supported each other in this difficult life. We see this relationship now in young teenagers experimenting with clothes and make-up; friends sharing the joy and perhaps hurt in love affairs and marriage; frustrations with parents and ultimate grief at their death and times of great sorrow which can only be shared with a another woman—their own family is in too much pain. Women need their women friends to help them through life. This was the relationship between Kay Thompson and Judy Garland—a true woman's friendship.

The Lufts did not live a frugal life. Sid was constantly remodeling the house, and they had many more staff members than most of their neighbors; a butler, gardener, cook, two maids, nurse, nanny and a handyman. Bogart, who was cautious with money, advised Sid to use his business manager, but nothing changed. I had met Sid many times in England and observed how he was always immaculately dressed. In Grand Rapids, 1997, I noticed the addition of many gold chains. I sensed that not all of Judy's friends approved of Sid and his life style, but Judy loved him, and so what could they do? They knew that Judy worked very hard and felt Sid spent too much time at the racetrack and gambling. Lauren Bacall said of her

> She was a complicated woman of tremendous wit and intelligence who had survived a distorted childhood and distorted marriages and relationships that had left their mark. ....She was fun and, when we'd sit quietly of an afternoon or evening, great company.[16]

A STAR IS BORN

We in England were starved for news of Judy, apart from the four songs from Columbia, which I still have. We heard about the movie she was making, *A Star is Born*. I remember the first time I heard Judy singing "The Man That Got Away". I was home ill with the flu, and suddenly blaring from the radio was this magnificent voice thundering around the room, and I stood holding on to the back of the sofa. It was Judy, not as I had heard her before, but with the full power of her stage performances.

Eventually the *A Star is Born LP* was released and we listened to it, trying to imagine the scenes we would see on the screen. We did not know then about the problems during the making the movie. I went up to London from the suburbs to see it. Everyone applauded as her name came up on the screen; it was thrilling and magnificent. Later we learned about the massacre, which inflicted on the film.

In August, Transcona Enterprises was formed with Judy and Sid owning 75%, Ted Law 5% and Eddie Alperson, 20%. Vernon Alves became Production Assistant. It was Eddie Alperson who had originally bought the rights of *A Star is Born*.

During the spring and summer of 1953, Moss Hart revised the 1937 version of the screenplay by Dorothy Parker, Alan Campbell and Robert Carson. Harold Arlen and Ira Gershwin composed the songs.

The movie had some stops and starts because the studio was not certain which filming processes to use. It started in August and took ten months to complete in part due to a decision in early October to film the movie in Cinemascope, which meant they had to re-film what had been shot up to that point. Filming finally finished in July 1954.

At the world premiere at Hollywood's Pantages Theatre on September 29, 1954, everyone was foretelling success. The premiere was broadcast live on NBC-TV and is still available on video. It was a big old-fashioned opening with an after-party held afterwards at the Cocoanut Grove. The movie premiered in New York on October 11.

This masterpiece lasted (in its original uncut form)3 hours and 16 minutes, and one could guess the length itself would lead to trouble. The theatre owners complained that the movie was so long that they could not make money from concessions. This caused Harry Warner to hack the movie to pieces. Sid and Judy were on vacation when they should have stayed and tried to control what the Warner brothers were doing to their masterpiece. It was reduced to a 181-minute version, which played until October 1954; then Harry Warner ordered more cuts so the movie could have more showings a day. A further twenty-seven minutes were cut from the movie. Eventually, most of these cuts were restored in the 1983 version.[17]

Judy also talked about the movie and how much money it cost to make when she thanked readers of the *Picturegoer* magazine for voting her the best actress of the year in 1955. She wrote to thank them, and the following are extracts from this article, which appeared June 9, 1956:

When I was told in Hollywood that you, the readers of *Picturegoer*, had voted me the best actress of 1955, I wanted to cry with gratitude. But I hope my crying days are over. I've already cried too much during my career. But I am deeply and humbly grateful to all of you....Once again I was the butt of the columnists who claimed I was temperamental. I failed to show up on time. I walked out during scenes. I fought with the director. I fought with the dance director. I fought with the cast. I missed one and a half days work due to a cold....I got on famously with George Cukor, the director, and James Mason and everyone else who was in the cast. The trouble was that for weeks on end there were constant changes to the script, decisions about dance numbers, sets and routine. Then after shooting the film in Warner Process they decided to begin all over again in Cinemascope. Everyone was on full salary all through these wretched delays. Yet they were all blamed on me! But, because of the days back in 1949 when I was replaced in *Annie* and later the *Barkleys* due to illness, and was finally dropped by the studio where I had worked for almost sixteen years, I was said to be 'temperamental', 'impossible to work with.'

On February 24, 1955, Judy was honored by the foreign press and received a Golden Globe award for Best Performance by an Actress in a Motion Picture Musical or Comedy. James Mason received a similar award for his work as Norman Maine. She was honored with the Award for Best Actress from *Look* magazine around the same time. Sadly, she did not receive the Academy Award in March, 1955.

Judy's son, Joey, was born the night before the ceremony. Betty Bacall reports that she and Frank Sinatra to see Judy at the hospital (Bogey was filming the next day.) Frank took a fussy toy: "It was a lovely moment, very sweet and thoughtful of Frank, and it meant a great deal to Judy."

The TV networks sent crews to catch this moment when Judy would receive the Academy Award, but Grace Kelly won. Bacall said:

> She carried it off beautifully, saying her son, Joey, was more important than any Oscar could be, but she was deeply disappointed—hurt. It confirmed her belief that the industry was against her. She knew it was then or never. Instinctively, all her friends knew the same. Judy wasn't like any other performer. There was so much emotion involved in her career—in her life—it was always all or nothing. And though she put on a hell of a front, this was one more slap in the face. She was bitter about it, and for that matter, all closest to her were." [18]

The making of this movie is fully documented in the excellent 2002 book, *A Star is Born: The Making of the 1954 Movie and its 1983 Restoration*. Ronald Haver, head of the film department at the Los Angeles County Museum of Art was a part of the film's 1983 restoration and emotionally involved with effort to bring the movie back to its original state.

On Saturday 16, 1983, I attended the restoration presentation at the Paramount Theatre in Oakland, California. James Mason also attended the showing, among others, and it was an emotional occasion. James Mason said,

> I thought the film was something special when we were making it. But I think Warner Brothers lost some confidence in it and didn't push it as hard as they could have. [19]

I feel James Mason's performance was one of the best of his career. I had been an admirer of his since the early years in England when he made many films, notably, *The Wicked Lady*(1945).

Often during the years Sid and Judy lived on Mapleton Drive, Judy was alone during the evenings. One wonders where Sid was. June Allyson, Debbie Reynolds, and others talk about Judy calling and begging them to come around and visit because she was lonely. By 1959, Debbie's marriage to Eddie Fisher was over; she lived just two blocks away from Judy and Sid. If Sid was not at home Judy would call her, and Debbie would go over and visit her after putting the kids to bed. Debbie said Judy didn't like being alone and complained that Sid didn't like her having friends around. He could be very domineering; his harsh treatment made her lonelier and more depressed.[20]

Judy counseled Debbie on the pitfalls for women in show business. Debbie was lucky, she says in her book, *Debbie My Life*. After the big dance routine for the song "Good Morning" in *Singing in the Rain (1952),* she was exhausted.

Her doctor, Dr. Levy, said she needed to stay in bed for two days. The studio sent over the so-called Dr. Blank, who wanted to give her some vitamin shots. But her mother and Dr. Levy would not allow it; they insisted that all she needed was rest. Debbie felt this decision saved her life. "Dr. Blank" administered all the vitamin shots that Judy got.[21]

But there was also fun. Debbie says,

> Judy was a great storyteller. She'd get up and sing and dance around the room. Then it was wonderful and great fun. She loved performing, *loved* it. I'd get up and we'd both dance, like two kids in high school." [22]

Debbie said that Liza, who was about ten at the time, would sit on the stairs listening to her mother, and she never wanted to go to sleep. The smaller children were in bed. Debbie and Judy remained close friends for about two years. *In October, 2004, Debbie came to Vacaville to give a concert I attended; she talked a lot about her friendship with Judy and how Judy had helped her as a newcomer to Hollywood.*

THE RAT PACK

Noël Coward came to Las Vegas in early 1955, and Frank Sinatra organized a group trip to Noel's show. The group included Judy and Sid, Mike and Gloria Romanoff, David Niven and his wife, Hjordis, and others. After four days of partying Betty Bacall named the group with her declaration, "You look like a god-damned rat pack". Bacall writes of the rules of the Rat Pack: "One had to be addicted to nonconformity, staying up late, drinking, laughing, and not caring what anyone thought or said about us." [23]

Sid would later say, "Bogie never locked his doors. They were always open, and his friends could just walk in and make themselves at home. You'd pour yourself a drink, then others would join you and you'd be there for hours."

Frank was the Pack Leader, Sid the Cage Master, Judy First VP, Irving (Swifty) Lazar the Recording Secretary, Betty the Den Mother, and Bogart was in charge of Public Relations. Nathaniel Benchley, the Group Historian, prepared an insignia for the group consisting of dozens of rats of different sizes going in every direction. Others in the pack included Sammy Davis Jr., Tony Curtis, David Niven Dean Martin, and Kay Thompson.

When there didn't seem to be any more movie projects from the Warners Studios, it was time to send Judy out on tour again to make some money. Roger Edens put an act together, and in April, 1955, Sid organized a seven-city tour. Judy wanted to re-capture the fun and excitement of the Hollywood Cavalcade of Stars in 1943 when she and many other stars went out to entertain the troops. She premiered her new show in San Diego on July 5 and then opened at the Municipal Auditorium in Long Beach on July 9, with the proceeds going to the Exceptional Children's Foundation.

Sinatra hired a bus and took a crowd of Judy's friends to the show in Long Beach, including the Bogarts, Debbie Reynolds and Eddie Fisher, Dean Martin, Van Johnson, Sammy Davis, Jr., June Allyson and Dick Powell. Unofficial audio records of this event exist and one can relive the atmosphere and excitement of that time. Frank Sinatra, Dean Martin, Sammy Davis, Jr., and Humphrey Bogart joined Judy on stage. Sinatra had been a friend from his early days in Hollywood. Debbie said;

> She was brilliant and great and she brought down the house. Everyone cried. She generated such joy and excitement. It was after seeing Judy that I knew one day I wanted to act an act. [24]

But Judy ended up completing two performances if the planned seven-city tour. Sid felt there would be heavy costs and no guarantees that it would make money. There was one way to get out of the contracts—if a movie or television show came up. As luck would have it, CBS wanted Judy for its *Ford Star Jubilee* special, the first one to be shown live and in color on September 24. CBS would pay Judy $100,000 and Sid 10%. Judy was scared — her first television special. There would be 40 million viewers, but even after problems with her throat and nerves, it was a success with Judy singing many of the songs on her Capitol *Miss Show Business* LP, which was released two days after the special aired. Judy went on to sign a contract with CBS TV for five yearly color specials from 1956 through 1960. Also in December, she renewed her contract with MCA Artists as her agents.

The same day as her television special, a teenager named Alfred Poland contacted Judy and asked if he could start a fan club for her; Judy responded warmly. Later Poland passed over the club duties to Pat McMath of Richmond, Indiana, who ran the club until the spring of 1966.[25]

Judy signed a five-year recording contract with Capitol Records in August 1955 and stayed with them until 1966. *Miss Show Business* was the first album recorded, followed in March of 1956 with *Judy* album, which is perhaps one of her most beautiful and well-balanced LPs, arranged and conducted by Nelson Riddle. Judy stayed on the Top 40 charts for five weeks. In February and March of 1957, Judy recorded her third LP *Alone*, with Gordon Jenkins arranging and conducting. Alone contains all beautiful, sad, heart-breaking songs. Jenkins later went with Judy to London. Many other LPs followed over the years. One of the last Capitol LPs, *Judy Garland Live!* was released in 1989 and included nine tracks recorded during a 1962 midnight recording session at Manhattan Center in New York City, and five additional tracks from the *Just for Openers* LP, consisting of songs from Judy's 1963-1964 CBS TV series.

On February 4, 1956, Judy filed the first suit for divorce from Sid Luft, but later dropped it. On April 8, 1956, she did her second CBS television special for *The General Electric Theatre,* using many of the songs on her recent *Judy* LP. These songs would remain with her for the rest of her life. Among them: "I Feel a Song Comin' On," "Maybe I'll Come Back," and "Come Rain or Come Shine."

Las Vegas came next, from July 16 to August 19, 1956, with shows at The New Frontier Hotel. Judy earned $275,000 for this engagement, and she did seventy shows. *Daily Variety* said,

[She's] a singer's singer. Her style, her voice, and her delivery are the pride of her profession. There is no way to draw comparison between (her) and any of her contemporaries, male or female. [26]

Even with the high temperatures and air conditioning causing Judy's throat to dry out and laryngitis to appear, there were good times. The expenses were low and the children were happy swimming in the pools all day. Jack Cathcart was the conductor, so her sister, Suzanne, was there. Judy invited her other sister, Jimmy, her husband, Johnny, and her 18-year-old niece, Judalein, to come in from Dallas, so the three sisters were back together again.

It was more expensive easy in New York when Judy returned to the Palace Theatre on September 26, 1956. The family had to get expensive accommodations at the Park Lane apartments. The initial four-week engagement extended several times, finally concluding seventeen weeks later on January 8, 1957. Chuck Walters arranged a new introduction with eleven dancing boys and Alan King joined her in the act. Brooks Atkinson of the *New York Times* wrote on September. 27, 1956 that

> [h]er boyish grin, her pumping bows to the audience, and her breathless patter between songs complete the portrait of a wonderful singer who is also having a good time...[27]

Liza, who was 10 years old then joined the show and danced while Judy sang "Swanee."

On May 1, 1957, Judy went back to Las Vegas, this time at The Flamingo Hotel. It was a ninety-minute act for a three-week engagement with Liza and Lorna both singing songs, too.

On May 30, Judy performed at the Riviera Theatre in Detroit for a week and then went on to Dallas to perform at the Texas State Fair for two weeks, where she was reunited with her sister, Jimmy, who lived in Dallas. Unfortunately, Judy was not able to complete the last show because she heard that Bob Alton, her friend from MGM days, had died. This meant much of the profit from the entire run was lost because she was too sad to perform.

However, Judy kept going. On June 25 she was back in California for a two-week engagement at the Greek Theatre in Los Angeles where she broke all house records. MCA took $3700 in unpaid commissions, which must have been unsettling. Who was looking after Judy's business affairs?

Judy was tired of all the traveling around the states and wanted to go back to London. Sid felt it would be impossibly expensive to take 25 people over to London—the eleven dancing boys, Gordon Jenkins, and staff to look after the three children. He thought the only way it would work was if Judy could do two shows on the east coast to finance it. Judy was not enthusiastic; Sid was aware that if Judy were forced into doing something she did not want to do, there would be trouble. This is something I theorized about in earlier chapters—going back to those days in Lancaster when Judy was forced to audition against her will. When this situation occurred again, Judy would find a way to retaliate — all subconsciously, of course, but nevertheless effective. Sid understood, but felt had no choice because they needed the money. He planned a week in Washington at the Loew's Capitol Theatre starting September 16 and another at the Mastbaum Theatre in Philadelphia starting September 26. He figured these two weeks would cover the costs to take the show to London. The night before the opening in Washington, Judy began complaining of a sore throat and asked for a doctor. The doctor came and gave her some pills. The next day the throat was worse; honey and tea did not help. She was not able to complete the final night, so there was no profit. Judy continued with the Philadelphia run, even managing to twist her ankle, and appeared one evening with her leg in a cast and hobbling. There was nothing dull in the life of Judy Garland! Again, the last night was cancelled.

There was more juggling of money, but as luck would have it, one of Sid's horses broke a leg, and he was able to collect $30,000 insurance money, so one way or another the family left for England. They sailed on the liner *United States*.

Chapter 12

The Dominion, London 1957

Judy Comes Back to London

We, members of Judy's fan club, were all so excited; Judy was coming to the Dominion in October. It was 1957, Judy had not been with us since 1951, and we had really missed her. By then I had joined the Judy Garland Fan Club. Our small group was cohesive, and we met regularly to listen to the new Capitol LP records, "Judy," and "Alone." Gordon Jenkins was the conductor and arranger on the last LP and came to London with Judy. We had listened constantly to these LP records and saw the movie, *A Star is Born*, but there were no television programs for us in England, so we missed the CBS Ford Star Jubilee with the Jack Cathcart orchestra in 1955 and The Judy Garland Show in April 1956 with Nelson Riddle at the helm.

The Rank Organization owned the Dominion Theatre, which had recently been used as a cinema, but knowing Judy would come for a month they refurbished the 3,000-seat theatre at a cost of $180,000 and made a lovely dressing room for her.

Judy insisted upon coming back to London even though Sid had complained it was too expensive. She was tired of racing around the States and had an emotional need to come back to England just as much as we had an emotional need to see her again. Remember Judy's grandparents on her mother's side were Scottish and Irish and she felt at home in the British Isles. She grew up with all the traditions and customs of Britain.

Judy was coming—we could not wait and ran off to get as many tickets as we could afford for the duration of her run. Opening night was October 16, and we were all there, plus most of the celebrities in London. The London theatre scene is a very special time in the autumn when the streets fill with excitement, and the return of Judy Garland certainly added to the magic around Tottenham Court Road, where the Dominion is located.

This opening night atmosphere was like no other opening night. Excitement went through the audience in waves. One did not need to see Judy; the mere thought that she would be walking out of the stage had everyone sitting on the edge of their seats ready to burst into applause. However, the show was a few minutes late in starting because Lana Turner was there sitting on the lap of her boyfriend, Johnny Stompanato, in front row center and refused to move. Finally, someone gave up a seat farther down the row, so she and Johnny were able to sit together, and the show started. Lana was in England filming *Another Time, Another Place* (1958). I noticed Judy giving Lana many smiles and grins during the show. *(Later I remember feeling such a fool asking for Lana's autograph when I did not have a pen!)*

This was the first time London discovered the humor of comedian, Alan King. King strode out on the stage in his dark green silk suit, the epitome of New York sophistication. With no introduction, he started his patter with words like, "I know you are waiting for Judy—hanging from the balconies, and all you have got is me." We loved him. King's New York Jewish humor was not that much different from the London Jewish humor that we were familiar with.

In 1998 two-night event, *Carnegie Hall Celebrates the Music of Judy Garland*; Alan King explained how he came to be in London that year. He had been touring with Judy in the States, wanted a break, and was on vacation with his wife in Italy when Sid and Judy called him and said they needed some help with the opening night; he came, reluctantly, to London. When he arrived, the driver asked if he would like to drive by the theatre,

and he replied that he didn't think it was necessary because he knew what theatres looked like! They drove by anyway, and he saw the sign outside the theatre, "Judy Garland and Alan King," and he knew he was stuck with a four-and-a-half week run in London.

We loved Alan King and later during the run, I can remember sitting in the front row and bursting out with laughter anticipating his punch line before he came to it. He used to give me a very odd looks!

The following is my write-up of the concert:

"Gordon Jenkins had put together a magnificent opening medley including "The Man That Got Away," "Trolley Song," and "Rainbow." Judy was to use this medley for all her shows from then on. The show started with ten dancing boys wearing black jackets, pinstriped pants, bowler hats, and rolled umbrellas. (Richard Barstow did the choreography.) Their opening  song was about some of the great falls in history and "how she fell on the Palladium stage." The curtains opened and we saw Judy seated in the middle of the stage wearing a dress with black top and frilly white skirt spread out around her. The boys helped

 her to her feet and the audience went crazy, cheering and applauding. People called out, "Welcome back, Judy! Why did you stay away for so long?" Judy appeared to be overcome and speechless; she finally said something like, "I don't know whether I can sing after that reception; I'll see what I can do". She then went into "It's Lovely to be back in London/Just to feel the thrill of London, I always come undone/I'm so glad I'm back" written specially for her by Roger Edens. Her voice was husky from the laryngitis she had been suffering from but so attractive, nonetheless. I was lucky enough to get one of the 45-rpm records given out at opening night, and it brings tears to my eyes whenever I hear it.

Other songs included "I Feel a Song Coming On," "Minstrel Girl," "Get Happy," "Lucky Day," "Rock-a-Bye," "How About Me?," and "The Man That Got Away." I remember Judy wearing the tomato-red frilly lace dress belting out "Come Rain or Come Shine" with the bongo drummer sitting with her at the

front of the stage. I don't think there has been a more exciting theatrical performance on any stage at any time! She changed into the tramp outfit for "Swells" and Jimmy Brooks, one of the dancers, joined her.

We understood that when she started on "Rainbow" the show was nearly over, so it was doubly nostalgic. No one wanted the evening to end, and we begged for more. I remember Judy wandering around the stage with her blackened front tooth removed, singing gently, "Me and My Shadow." The audience called out for another song; she waited a while and finally said, "I'll do 'Swanee'." There were roars of approval.

Many of Judy's friends from Hollywood were there: Janet

Blair, Donna Reed, and Rod Steiger, along with Richard Attenborough and others from the British stage and cinema. After the show Donna Reed, Petula Clark, Alma Cogan, and Vera Lynn came up onto the stage and presented Judy with baskets of flowers."

The *News Chronicle* reported that there were five changes of clothes. I actually only remember the black top with frilly white skirt, a red tomato-colored feathered dress, a simple black dress with sequined long jacket, and the tramp outfit (but maybe there was a "Get Happy" outfit.). At the Palladium in 1951, the song

"Rock-a-Bye" stands out in my memory. This time it was Judy and the bongo drummer, belting out "Come Rain or Come Shine." I went as many times as I could afford, and later Lorna Smith were able to get front row seats—which I must tell you is exactly the most perfect place to be when Judy is on stage.

During the 4-week run, Judy's laryngitis returned so that it was difficult for her to get through some of the more demanding songs, and she substituted others, but she always performed well. What I did notice in the later shows was that some of the costume changes were cut down, and I believe the last show had her coming out in the black dress and sequined long jacket, which she generally wore towards the end of a show.

Lorna Smith writes about one particular evening:

> Judy is a born clown, but some days she can be just as sad as on other days she is happy and sunny....Judy's encores were set, of course, and we were due to get "Me and My Shadow." Someone called out, amongst all the other 999 titles,... "Happiness." Judy stopped dead in her tracks. "Would you like that?" She asked in a quiet little voice. Yes, we would, "Gordon, would you mind if we don't do your song tonight?" She murmured down to Gordon Jenkins who was in the orchestra pit. It had been one of those evenings when Judy had seemed a little nervous and the sadder songs had been more poignant. She sat down on the stage, in her tramp outfit and grubby face, and sang that song as I've never heard her sing it before or since....Halfway through, the voice faltered and the tears began to trickle down Judy's cheeks. That finished me completely—and I joined her! If it were planned on this occasion, I'll eat my hat. The next performance I saw the happy songs come bouncing over and Judy was reduced to helpless giggles by the remarks the orchestra were calling up to her. [1]

During the engagement, Judy brought her young children, Lorna and Joey, onto the stage to introduce them to London audiences.

Contemplating Judy's talent seemed to bring out the eloquence of British news writers. There were excellent reviews in the newspapers. Richard Finlater of *The Observer* ends his piece with these words:

...it is in the girl-tramp's patched and baggy trousers...that Miss Garland gets her freedom and demonstrates that heart-warming strength and energy and exuberance in which our own songstresses are so sadly lacking, however tasteful their wardrobes, however slim their waist.

The News Chronicle (Elizabeth Frank) reported,

All that is the essence of real star quality now holds the limelight at the Dominion Theatre. It was a wonderful experience to feel a London audience of 3,000 give themselves in a flood of affection and warmth and, I like to think, a certain pride, to the miraculous, dumpy little waif, to whom they restored life and confidence six years ago. Judy is a great clown. That is why she can make you laugh and cry at the same time. The spotlight picked up the dirty little gamin's face, as she sang 'Over the Rainbow' squatting on the stage by the footlights, and we wondered at the strange guise in which genius can appear to us. [2]

The Record Mirror, London reviewer wrote, "She is a superb artist, a born trouper, an entertainer, a performer in every sense of the term. The quality of stardom emanates from her every movement, her every gesture..."

Gordon Jenkins wrote about this experience in the November 16, 1957, issue of *The Melody Maker* in an article titled "Miraculous Person":

...those electric crescendos are far beyond the scope of any mortal teacher; the talent of Judy Garland could never be learned. It must take a strange sort of person not to be moved by this great talent. I believe that people cry at Judy for the same reason that they do at sunsets, or symphonies, or cathedrals: when one is confronted with overwhelming greatness, it is impossible not to be touched....The most exciting thing about her performance is that it is completely different every night. There is never any fluctuation in quality or effort or presentation, but she seldom conquers a song in exactly the same way and is constantly inserting little joyful bits of business that makes every night seem new. [3]

Jenkins often said how much he loved the Tramp number, and one day he would start it again. He did just that on the final night (Lorna Smith and I were in the front row again, as seen in photo) and I remember the audience (including me) calling out, "More! More!," Jenkins raised his baton to start the number again, and Judy called out "Oh no! You don't really want it again?" The answering roar was in the affirmative. Judy and her partner, Jimmy Brooke, restarted the number again although they were breathless. The baggy suit, broken top hat, fright wig, blacked-out front tooth, dirty spots on the face and crowning features were the oversized shoes. Just the sight of Judy coming onto the stage around the curtains was enough to send the audience over the top. I think she understood how funny she looked and joined in the fun. From then on the show was euphoric; in the midst of "Swanee" she forgot to take mike out

of stand. In answer to Jenkins question, "From the top?" she replied, "We will not! Six Swells, four Swanees, we'll be here all night! We'll take it from 'I love ya.'" The last night ended on a very high note.

For me the evening continued to be even more exciting than the opening night, if that were possible, because after the show Judy invited us (about ten of us club members) backstage to attend the last night party on the stage of the Dominion Theatre. Lorna Smith, as a representative of Pat McMath's fan club in the States, had been to visit Judy on several occasions and asked her if she would meet members of our group after the last show. Judy had readily agreed. When she saw us waiting to speak to her at the stage door, she came towards us with her hand outstretched to greet Lorna and then, with a welcoming gesture to the group, said, "Come on in!" She twisted on her high heels and led us to the stage to the closing-night party where we mixed with the musicians and theatre staff who all spoke highly of her. Judy was wearing the simple black dress she had worn on stage, pictured in Watson & Chapman's book, Judy, facing page 1.

A British club member took some photographs, and we all managed to have a few words with Judy. I must admit I was completely tongue tied and only managed to get out something  quite inane. When Judy turns her serious enormous black eyes on you, it is very hard to concentrate and sound intelligent. After the thrill of the show and meeting Judy, it was very difficult to get on our respective underground trains and walk the half-mile home from the station and actually go back to humdrum work the next day.

Two days after the close of the Dominion run, Judy appeared at *The Royal Variety Show*. This annual show this year was for the benefit of the Variety Artists' Benevolent Fund. Fellow American performers were Count Basie and Mario Lanza. Judy wore the black dress and sparkling evening three-quarter-length jacket and appeared quite nervous in the first number of "Rock-a-Bye Your Baby". She changed and went into the tramp number, ending with "Rainbow." She stopped the show; it was difficult to go on with the final act of Tommy Steel. Afterwards the performers got to meet the Royal Family. The Queen told her simply, "We missed you. Don't stay away so long next time."

The Queen Mother commented: "I'm sorry you weren't allowed to sing another song." [4]

Judy left London on an emotional high; this second visit had cemented Judy's relationship with Britain. She felt at home in Britain and from then on until the end of her life she kept coming back because she felt safe and happy there. She loved being in the place of origin of all the influences of her maternal grandparents--Scottish and Irish music, song, and food. Moreover, she considered her father an Irishman. From then on, she would often comment when on stage, **"I am home now."**

Chapter 13

Judy and the musicians in her life

Judy Garland had many long relationships with musicians. Her parents were both musical performers-her mother taught her to sing and were her accompanist from the age of two. Music and singing with her accompanist were nearly her whole life. When she signed a contract with MGM at the age of thirteen, Roger Edens took over from her mother and helped to define her style, as would Kay Thompson later in her career at MGM. She worked with all the great orchestras and conductors at MGM, radio, and recording studios during those years, including Alex Stordahl (recordings in the 1940s) and Lennie Hayton (her conductor on MGM musicals) and her own first husband David Rose, not to mention Artie Shaw and Oscar Levant.

Judy formed great friendships with all the composers of the day—Cole Porter, the Gershwins, Richard Rodgers, Oscar Hammerstein. In fact, she changed her show at the Palladium August 28, 1960, when she learned of the death of Hammerstein to include "You'll Never Walk Alone". She had a special relationship with E.Y. Harburg and Harold Arlen, who wrote the lyrics of "Over the Rainbow." Johnny Mercer carried a torch for her for years. Irving Berlin was delighted that she would sing his songs in *Easter Parade* and was disappointed when she was not able to complete *Annie Get Your Gun.*

When Judy signed with Capitol Records, Frank Sinatra recommended Nelson Riddle as her conductor/arranger. Together they produced the wonderful *Judy* album. Riddle worked with her on many of her concerts.

Gordon Jenkins first worked with Judy when she was 21 in March, 1943, on a wartime show for Free World Theatre and again in July 1944 for the show "Everything for the Boys" for NBC with Dick Haymes. She also performed "When Somebody Loves Me," "Long Ago and Far Away," and "There's a Tavern in the Town."

They would go on to record the *Alone* album in 1957 and *The Letter* in 1959. Judy dearly loved the sad, sensitive songs in the *Alone* album. She felt "How About Me," written by Irving Berlin, was the saddest song ever written.

Someone once asked Gordon Jenkins if he would take two of a particular artist for one of Judy, and he replied, "I would not take two of anybody for Judy Garland. She was the greatest female entertainer ever." [1]

Gordon Jenkins performed with Judy in London 1957. I watched him love and admire her at the Dominion during the 4½ week run. (There are more comments from Jenkins in the "Dominion" chapter.) He also said,

> With Judy, she'd do something different all the time, and I always felt she got better with every performance. She was a joy to work with, because she had exceptional timing. If you looked out the window, you'd be lost. [2]

Later I would see Mort Lindsey with her, again at the Palladium, during the filming of "Hello Bluebird" in the movie, I Could Go on Singing, for I was lucky enough to be among the extras in the audience that day.

I was also present, as a guest of Judy, at one of the recording sessions in London in 1960 and watched Judy interact with the conductor, Norrie Paramor, and orchestra. There was no diva there; it was a collaboration of artists working together to produce a piece of art. Judy guided the orchestra, encouraging them to get the effect she needed. She recorded "I Happen to Like New York," "You'll Never Walk Alone," "Swanee," and "Why Was I Born?" She would record one song, and then we would go into the soundproof room to listen to playback. She guided the chorus and orchestra on how fast the tempo should be—the rhythm, pitch and volume. She was always very sweet, charming and funny; she also knew what was going on at every moment. She would sing over some of the lines for the chorus, conducting and leading, and wishing them to be perfect. "Could you sing a little louder there?" she inquired at one point to the chorus. There were only about ten chorus members but she said, "You have to sound like twenty-eight" and laughed with them.

Mort Lindsey was the first conductor on her first US concert after she returned from England in 1960. She was so pleased with him that she wanted him with her for all concerts including the famed Carnegie Hall event.

Mort was a great musician. Not only was he classically trained, with a BA and Master's degrees from Colombia (and a doctorate in Music Education in conferred in1974), but at his core he was a jazz musician. Says son Trevor, "He understood the mechanics of music from schooling, but he was still able to improvise freely on the piano."[3] This, along with his charm and sensitivity made him the perfect person to accompany Judy.

I was at many of the early season taping sessions at CBS of her 1963-1964 television series. Although generally one did not see Mort then because the orchestra was behind the scenes, one knew he was there. Later we were able to see him interact with Judy in her concert-type shows.

When the series ended, Mort and his wife went to Australia with Judy. I suppose key orchestra players went too. The Sydney venue management provided Judy an enormous orchestra for her show in a big sports arena holding 10,000 people, and in a couple of days Mort had them in magnificent shape. Unofficial copies of this concert exist, recorded by attendees of the concert. I encourage everyone to try and obtain a copy of this recording. On it, we can hear what Mort does for Judy. One can actually hear their relationship—Judy is messing around with microphone or spilling water while chatting to the audience, and suddenly her voice changes, and in a firm tone, she says something like, **"Let's go!"** and that is his cue that she is ready to sing again. They were perfectly attuned to one another.

Mort Lindsey told Larry King that working with Judy was one of the highlights of his career. He said, "Every time she sang, I got goose bumps....My back was to her, too."

Chapter 14

1958-59 in the States

After the successful Dominion run in London, Judy and family return to the States at the end of 1957. In the next two years there were the usual highs and lows, but eventually in July, 1960, Judy returned to London.

The year 1958 did not start well. Money was short, so Judy had to go back to work. There was a rough start in Las Vegas on December 26 with the dryness of the desert hurting her throat so that she missed some performances; then the clatter of waiters serving people and the general unruliness of the New Year's Eve audience caused her to cancel the run.

Difficulties started between Sid and Judy. *I had heard rumors of an argument between them at the Dominion back-stage party. Apparently, Judy had been annoyed about the many cash advances Sid had taken.* Judy hired Jerry Giesler and filed for divorce on March 4, 1958. There would be many reconciliations and separations before they separated for the last time in 1962.

Judy and the children went to New York for a run at Ben Masik's Town & Country Club in Brooklyn on March 21. Bobby Van had been with Judy in Las Vegas and continued performing the tramp number with her for this engagement. It seems sad that a thirty-five-year-old artist with three young children had to go back on the road again so soon. She had to get herself and her children across the country and find somewhere to live for four weeks.

146

Norman Weiss, the MCA agent, negotiated the contract with Masik. Judy was not good about reading and understanding contracts; she left her manager to look after these details. She was horrified to realize she was supposed to perform twice a day, particularly as she had developed laryngitis. Then New York State demanded back taxes from the 1951 run at the Palace. Apparently, someone had not prepared the proper tax returns for that year! One has to wonder about who was handling the financial matters for the family; these things should not have happened. Judy managed to get through about eleven days and the whole thing ended with a big row involving Weiss, Masik, Luft (he had joined them), and Judy.

As we see from the Apted study what is in the heart of the 7-year-old child remains with them into adulthood. So when Judy finds herself in an impossible situation the resentments she felt as a child forced to sing against her will returned. This time she had no mother threatening her; and so with her back against the wall, she refused to sing.

Judy always seemed to get the blame for any upset,

and often she was not responsible. What she did lack was an efficient manager with a clear vision of her plans. Luft managed to get them out of this situation by borrowing some money, and the family was back together again.

In May, Judy was back on top again performing outdoors at the Minnesota State Centennial Celebrations before 20,000 people. Later in May, Judy began to record, with Nelson Riddle, *Judy in Love*.

Judy completed three weeks in July at the *Cocoanut Grove* in Hollywood, and all her friends came out to cheer her on. In the audience were Lana Turner, Frank Sinatra, Marlene Dietrich, Lauren Bacall, Rock Hudson, Dean Martin, and others. Louella Parsons wrote,

> In the years I've been covering this town I've never seen such a turnout of stars, nor have I felt under one roof such an outpouring of affection and love as greeted Judy, What a show. Judy giving back all that affection by singing her heart out. I think we all realized we were enjoying an event that has seldom been equaled and will hardly even by topped.[1]

The final night's performance, called *Judy Garland at the Grove*, was recorded, complete with laryngitis!

In early September 1958, 17,500 people came to Orchestra Hall in Chicago to see Judy perform seven shows over six days. . This is when she sang the new arrangement of "Chicago." Nelson Riddle and Alan King were with her.

She performed at The Sahara in Las Vegas on October 1 for two weeks; many of her friends were there -- Debbie Reynolds,

Betty Hutton, and Shirley MacLaine. On the final night she finished the act singing with Frank Sinatra and Dean Martin.

Things continued to go well. There was a tribute to Judy at the Masquers Club with all her friends on October 24 and she was given a plaque, which read, "To Judy Garland -- *Over the Rainbow/A Star is Born.*" George Jessel was the emcee.

On November 15, Judy sang a benefit concert at San Bernardino Community Hospital.

The next LP was *The Letter* with John Ireland, beautifully written by Gordon Jenkins and recorded in January 1959. This was quite an unusual LP with narrative by John and Judy reminiscing about a lost love affair.

In February, she went out to Miami's Fontainebleau for two weeks with good reviews.

Judy appeared to be putting on weight; it occurred to Sid that she looked like an opera singer, so why not book her into some opera houses? Thus began the opera house tour. Many fans in recent years have told me about seeing Judy perform on these occasions, and they could tell she was ill. However, the trooper that she was continued the shows. On May 11, 1959, she opened at the Metropolitan Opera House for the benefit of the Children's Asthma Research Institute and Hospital of Denver. Nelson Riddle was her conductor, with a larger orchestra; Alan King there along with 100 more performers. Luft felt that these performances in an opera house environment—far from the usual concert scene, would give Judy a greater lift emotionally, which it did. Of course, the costs of putting on this type of show were considerable, around $150,000 to stage, in addition to the hotel, living, and entertaining costs, so there was not much money left for the family. Shows followed at the Stanley Opera House in Baltimore on May 5 and the New York Metropolitan Opera House May 11 for a week, with every seat sold out. Another week followed at Chicago Opera House, Chicago and the new arrangement of the song, "Chicago," went down well.

I always love to hear personal stories of friends who attended different concerts. My dear friend Jack Wood first saw Judy live at the Memorial Opera House in San Francisco where Judy performed in July that year for eleven days. He said that although she looked overweight, bloated, and very pale, her voice was memorable! Judy included the new arrangement by Roger Edens of "San Francisco," which poked fun at Jeanette Macdonald singing sweetly in the movie about the San Francisco 1906 earthquake. How important these two arrangements became for Judy! She would sing them for the rest of her life.[2]

Later in July, Judy performed at the Los Angeles Shrine Auditorium. The Shrine may have been emotionally uplifting, even if it did not bring any money into the family; one wonders why it did not. Judy was working consistently, so where did the money go?

Judy appeared to be even more overweight, but actually her body was waterlogged, and eventually Sid got her to New York in November where she was taken to the Doctors Hospital. She agreed to be treated by Dr. Israel Rappaport, Sid's uncle. He reported that her liver had swollen to four times its normal size and was pouring poison into her body. The diagnosis was acute hepatitis. The prognosis was not good; Judy would probably be a semi-invalid for the rest of her life, and she would not work again. She stayed in the hospital for seven weeks and returned to California on January 5, 1960 to recover.

After several months, with time to meditate and think about her future, Judy returned to the world. In early July, she sat between Senator John F. Kennedy and Adlai Stevenson at a Democratic fundraiser at the Beverly Hilton in Beverly Hills, and then on July 11 left on her own for England. She seemed to understand that she needed a change in her life; it was most likely that she could sort this out in London, where she was the most at ease. I imagine that she finally understood that relying on Sid as her manager and husband was not working; she would have to make some changes.

Chapter 15

Judy comes back to London - 1960

In England, we were desperately worried about Judy. She had been very ill with hepatitis and there were rumors that she might not work again. Judy had recovered but felt that nobody needed her in Hollywood; the telephone never rang, so she felt it was time to leave. Where would she go? To London, of course -- this is where she felt safe. The Palladium audiences had taken her to their hearts in 1951, brought back her confidence, and this had led to her concert career. The 1957 Dominion run had also been uplifting, and she had made so many friends in London. She told Sid she needed time to think. She took off by plane on her own; perhaps for the first time, and on July 14, 1960, at 7:30 a.m., she arrived at London airport. This was something she had never done before. She seemed to be physically well; the only medicine she was taking was Ritalin.[1] (*Ritalin* is a trade name for the prescription drug methylphenidate, a central nervous system stimulant. Its effects are similar to, but more potent than, caffeine and less potent than amphetamine. Ritalin is both a stimulant and appetite suppressant, causing wakefulness, euphoria, and increased focus and attentiveness.)

There were many reasons to come to Europe. Liza was in France for the summer with other students to practice their French, and Judy planned to visit her in Rome after two weeks. Rossano Brazzi had lent Judy his house; Ethel Merman and Kay Thompson would join her there.

Lorna Smith, who ran the U.K. fan club, heard that Judy had arrived. There was a press reception for her at the EMI, Abbey Road studios (EMI was the parent company of Capitol Records), and Lorna and I were invited to attend. We were glad to see Judy and welcome her back to London.

Lorna sent Judy some flowers on arrival and Judy greeted us warmly. I never will forget that firm handshake. Judy wore a slim black dress and turquoise jacket. Judy was to joke later about this press conference with Terry Thomas on her CBS-TV show in 1963.

As Judy entered the room, "Over the Rainbow" was playing and someone escorted her to a small platform with spotlights, made a speech, and handed the microphone over to Judy. She looked quite surprised. "Well—I didn't expect a speech. I— er— what can I say? It's wonderful to be here. Er—". Then a television program interview took place. As soon as she could, Judy got off the stage and came

down among the reporters. This is when Lorna and I greeted her, and I remember her first words were to thank us for the gifts and flowers fan club members had sent her.

Judy looked well and relaxed and handled the questions from the press well. We tried to stay near to her offering our presence

153

as support to her. She told the press representatives that she was on holiday and would make a recording. They asked about stage fright, and she replied that she was learning to live with it. In

reply to how she felt, she said, "I have not worked for about a year (I have had this hepatitis) and I feel good."

They asked her about plans and she mentioned *Born in Wedlock.*

They rudely changed the subject and asked about her weight. She jokingly said to one reporter, "I'm quite a bit slimmer than I was and if you haven't noticed, you'd better (taking his glasses off and putting them back with a chuckle) get some new glasses."

When asked about her being late on a movie set she said, "There are some very interesting trends in the movies now. Times have changed. If I was half-an-hour or 45 minutes late, I was crucified. But now, I read that "Marilyn Monroe is six-and-a-half hours late—and isn't she adorable!" (Judy lifted her hands and laughed. There was

no bitterness in the comment.) "I guess I worked at the wrong time," she added ruefully.

When asked about England, Judy replied, "I love it here. I would like to live here, if I could." and went on to say that she owed England an awful lot. "English audiences are very loyal— no matter how long it is since they have seen you. They are very demonstrative and they give you a lot of love." Another comment was, "I'm so damned calm these days; I guess I'm a pretty dull person. I go along the same old line all the time—no highs, no lows. I never lose my temper anymore and I never throw tantrums. When something happens to annoy me, I just walk away and forget it." Regarding living in England, she said at that time, "The tempo is slower, yet it stimulates me and puts me in a VERY happy frame of Mind."

The press often hemmed Judy into one corner or another, but finally she was able to leave. Then she went to stay with Dirk Bogarde at his house in country.

During the next month, before she began her concerts in August, Judy recorded some songs at EMI.

RECORDING STUDIO

Lorna Smith called Judy and spoke to her on Sunday, 31 July, at 1:15 p.m. while Judy was at the Westbury Hotel, London. Lorna inquired how she was and chatted about her recent trip to Rome and diets; both were trying to lose weight. Judy asked how the club members were, and she thanked Lorna again for the lovely presents and flowers and for thinking of the children. Lorna replied that Judy had given the fans lots of pleasure, and this was the only way to show it. Judy commented that it was very sweet and she appreciated it.

When asked about the children Judy told Lorna that she would stay in Europe for a while and that the younger children would join her soon. She said that Liza was in the French Alps now with six other girls learning the language. Judy said she would join her the Sunday after the recording sessions and go to

Geneva, where Liza was, for a while. Then they would spend two or three days in Paris before returning to London.

Lorna then asked Judy if it would be possible for us, Lorna and me, to come to one of the sessions. Judy replied, "Why, of course. I'd be delighted to have you come along. I'll leave word at the door." When Lorna asked which day would be convenient, Judy replied, "Any time you like. I'm recording Tuesday, Wednesday, Thursday, and Friday at 7:30 p.m. Any evening you come along will be all right. Do you know where it is? Abbey Road? That's right. St. John's Wood." Lorna thanked her and said, "It'll be lovely to see and hear you sing again." Judy thanked Lorna for phoning, called her "dear", and said she looked forward to seeing her sometime the next week.

I consider this time when she was happy, well, and singing at the studio to be my favorite memory. I was terribly shy at that time and in great awe of her. We did not take any cameras because she was working, and we did not want to distract her. The first day we were unlucky because the guards would not let us into the studio, so we stood outside, and Judy waved to us from the steps, probably wondering why we were not in the studio. Lorna called her the next day and explained. Judy said she would make sure that we got in the next day. As the limo drove up, Judy talked to us from the open car window and we walked alongside the car through the gates. Sid had just arrived from the States. As Sid, Lorna and I tried to keep up with her, she scurried (there is no other word for it, Judy walked fast) down the corridors. She kept turning back to us saying, "I don't know why you want to listen to this—it will be so boring." Judy could draw out the words and emphasize them. We insisted we would not be bored— we were in seventh heaven. Judy was unfailingly polite, seeing that everyone was introduced to everyone else; this was how she was. Sid was charming, as he always was to the fans, and he looked very handsome in a beige suit, always well dressed.

Before the session began, the recording manager had strolled over to tell us Judy's voice was better than ever, and she had made five wonderful recordings the night before. (These would later to be on the London Recordings.) The staff at the studio wanted to seat us away from the recording area, in case we made a noise and spoiled the recording, but Judy would not have it. "I want the girls up here with me," she insisted, and we were given two chairs about three feet away. We sat there like two very small mice, scarcely breathing. She told us she preferred that we did not face her, as this would distract her when she sang.

The songs she recorded that evening were, "I Happen to Like New York," "You'll Never Walk Alone," "Swanee," and "Why Was I Born?" She would record one song, and then we would go into the soundproof room and listen to it in the playback. After one version of "I Happen to Like New York," another guest, an English girl pop singer, made some disparaging remarks about New York, along the lines that it was a dirty smelly place. Judy stood looking down at sheet music on a table, said quietly and very firmly, "**I** happen to **like** New York!"

Norrie Paramor, was conducting the orchestra, for the session with about 8-12 people in the chorus. She told them they had to sound like 50—so "sing big," or something like that. Another time while she was doing "Swanee", the orchestra did not know how to deal with the pauses, and changes of tempo, Judy went through it with them, encouraging them and showing them exactly how she wanted it to go, guiding and advising the chorus and orchestra on how fast the tempo should be—the rhythm, pitch and volume. During the end of one recording of "Swanee" Judy realized she was not going to make that last note perfectly and so she finished with a great comic yell. The next take was fine.

When we heard the play back of the faulty take, Judy laid back in her chair, laughing so hard she was horizontal. It was at this point that I noticed she was wearing nylons under her pants. I had not met many American women; we always wore ankle socks with sneakers and pants, and I doubt we even had jeans then. I considered her extremely elegant.

She was always very sweet, charming and funny; she also knew what was going on at every moment. Even when concentrating on her singing, she knew if there was something wrong in the orchestra or chorus. She would sing over some of the lines for the chorus, conducting and leading, and wishing them to be perfect. "Could you sing a little louder there?" she inquired at one point to the chorus. "You have to sound like twenty-eight," and she laughed with them. The leader suggested at one point that he stop his note when Judy stopped. "I don't stop," smiled Judy, "I hold it through to the end." (The chorus collapsed in laughter.)

Sid and Judy seemed to be on good terms. He would give inputs on the recordings, and she would good-naturedly do it again. At one point she turned to us when Sid was rubbing his eyes and said, "He is suffering from jet lag!" Later, she would say to us, "Would you like some tea?" She was wearing flat shoes, black pants and a lovely blue shirt she had brought back from Italy. She was not heavy but at the weight, which was correct for her, and she looked comfortable. She wore lipstick and little other make-up, and her hair was just normally curled

Many years later Lorna Smith asked Judy about the recording she had made that day of "Why Was I Born," commenting how beautiful it was. She wanted to know what they did with it. Judy laughed and said, "I expect they lost it." That is how she was, a funny, charming woman. It is nice to know that these recordings are being re-issued.

Judy rented Carol Reed's house in King's Road, Chelsea, and the children joined her.

PALLADIUM CONCERTS

The format for the two concerts Judy would do at the Palladium in the 1960s came about after a discussion with Dirk Bogarde when she stayed with him soon after arriving in London. She him that she was planning a concert, just two nights, at the Palladium and she warned him that he'd better be there.[2]

He records that it was a wonderfully happy time. They went for long drives into the country:

> [W]e talked and laughed. She was without doubt, I suppose, the funniest woman I have ever met. We seemed, in that July, to laugh endlessly." [3]

It was at this time that Judy asked him never to leave her.

They planned the show and he insisted that she didn't need a warm up act: "You don't. And you don't need those Dancing Gentlemen to spell out your name. They know who you are." He asked her how many songs she knew, and she replied about 200. He replied, "Just sing them all." She burst out laughing. "All of them! Are you out of your mind?" Dirk replied, "Just you and a whopping big orchestra and just go on singing." Judy responded, "You mean start cold? Cold! And just sing?" "A tremendous overture and just you in the spotlight. Cold." Her  eyes were suddenly interested. Not a spotlight....The conversation went on. "I just holler. And I can't holler for two long hours." "Try." Dirk replied. "My best friend and you want to ruin me....I'm going to see Kay Thompson in Rome and I love her and trust her too. I'll maybe kick it around with her."[4] So we can see that Dirk Bogarde instigated these one-man concerts, no doubt with the help of Kay Thompson.

Suddenly we heard that Judy was doing a concert at the Palladium on Sunday evening August 28. Lorna Smith managed to get two tickets center front row, and this became one of our favorite Judy evenings. Judy did the show on the following Sunday also.

I have seen Judy many times, but never, never quite as happy and relaxed as she was tonight. Never have I seen her so relaxed and happy on stage right from the word "go," nor, and I don't really mean this as an afterthought, has her voice been so marvelous. I made some notes of Judy's comments and the songs she sang; 28 in all (is that an all-time record?)

Just after 8 o'clock the show started with Norrie Paramor and orchestra on stage playing a couple of warming-up numbers and then they burst into "The Man That Got Away" amidst tremendous applause—but no Judy. "The Trolley Song"—wild applause—no Judy. "Over the Rainbow"—still no Judy. Then at last, there she was. A small figure dressed casually in cocktail clothes (straight black dress/turquoise jacket) with hands thrust into her pockets standing a few paces from the side of the stage while the roar of applause welcomed Judy back to London. Always on Judy's first nights, I want to cry and tonight was no exception and I expect there were many others feeling the same way. After a minute or two I thought Judy's eyes glistened, and then she grabbed the mike and went into "I Happen to Like New York"" (revised words including London Bridge and Brighton Pier) then "Almost Like Being in Love" and "Do It Again"—stage version.

After the third song, Judy stopped to say a few words about the fall she had had in 1951 on the Palladium stage. "I don't think I've ever told you this. When I came here nine years, was it nine years? (in mock horror) I was so nervous on the first night while waiting in the wings that my knees completely locked and I had to walk on stiff-legged" (demonstrating amidst laughter).

Songs 4 and 5 were "You Go to My Head" and "Alone Together" and the lights dimmed during the last number. Judy: "I usually have such big bands–and by the way, isn't this a wonderful band! (Applause for band), but we are going to try a few numbers with a small group. It has been said that I can only sing melancholy songs or [dramatic] songs (Judy throws her right arm out as she does in her BIG numbers) but I want to show I can sing jazz."

A screen came down cutting off the big band and as the small group got ready on the right of the stage; Judy jigged around like a kid getting ready for a party. "Let's pretend this is a jam session—with music! I'm the leader" to group—aside to audience shrugging, "I can't even remember the song!" and then "You start <u>now</u>," to one of the musicians and away we went into a very hot jam session. "Who Cares," "Puttin' on the Ritz," "How Long Has This Been Going On?" and "Just You—Just Me." Somewhere along the line, Judy commented that she had come home: "England's my home now."

At the end of the session, Judy paid tribute to the late Oscar Hammerstein II who had died five days before and sang one of his songs, "You'll Never Walk Alone."

The first song after the interval was "When You're Smiling," and some people were still returning to their seats as Judy was singing, but she said afterward, "I don't think I gave you enough time to get back to your seats, but that wasn't a very good song anyway—just one to get started." Which I thought was pretty nice of her. After the next song, "I Can't Give You Anything But Love," she explained about the change of outfit (tapering black slacks and sequined blouse). "It's more comfortable; I'm not strapped," and then she told a story about a recent press article with a certain amount of wonder and humorous indignation: "I was at lunch with a man the other day and he kept saying, 'Won't you have some more dessert? Won't you have some more cheese?' And then he wrote (said in a Garland dead-pan voice), 'SHE LAUGHED WITH BOTH HER CHINS.'" As the laughter subsided, "But you should have seen him!" Then under her breath, "I'm going to get into trouble—I'm naughty," chuckling. The 14 song was "Come Rain or Come Shine." Surely one of my special favorites and sung magnificently. Afterward Judy said, "That was a loud one!" A pianist came out to a piano at the front left of stage, and after Judy had introduced him she sat sideways on the piano stool and said, "So many people have told me that they listen to my records at home, and as I usually sing such loud songs I thought

I'd sing some quieter songs for a change. There was an old film in which "September Song" first appeared (applause). This isn't it! (laughter) And this is one for Dirk and Tony." Then, suddenly, as if the idea had just occurred to her, she rushed to the footlights and peered into the audience calling, "Where are they? Where are you, Dirk and Tony?" Dirk Bogarde came forward and kissed her, and before he could escape, Judy had pulled him up on the stage with the announcement that he was her friend. He sat on the stage at her feet while she sang, "It Never Was You," and as the last note died away, she bent and kissed the top of his head and said: "You see, I can thank you." Dirk left after this song, and Judy then sang, "You're Nearer" and "One for My Baby." Everyone had been requesting titles before this song, and I think Judy misheard a request for "Rock-a-Bye," but what does that matter, I'd never heard her sing this song before, and like every new song Judy takes on, she brings to it a new and wonderful interpretation.

The band came back, and Judy sang, "Zing Went the Strings of My Heart" with a little dance routine in the middle, of which she said after. "I'm really too old for this," and then after a pause, "Two chins—she laughed with both her chins!!!"

After the next song, "Stormy Weather," Judy said to the audience, "I must say that it is lovely to see you. It is lovely to be home (and a little shyly) because this is my new home." Everyone showed her how pleased they were.

Then "You Made Me Love You," "For Me and My Gal," "The Trolley Song," "The Man That Got Away," "Rock-a-Bye," and "San Francisco" with its new introduction verse, in truly Garland emphasis and humor.

Judy then said that Sid wanted her to sing, "It's a Great Day for the Irish." As she started, my husband whispered in my ear, in wonder, "She has just dropped 20 years—she is singing just as she did as a teenager—and she still can," in even more wonder. (From the second show in September.)

The show ended with "Swanee" and "Over the Rainbow" amidst many flowers and a standing ovation from the audience, which went on and on and on. As one critic said the next day, "And yes – my hands were sore too." So were mine."[5]

She was later to do shows in Birmingham, Leicester, and Manchester and also for the American troops stationed at Wiesbaden, West Germany—she also attending a Kennedy Rally in Germany.

It is interesting to read Lorna Smith's comments in her book, *Judy, with Love* about the Birmingham show. Initially the audience was more reserved than the Londoners, but by the intermission they were cheering and by the end of the second half, the audience rose to its feet and were standing in the aisles. Judy said she had no more songs except a slow one and they insisted she go ahead with "You'll Never Walk Alone." The audience joined in picking up the passage usually sung by the choir. Finally she offered to repeat something she had done

earlier and the audience called for the "Trolley Song".[6] A man commented afterward, 'I have never seen anyone work so hard!"

It is strange to think of a Judy concert as "work." I remember Judy once saying, I've loved *working* for you tonight!" and I thought at the time, "Work?" We in the audience had been in heaven, but Judy was working.

On October 5, she performed a similar show at the Palais de Chaillot in Paris and a second night on October 7.

On December 1 she performed for the *Gala Performance* before Her Majesty, the Queen Mother.

Judy did 25 minutes of a three-hour show and won the ovation of the evening, as usual!

In Amsterdam, she performed at midnight at the Tuschinski Theatre on December 10; it was broadcast live on the radio and recorded. Norrie Paramor conducted the Cosmopolitan Orchestra, and Judy sang 28 songs. This is perhaps one of my favorite recordings of this era, even more so than the Carnegie Hall recordings by Capital made the following April. I feel she was more relaxed and more like the "Judy" I had seen at the Palladium.

She returned to the USA for a short visit which became extended after the many concerts and film work organized by her new agents, Fields and Begelman. She would come back to London to work on the movie, *Lonely Stage* (later called *I Could Go On Singing*) in 1962 with Dirk Bogarde.

PART FIVE

Final Years

Standing Alone

1961-1969

Chapter 16

1961- Creative Management Artists, Fields & Begelman

When Judy returned to the United States after being in England for six months, her relationship with Sid became very fragmented. The family never seemed to get ahead financially; perhaps she needed new management. Sid had introduced Judy to Freddie Fields, who was leaving MCA and starting his own agency, calling itself Creative Management Artists, with just a few artists. Sid was going to work on his own projects.

Judy and children returned to the Carlyle Hotel in New York where she signed a contract with Freddie Fields, who had added David Begelman to his crew. John Springer was set to handle publicity.

Fields sorted out a dispute with CBS and in January Judy performed a concert in Miami. Judy, Fields, and Begelman set up Kingsrow Enterprises, and Judy gave them power of attorney to write checks. Begelman was set to concentrate on Judy's career while Fields went back to California. She moved into an apartment at the Dakota. The children enrolled in schools, and Liza attended the School of Performing Arts.

The following year brought varied work, high salaries, and many awards. There was no question that Judy was back in top form, feeling well and working incredibly hard.

She basically did her Palladium show for the next year. The first concert was Concord Hotel in the Catskills on February 12; the State Fair Auditorium, Dallas, on February 21 came next, where Judy had a reunion with her sister Jimmy. Stanley Kramer was in the audience. Followed by a concert in Houston on February 23.[1]

Fields and Begelman arranged for Judy to play the role of Irene Hoffman in *Judgment at Nuremberg*—this gave her $50,000 for eleven days work in March. Judy went to Uta Hagen, a German coach and actor, to get the accent. That year she received an Oscar nomination for Best Supporting actress.

Judy and Sid got back together again on Joey's birthday, March 29, and they spent Easter together in Palm Beach.

On April 6, the tour continued: Kleinhans Music Hall, Buffalo, New York, then on April 8 at Constitution Hall, Washington, DC. Sid was still around because Judy and he had dinner with Robert and Ethel Kennedy at the White House on April 9.[2]

She performed in Birmingham on April 11, Atlanta on the 13th, Greensboro and Charlotte, North Carolina on the 15th and 17th.

The famed Carnegie Hall concert came next, on April 23 and thanks to Wayne Lawless, I now have Sonny Gallagher's excellent memories of this concert from the article he wrote towards the end of his life: "Judy and Me." [3]

> The most exciting and vivid evening I ever spent in a theatre with Judy would be the April 23, 1961 Carnegie Hall concert. The force, power, and complete authority of Judy's work during that period of her life will always be with me. For me the experience amounted to seeing her in total and complete command of her craft giving the ultimate performance that I knew she had always been capable of, at the very top of her form. The terrifying outpouring that she gave of herself during the 1960-1961 period and during this particular concert was such a tangible thing that for me it was as though several times during that magical two hours for an instant or two the earth actually stood still, stopped revolving on its axis, lightning stuck, and my heart stopped beating. There was such a force and power on that stage and so much effort, love, and talent being

unselfishly given that the effect was awesome. The love that poured back to Judy from audiences during this period of her life was a natural response to all that she was giving us of herself and to her God-given talents. As that particular evening came to an end I found myself at the stage apron. I have no recollection of getting up from my seat and gravitating to the stage. I only remember being at the stage, rather stunned. At this point in Judy's career the rush to the stage at the conclusion of the performance was not part of the accepted routine. The Carnegie Hall concert helped formulate it, as did other concerts of the same tour.

There a few feet in front of me was this woman that I felt I had known for a long while. By now she was totally devoid of makeup, her hair was in strings, and her costume was drenched in sweat. The woman had laboured for two hours at the thing that she did better than anybody else in the world, and as she kicked, pranced, and sang her way through the closing numbers on the program I stood there with my mouth open and an endless chill going up my spine, realizing that I was witnessing a historic and classic performance. The force of Judy's work during that period is something that I can never forget, and that particular evening would rank as the greatest one I ever spent in a theatre. I don't mean to suggest that the performance by Judy that night was the only great one I saw her give. I was fortunate enough to see many of her memorable performances, and much of her concertizing during 1961 was of this caliber. It's just that the first Carnegie Hall concert is my all-time favorite, and a variety of reasons. When I remember her now and talk of Judy, for me the Judy Garland that I see in my mind is

eternally the Judy Garland of the 1961 era. It is how I choose to remember her, and there were many different Judys that I knew. If you could have been given the choice of seeing her perform just once during her lifetime, 1961 would have been a very good year to choose.

Gordon Stevens shared his photo with Judy that night.

Much is written about this show, but I felt I must add some thoughtful comments by Camille Paglia, Professor of Humanities at the University of the Arts in Philadelphia. She wrote in the New York Times on Sunday June 14, 1998, soon after the two-day tribute to Judy at Carnegie Hall organized by John Fricke:

> Overprotected by her domineering stage mother and a series of paternalistic caretakers, beginning with the MGM mogul Louis B Mayer, Garland obediently performed on cue, swallowed pills issued by the studio to wake her up or put her to sleep, and collapsed into vacillating misery offstage. She was addicted to chaos. But she came alive through music, which throughout her life she would happily sing for hours at any party with a piano....As the decades passed..."Over the Rainbow" became her tragic anthem. It accumulated more and more meaning, until it broke the audience's heart. Like Tosca's aria "Vissi d'arte" (I Lived for Art), the mature Garland's "Over the Rainbow," sung at an eerily slow tempo, was an operatic lament.... [4]

On April 29, she performed at The Academy of Music, Philadelphia. She went on to Newark, New Jersey on May 2. the Civil Opera House in Chicago May 6, the Music Hall in Dallas May 8, and The Sam Houston Coliseum in Houston May 10th. On May 12, there was a concert at the Masonic Auditorium in Detroit, then on to Cleveland on May 14. Lorna and Joey were at this concert for Mother's Day. May 21 saw Judy back at Carnegie Hall for a single night and Liza was present.

Judy invited Dirk Bogarde to come to Carnegie Hall, but he could not make it. Soon after the concert, she arrived at his house near London in June bringing a recording of that night. She told him that towards the end of the show, her voice was nearly gone and she had got to

> And you will never guess where?...right there, in the silence, one voice from way, way out in the dark, called out "Where?"...right on beat...and he saved me. I took it from him and I went, brother I went....thank him." [5]

She was exhausted; Dirk drove her around the countryside until she relaxed. She was still at his house when she got the call from Kramer to do a *Child is Waiting*. On the last night, they gave her a great party, she made out a list and everyone accepted. After supper everyone sat around the grand piano where she and Noël Coward sang for their suppers. She knew all Noël's lyrics. It was a shimmering evening; Judy wrote him this note:

> What you have given me is something I will never be able to explain to you, ever. I honestly don't know what I would have done without you. You always give me pride in myself and belief in myself…and that's the loveliest gift of all. How I will ever repay you, Heaven knows! Thank you for my shining new life. I won't fail you, and you have made it impossible for me to fail myself. God bless you. Forever Judy."6

The next few months Dirk was at the end of the telephone whenever Judy called him, even in the middle of the night. They talked of working together, so when the opportunity arose to make *The Lonely Stage* , they were happy.

Judy rented a house in Hyannis Port, and the children joined her.

Forest Hills Stadium, New York, came next on July 1 with about 14,000 people present with a gross of $54,621. The party afterwards went on until 3:30 a.m.

James Goode spent many days with Judy prior, during, and after Forest Hills and wrote a 3-piece article for *Show Business Illustrated* October 31, November 24 and 28. At one point, she coyly asks Goode if he liked Begelman. One can assume Judy was already emotionally involved with Begelman. One can hear from Goode's reporting that Fields and Begelman were giving Judy lots of tender loving care, and all was well. They were keeping her laughing. Judy told Goode that she felt that she was at the best time of her life. "I'm terribly healthy. I have three marvelous children, and I think I have a brand new career opening up."7

Judy talked to Goode about Liza and her summer stock:

> …When summer's over, she'll go back to school. I think it robs a youngster of too many things. It's too competitive. I don't think children should be thrown into that at all. They should have proms and football games and all of the fun of growing up. I was on sage from the age of two. I don't regret it. I learned a lot, and I've been successful. But I do think I missed a lot. It's a very lonesome life…[8]

On July 3 Judy performed at the Newport Jazz Festival in Newport, Rhode Island followed by a return concert at Forest Hills on July 30. By August 4 she was performing at Convention Ballroom, Atlantic City, New Jersey.

On August 11, Judy went to Boston for the opening of Noël Coward's play *Sail Away* (on its way to Broadway after a run in London) with John Springer and Kay Thompson. Elaine Stritch would tell stories in her one-man show *At Liberty* about Judy coming to this premiere, and how they would later become very good friends. (Stritch was anxious to know how Judy liked her performance, but Judy wouldn't comment and Stritch ran after them down to the elevator. As it closed Judy said "About your timing….") I spoke to Elaine after her show in London a few years ago and we talked about Judy. She told me she could have done a whole show about Judy![9]

Around this time Judy and Coward tape recorded a conversation which appear in Redbook magazine and well worth reading.[10]

Luft tried to hold on to the Mapleton Drive house, but he had put so many mortgages on the house that it was impossible. He sold it for $225,000. Judy was earning good money then, but I assume she did not want to put any more money into a house, which could be re-mortgage.

Judy went on to do shows in Atlantic City, New Jersey on September 3 and San Francisco on September 13. My friend, Jack Wood saw her there and told me the audience requested that she her sing the full number of "San Francisco," twice, and she did![11]

The report from the San Francisco Examiner was excellent.

> ...BUT THE CONCERT was memorable on several counts-for the astonishing slickness of Judy's vocal artistry: for her fantastic, inexhaustible energy: for her ability to hypnotize an enormous crowd or churn them into a mass hysteria that was almost unbelievable.
>
> When Miss Garland sang "San Francisco," for example, the frenzied shouting and foot-stamping made her all but inaudible and one was reminded of a giant political rally.
>
> THE STAR was in rare high spirits and, by and, by the second half of the evening, she had reached her top form. Her mood throughout was informal and infectiously uninhibited. She loaned, ad-libbed, told personal jokes, danced a little and conducted the concert like a house party, even to her costume, which consisted of a short silk jacket and black trousers...[12]

A memorable September 26 concert at the Hollywood Bowl, in the rain yet, grossed $74,400. She then went to Denver on September 20 and back to White Plains, New York, on the 29. Hartford, Connecticut, came next on October 1 and then to Newark, New Jersey, on the 7.

On October 13 she recorded, "Comes Once in a Lifetime" and "Sweet Danger" in New York City, followed by concerts in Rochester, New York, on October 17, Pittsburgh, Pennsylvania, on October 19, New Jersey on October 21, and then the famed Boston Garden concert on 27 October with 13,909 people grossing $52000. Judy then went to Montreal, Canada.

Judy spent three weeks in Los Angeles recording for the animated film *Gay Purr-ee* (1963) with Kay Thompson at her side. A concert at the Beverley Hills Hotel in Los Angeles on November 20 came next, then to Miami, Florida, on November 25th. New Jersey on November 28 and back to Toronto, Canada, on December 3.

A review from the December Toronto concert captures the heart of the Judy thing with her audience: "Any cool investigation of the Garland mystique goes by the board after you find that unexpected moisture in your eyes. All you wonder at is how, in that great, big, crowded, noisy house, Judy Garland can find you out and sing directly to you." *The Telegram.*[13]

Another concert took place on December 5th at the O'Keefe Center in Toronto. Gordon Stevens, who saw Judy over thirty times, (and shared his photograph), told me a delightful story about Judy's bracelet falling off as she was running along touching hands at the end of a concert. A man picked up the bracelet and managed to get it back on Judy's wrist as she passed by a second time. Judy thanked him gratefully after the show and told him her children had given her this charm bracelet.[14]

Next was a concert on December 9 at the Armory in Washington, DC. Less than a week later, Judy flew to Berlin with Kay Thompson for the December 15 premiere of *Judgment at Nuremberg*. She went on to Rome completely exhausted, returning to New York for Christmas with Sid and the children.

No wonder she was tired: just to document all the concerts and movie work Judy did this year is exhausting. She earned an incredible amount of money; one wonders where it all went.

The year 1961 ended on a high note, however. In December, she was voted Show Business Personality of the Year, Female Vocalist of the Year, and Best Popular Album of the Year.

Chapter 17

I Could Go on Singing–1962 until mid1963

The year 1962 started well with rehearsals for the television special *The Judy Garland Show* on January 5, 8, and 9 with Frank Sinatra and Dean Martin. Kay Thompson was on hand to keep things rolling smoothly. I feel Judy was at her healthiest and most comfortable weight then, but I suspect she wanted to be slimmer.

From January through April, she worked on Stanley Kramer's *A Child is Waiting* (1963). This is a beautiful movie about handicapped children, which was not given sufficient attention when it was released and is now very hard to find.

In March, Judy received the Cecil B. DeMille Award for outstanding contributions throughout the world of entertainment, given by the Hollywood Foreign Press at the Golden Globe Awards. She was the first woman to receive this honor and the youngest at 39 years old. No one has beaten her record so far.

Judy was considering the script for a movie, *The Lonely Stage* (later the title changed to *I Could Go On Singing*). She asked the producers whether they would offer Bogarde the role. She was not happy with the script, so he took it and tried to get it re-

written. They agreed to make the movie together.[1]

Unfortunately, by the time the movie was about to start, Judy and Sid had become embroiled in their latest divorce fracas. He tried to take custody of the two younger children, and Judy flew to London on April 12 in a panic. She had the children made wards of the court in Britain. I feel this was the beginning of the end for Judy's health. She was continually worrying whether Sid would take the children; the thoughts of an unpleasant divorce suit would be enough to stress anyone out, even without having to appear on the set and sparkle. *(Anyone going through this would understand the anxiety. When I returned to California in 1973 with two small children, 8 and 6, I was obtaining a divorce from my husband; he made the children wards of the California court, so I could not take them back to England, even if I wished. I was not working then, and I doubt that I could have emotionally managed to do so. I felt sorry and completely understood how Judy must have felt a decade earlier. Later I heard that she had been awarded $150 a month for each child, the same amount as I received. I wonder how much of those $300 a month she received!)*

Although there were difficulties in making the movie, there were some marvelous times, too. For example, May 7 Judy recorded "Hello Bluebird." Then between May 14 and 16 there was filming

at the Palladium. Members of the London fan club (now known as The

175

International Judy Garland club**Error! Reference source not found.**) attended, as extras, in the dress circle. I remember spending a lovely day sitting in the audience listening to playbacks of "Blue Bird" and watching Judy come out in rehearsal clothes with her hair in curlers. In between, Liza would come on the stage and go through her mother's motions to the playback. My one claim to fame is that I can be seen in the second row of the dress circle in both these shots.

Then Judy would come out again and talk to the audience, hoping they were "not too bored". Finally, she came out and it was filmed. Apparently, there was something wrong with the camera, and it had to be reshot, but we had a lovely experience. Another day Lorna Smith and I were there for the filming of the song, "I Could Go on Singing", and my dear friend, Steve Jarrett

recently found this photograph of Lorna and me looking over a box onto the stage. When filming was done talked to Judy for a few minutes backstage, and she introduced us to the children. Later Lorna was at the studio on Judy's birthday; many photographs recorded the event.

Director Ronald Neame writes in his memoir, *Straight from the Horse's Mouth* (2003) about directing *I Could On Singing*. The plot involves an American singer Jenny Bowman (Judy) visiting with her ex-lover David (Dirk Bogarde) and their now adolescent son Matt (Gregory Phillips) at the King's School, Canterbury, where they shot the school's production of *H.M.S Pinafore*. After the show the boys put on, Judy got together with them at the piano and sang "I Am the Monarch of the Sea." Neame writes that this was shot live with no playback. It was incredibly natural with Judy laughing and encouraging the boys on. I have always felt that if people wanted to know what Judy was like as a person, they should watch this segment. She was so jolly and relaxed having fun with the boys. [2] This was "my Judy".

Another time a group of us, about 80, were invited to watch Judy record "I Could Go on Singing." Judy arrived at the recording studio with Dirk Bogarde. Apparently she had not been told there would be an audience and was slightly disconcerted, saying, "Give everyone some refreshments," and we went off to get a drink. Finally, the recording started—you get the picture, about eighty people sitting in some bleacher seats at the side with Dirk Bogarde. Judy, in a black straight dress, kicked her shoes off and she was away…

Dirk and Judy wrote the final scene of the movie, which Dirk included in his book, *Snakes and Ladders.* Judy and Dirk rehearsed

it together at her home at the weekend (when the unit was not working) and it was filmed the next day at the studio in one take and without any rehearsal there, following by spontaneous applause from the film crew. [3]

During July and August there were custody hearings about the children, a settlement arranged for Sid, and the "ward of court" status removed from the children.

On August 12, Judy flew to Los Angeles. Then she went to Lake Tahoe, Nevada where she filed for divorce. This is when Judy went on a crash diet and only drank two cups of tea day.

She went down with acute pyelonephritis of the right kidney, in the hospital again, but she got down to 100 lbs.

There was a six-week season at the Sahara in Las Vegas from September 18 to October 29. Mort Lindsey was with her.

During her opening night on September 18 Judy received a 2-minute and 18-second standing ovation and a Gold Record from Capitol Records for *Judy at Carnegie Hall*. On November 7 she performed in a concert in Chicago scheduled associated with the Chicago world premiere of *Gay Purr-ee* was on November 9. Then came a television show filmed in New York with Jack Paar on December 2 where we all saw the beautifully slim Judy.

On December 6 Judy got to sing for Jack Kennedy at the White House.

In December, Judy signed a contract worth $24 million with CBS for her weekly television series, which sounds a lot, but this would be if the series went for four years. $6 million was the outlay for the first season with options—with Judy being able to cancel after the first thirteen weeks.

On January 18, 1963, Judy appeared at the White House Inaugural Anniversary Salute to Kennedy and Johnson. Between January 30 and February 3 Judy recorded a television special with her friends, Phil Silvers and Robert

Goulet. This television special gave Judy the opportunity to play many different and funny characters.

February 7 found Judy at the Harrah Resort in Lake Tahoe. There were health problems, and by the 13 Sid is back with her.

There were reconciliation weekends in Las Vegas and San Francisco. They went to the Kennedy compound in Hyannis port.

In March, Judy flew to London for four days to do a show at the Palladium and attend the premiere of the movie. At the Palladium show, which was live, Judy sang "Almost Like Being in Love" and "This Can't Be Love" (which must have brought back memories to her of the first time she sang them at the Palladium in 1960). Among the other songs she sang was "Smile," which was broadcast on The Ed Sullivan Show on April 13, 1963. Judy received £3,000 for this performance, which she quickly donated to Lady Hoare's Fund to Aid Thalidomide Children.

Lorna Smith told me a lovely story about those four days in London.[4] This was the official beginning of the Judy Garland Club in Britain. Pat McMath, who ran the US club, had asked Lorna to pass Judy a letter—which she did when she met her outside the Palladium for rehearsal, and Judy put it in her evening bag. She put her arms around Lorna and took her backstage asking if there were any other club members outside.

Lorna said, "Yes, a couple."

"Well, go and get them," said Judy.

When Lorna came back with the club members, the stage door attendant refused to let them in, even though he had seen Lorna going in with Judy. Lorna was very upset because she knew Judy liked to see friendly faces there when she rehearsed.[5]

The next day Judy asked Lorna to write to Pat McMath and ask her to disband the club, which she did. I believe Pat continued with the club for a few years.

After Judy returned to the States Lorna wrote to her asking if she could run The Judy Garland Club and Judy gave her blessing. This is when the current club, which is now called the International Judy Garland club, came into existence.

During the last two weeks in March the family was back together again for a vacation in the Caribbean.

The family went to see Liza in *Best Foot Forward* on April 3.

The Garland 1963-64 television series was originally planned for New York, but the venue was changed to CBS Television City in Hollywood. Judy appeared at social functions with Jim Aubrey and his family, and all seemed to be well, but later the relationship seemed to cool.

A house in Brentwood on Rockingham was purchased, and a housewarming and birthday party for Judy's 41st birthday was held in June 1963 with Sid present, but soon after the couple separated for good.

One of the issues between them was that Sid suspected that Begelman was stealing money from Judy. He got an accountant, Oscar Steinberg, to audit the accounts. He found 13 checks paid out to cash for $35,714, another $10,000 unaccounted for, and a 1963 Cadillac given to Judy for partial payment for her appearance on the Jack Paar show but registered to Begelman. When Sid brought this information to Judy, she said, "Look, suppose he did steal $200,000 to $300,000 and swept it under the rug. Now I'm going to make $20 million on these television shows, what is $300,000?"

In many senses, Judy was right about this decision. Later Begelman cashed a check made out to Cliff Robertson. Robertson and his wife went to the Wall Street Journal about it but Robertson found himself blacklisted and did not act in movies for several years. The entertainment industry does not like someone to report the wrongdoings of another!

Chapter 18

CBS Television Series–1963-1964

By October 1962, I was living in Los Angeles with my husband. In the spring of 1963, I started work at CBS studios in the Business Affairs Department on Beverly Boulevard. Judy signed a contract for her CBS television series in December, 1962, and we would both be working at the same location!

The studio provided a portable dressing room with a yellow brick road leading to Studio 43 where Judy would be working. There was a lot of positive publicity initially with regard to the series, but later that changed.

The first episode of *The Judy Garland Show*, taped on June 24, 1963 was full of optimism. Mickey Rooney was her first guest. I was at that show and the party afterward. There was so much excitement, joy, and hope for the future amongst her friends and loved ones. It was sad that forces would soon turn against her.

My write-ups appeared in 1963/65 issues of the 'Rainbow Review' and 'Garland Gazette,' and in Rainbow Review, Autumn 2004.[1]

"My husband and I arrived at CBS Television City at 7:30 p.m. The doors closed at 7:40 p.m. There were two entrances to the studio, one from inside CBS and one from outside. As I had seen just how few seats there were—about 250-300—and as dozens of VIPs and stars were arriving and going in, I thought it best if we went in from inside the studio. We found ourselves mingling with the stars outside the set, and when the doors opened, we found raised seats near the back. I noticed Lucille Ball, Natalie Wood, Hedda Hopper, and her son William Hopper, Louella Parsons, Dick Van Dyke, elder brother of Jerry

Van Dyke, Van Heflin, Glynis Johns, and a number of other American TV personalities, along with most of the Hollywood press. Liza was sitting in the row in front of us.

Probably because of the fame of his brother, Dick, Jerry Van Dyke gets a break and joins Judy as a regular on her show. He came out for the warm-up and explained that because of the complicated nature of the set, a sketch would have to be shot first, and then the show events would run through in proper order. He introduced Mickey Rooney, played the part in this sketch of a German doctor living in an old castle-type place with walls covered with heads of stuffed animals. Mickey was watching The Judy Garland Show on a TV on this set. Judy started her number by commenting on the difference between concerts and nightclub appearances, but she hoped that no matter what the TV audience was doing, they would welcome her into their homes. The TV screen enlarged several times to show different amusing home situations and settled in Mickey Rooney's room. Just at that moment, Mickey's TV set broke down and he called for maintenance. The TV was repaired as Judy was finishing her number!

Then, the set was cleared and prepared for the beginning of the show. The stage was completely empty but for an enormous spotlight standing near the back of the set. The show started with shots of the orchestra playing excerpts from her numbers and finally Judy walked out from the back/left of the set towards the camera and sang "Keep Your Sunny Side Up." During this song, Mel Tormé stood alongside the camera mouthing the words to Judy. He later told my husband that he had written some new words for this song, and Judy had asked him to give her encouragement with this first tricky number, as she was nervous. She was incredibly slim and wore a sleek black crepe or silk dress with a black velvet border on the V-neck, which crossed with a diamond clip at the waist and went on to the hem line. The dress was sleeveless and split up the side.

The applause went on long after the cameras had finished rolling and Judy had left the stage. Judy, who was in a gay mood, popped out from the side and edged the applause more until a spotlight caught her and she ran off. Mickey Rooney came on—acting as if the show had not yet commenced, and talked about Judy and old times, and a few seconds later Judy joined him and he showed her a sign which read "Mickey Love Judy...still." They talked about how good it was to work together again, and then Judy dragged him off into her dressing room, saying they still had a few minutes to go before the show started. Cameras then switched to Jerry Van Dyke, who was trying, unsuccessfully, to rehearse his introduction. He started taking some pills to calm his nerves, and then Judy joined him and warned him of the danger of taking pills. Judy began "I Believe in You," and he eventually joined her. She encouraged and coaxed him along until he felt wonderful, and then he fell flat on his face.

The next scene was a lighted staircase with Mickey Rooney in evening attire singing "When I'm Not Near the Girl I Love." Chorus girls join him as the song went into "Thank Heaven for Little Girls," and he finished with two six-and seven-year-old girls beside him on the set.

Judy arrived on same set in a black jacket with a white collar and cuffs over her dress. She sang "When the Sun Comes Out." Judy was in fine voice and the audience just adored her.

After this scene was finished, she ran across the stage and grabbed the wardrobe mistress, racing back with her across the set calling out, "Wardrobe, wardrobe!" As I said before, Judy was feeling just fine.

The next scene had flat screens showing Judy's and Mickey's films *Babes in Arms*, *Strike up the Band*, and *Girl Crazy*. Before the cameras started, Judy came out in a black dress with a fitted bodice and a very full stiff net skirt with many slits around it, showing glimpses of Judy's legs as she danced. She stood at the front of the stage with producer George Schlatter and introduced him to everyone.

As Judy was showing him that her throat was still fine, she nearly fell over backward. Lucille Ball, who was in the front row, jumped onstage and puffed up Judy's crazy skirt, and in retaliation Judy and Mickey, who had then joined her, tried unsuccessfully to get Lucy back up on stage.

The scene finally started with Jerry spoiling his introduction because he tried to tell the camera operator how to work the new camera, and he introduced "Two people who need no introduction as they've already met each other." The camera switched to the dancers, and Judy and Mickey joined them singing, "You're So Right for Me." They went into a mock comedy dance routine, and Judy kicked her shoes off. Finally, they flopped down into the canvas director chairs and looked through some old MGM stills from their films together, commenting and laughing about old times. Judy then asked Mickey to do his golf routine, and she gave the commentary, taking off on the usual golf commentary. They finished the scene with the last chorus of "You're So Right For Me."

The final scene was set very similarly to the last scene from her first special, with runway lights along the floor and a large trunk in the middle aisle. Judy stood behind the trunk and sings "Too Late Now," "Who Cares," a marvelous "Old Man River," and closes with "I Will Come Back."

After the show finished, Mickey came on and talked to all the old show business pros. "Have you ever heard anyone sing 'Old Man River' like that?" He brought Judy back on stage. He commented that  Judy was the love of his life; his wife knew it, and in fact all his wives knew it. Finally, Judy dragged him off. Judy did not fluff one number; everything went beautifully. There were no second takes on anything. It was unbelievable.

After the show there was a press party. As we were walking out, one of the ushers said to my husband, "Won't you go into the party, sir?" So we did. We had a couple of drinks and wandered around; everyone else seemed to know each other except us. Finally, we sat down at a table with a charming couple and quite enjoyed the hour we spent there. I

didn't intend on speaking to Judy with all my bosses and the stars present, but she stopped near our table to speak to Jerry Van Dyke. Another man, I think it was David Begelman, was trying to drag her away, and I couldn't resist the opportunity to

try and get a word in before she left. This man was pulling at her left arm like crazy, and I went up and took hold of her right hand. Her head was still turned looking up at the man, but she immediately grabbed hold of my hand, even though she had not yet turned her head. We must have stood like that for several minutes, and I

would have let go of her hand, but I couldn't. Judy held on fast! Eventually, her head turned sufficiently for her to see with whom she was holding hands, and I said something like, "Lorna (Smith) would never forgive me for not saying 'Hello' to you and giving you best wishes from the Club." She responded in the affirmative as she was being dragged away. I said, "You remember, in London?" Her face lit up and she said, "Yes, yes, I I remember!" The woman we were sitting with said, "Don't feel too bad about only getting a word with her—that man was dragging her off to Louella Parsons." There was so much happiness that night with Mickey Rooney and George Schlatter. They asked if I knew Judy, and I said I had met her several times. This was the last time I spoke to Judy.

On Saturday, July 6, we went to the dress rehearsal of "Episode Two" with Count Basie and his band, Mel Tormé, and Judy Henske. It started around 7:30 to 7:45 p.m., and it was finished by 9:00 p.m. The director was very efficient; everyone seemed to know exactly what they were doing. Overall, it seemed a very happy set of people. Judy looked fine again in a black sparkling outfit.

Jerry Van Dyke asked the audience not to applaud at the beginning, as the show would start quietly. Judy walked out onto the empty stage with chairs and cables all over the place and softly started to sing "I Hear Music." The Count Basie Band gradually joined her, finishing up with "Strike Up the Band." Mel Tormé was rehearsing his bit with the drums and then went into "Fascinating Rhythm," which Judy watched intently. Then Judy sang "Memories of You" with Count Basie at the organ. Some scenes with the Count Basie Band had been taped previously. There were three or four numbers in all, one with the band alone, one with Judy singing, one with Mel, and then "April in Paris" with Judy, Mel, and the band.

To be honest, I cannot remember Judy and Mel's singing numbers because I was watching Judy watch the monitors! First of all, she came out wearing her sparkling pants for the first time, and sat down at the edge of stage next to Lorna and Joey (who were at the corner of the stage), kissed Lorna's hand, and intently watched herself singing on the monitor, clapping madly at the end. This caused a laugh, naturally! During Mel's number she danced with any member of the crew who would agree to make a fool of himself, then finished with Mel Tormé—dragging him out to sing their duet for the audience with each other on the monitors. So we had two Judy Garlands and two Mel Tormés to watch. I think Judy felt the audience was not getting a full show because of the way the monitors were used during the numbers, and she wanted to make it up to them. It was certainly her idea, for it was obvious Mel knew nothing about it until then.

After this, Judy went into a cute dance routine in which she wore a pink bowler hat. Then the set was changed for the finale, which seemed to be the same each week: edge-of-the-stage runway lights and a trunk. Judy sang the sad "A Cottage for Sale," then "Hey, Look Me Over," finishing with "I Will Come Back." There was a lot of fooling around as the credits rolled. After the usual ovation and the "applause" lights went out, and after the cameras stopped, applause started over again as if it had just occurred to everyone that it really had been a good performance. It was nice to hear because it was genuine. Judy had fluffed her lines in the first and last songs, but she gagged her way through them. Afterwards, she went anxiously around the audience, thanking them and apologizing for all the mistakes, which were only very minor due to the tricky new words put into the songs. She was extremely sweet to the audience full of out-of-town holidaymakers. The girl I went with had never seen Judy before and thought she was wonderful.

I was on vacation and missed "Episode Three" with Liza and "Episode Four" with Lena Horne, but I got tickets for "Episode Five" with Tony Bennett and Dick Shawn. The show started with Judy coming out singing "If Love Were All," then later the big production number "Yes, Indeed" with Judy and chorus, and at the end Tony and Dick finished with Lena, and Judy. The set -- railroad and signposts -- was very attractive for Judy and Tony's medley. The songs here included, "Lullaby of Broadway" (Tony), "Carolina in the Morning" (Judy), "Kansas City" (Tony), "When the Midnight Choo-Choo Leaves for Alabama" (Judy), and "San Francisco" (Tony, later joined by Judy). Towards the end of the show Judy told the audience that she always ended with a miserable song, so no need to change the rule now, and then she went into "Stormy Weather." finishing, as usual, with "I Will Come Back."

We noticed that Judy had begun to look directly into the camera, an improvement over the first show when she wouldn't do that—the same as for talking to the camera! She said 'they' had told her she should talk more to us (the audience at home, I suppose), so we would get to know her more. "Might be disastrous, of course," she wickedly added to the studio audience!

I did not really feel Judy was quite as on top as on the other shows. The only song she really got her teeth into was "Stormy Weather." Her frame was so slight in those days. I wished she had started eating again and put on a little weight.

Joe and Lorna were both there again with many of their friends. Judy watched the other artists very intently, and at one point in a swinging number of Tony Bennett's, she started clapping a couple of times accidentally. She also watched Dick Shawn and laughed a lot at his act. She seemed to get real enjoyment out of these acts, which she must have seen before, and always made a lot of fuss over everyone.

An interesting point was that during the "Tea for Two" segment, Judy was supposed to have a chat with Roddy McDowell, but instead Steve Allen was sitting on the set when she arrived. She seemed surprised and insisted she didn't know he would be there.

Unfortunately, there did not seem to be the usual breaks between the shows. I began to worry; I hoped the going was not too tough for her."

On August 5, *The Hollywood Reporter* stated, "George Schlatter withdraws as Garland Show Producer," and so it started. Coyne Steven Sanders' book *Rainbow's End* (1990) documents all the difficulties.

From that time on I remember as the weeks went by the many negative comments coming down from management about her show. I was so distressed about the treatment Judy received at CBS that I left their employment in the autumn of 1963.

Fields and Begelman focused on many other artists gained from their association with Judy—Barbra Streisand, Marilyn Monroe, Liza Minnelli, Carol Channing, and others, and they left Judy at the mercies of CBS.

There were several romances while making the series, but Mark Herron was the one person who accompanied her to Hawaii and Australia when the series ended in late March of 1964.

Through the years, after the television series, Judy would often talk about it. She talked to Judy Philipson of the *Miami Beach Reporter* who reported on March 11, 1965:

> There were so many switches. I didn't care to be caught in the switches. It was agony. I can't read music and I had to learn 12 new songs for each show. And, they were always changing producers and format and writers. It was just awful. I just thought it better that I resign. I wanted to just sing…what I do best is just to sing…but they wouldn't let me. I couldn't make them understand.[2]

Judy in Hollywood 2010

In April of 2010, I was lucky enough to be in a group, organized by Jan and Richard Glazier to visit CBS studios. Eleanor Lyon was one of the then young people who waited patiently outside the studios for Judy before and after takings for each episode all through the series. Through the years, Eleanor and other members of the gang have told stories of Judy greeting them and chatting with them, even taking them into shows. Eleanor met George Sunga, Production Supervisor of the series, during a small reunion of "Judy's Gang" in 2003 for the 40th anniversary of the first taping of the Judy Garland Show, and she arranged the 2010 tour for us using that same connection.

George Sunga met us at the Artists' Entrance and talked with Eleanor Lyon and Coyne Steve Sanders, who had written the already referenced book *Rainbow's End*, about Judy's time with CBS. We went into the building and took an elevator up to the next floor. As we entered Studio 43, I felt shivers up and down my spine; several other people felt the same way. This was a special place. At this time, it seemed to be a warehouse for unused lights and equipment with just a couple of small sets on the side. George is a very

quietly spoken and gentle soul who has a great love for Judy, often using the expression "perpetuating the memory of Judy".

George explained that Studio 43 could accommodate only 275 people at most, but this did not matter because Judy's audience was dedicated and could make more than enough noise. During her series, Judy had both looked and sounded great. He explained about the sound systems -- they used an A7

mobile speaker to focus the orchestra sound directly at Judy on stage. Even though the orchestra was in the same studio, it was in a band shell surrounded by heavy drapery and large Plexiglas walls some distance from the stage. Without the A7 playback speaker close enough to Judy, she would have been bothered by a time lag in the orchestra sound.

Judy sang using a hand microphone, but when it was  important for her to have her hands free, they used a boom mike. Because the A7 speaker could surround Judy in a narrow cone of music, the boom mikes could operate with little fear of feedback. Murdo MacKenzie, Bing Crosby's audio expert, came over to help solve any audio and musical balance problems. All the crew wanted her show to be a success.

George showed us where the runway was, and the raised stage with the turntable that was sparingly, but tastefully used. Eleanor said their favorite place to sit was next to the runway off by the portable dressing room. She questioned where the dressing room was—usually at stage left, but sometimes on the other side for quick costume and make-up changes.

Steve asked him to tell the story of when Judy sang to him. George explained he was the production supervisor assigned to *The Judy Garland Show*, which meant he was wearing two hats, one for CBS and one for George Schlatter and Judy.

My responsibility was making sure we could deliver everything the show required. It was early evening of the first orchestra reading and music rehearsal of the very first show on Judy's stage. Mort Lindsey, the Music Director, is running music cues and production numbers for Judy and her guests. Judy is sitting on the edge of the raised stage and she caught my eye and beckoned me to join her. She indicated I should sit next to her. As Mort started to play one of Judy's ballads, she put her arm through mine, and started singing to me. Now, you would think that I would remember every note and every lyric but I can't...I was in a haze. My cohorts and crew were really enjoying my discomfort. Guess I was gone. I really didn't have to reaffirm that I was a Judy fan...forever.

George talked about the first Judy Garland Show episode. He commented that it was electric.

> First of all, we had to beat off Mickey Rooney with a stick! He had so much energy. Since it was Judy's first show, he took it upon himself to keep her energy up, and they knew each other so well after two decades of working together. Mickey was with us during a final note session one evening and he admonished us, "Please take care of Judy". We knew that it was from his heart. It affected all of us. It was a challenge and a half; how to do a credible Judy Garland Show, and how to meet the expectations of her audience.

George talked of the last show of the series. He told us that no one tried harder than Judy to finish that show. "It was her last episode, therefore, the last time she would use her trailer, or walk the yellow brick road." Earl Carson, prop manager, took care of her "under the radar". They were good friends. Earlier in the season, Judy asked Earl if he wanted to be stage manager and he replied that he felt he could help her more as prop master. Judy was caring and generous, said Earl. They had gone past the scheduled videotape time. It was late and Judy's voice was going.

George remembered the clown number. Judy would get up to a certain point, but she couldn't finish. It was sad. We took a two-week break and started the painful session all over again, but she still couldn't complete the number. Eleanor told how they went to Kelbo's restaurant/bar in-between takes. Back in the studio, Eleanor and the other "bench wenches" were shifted from one place to another in the audience to make it look like there were more people there. At one point, Judy was sitting on the edge of the stage talking to them saying, "It has been a disaster from the beginning."

"No, no" they insisted, "it has not been so."

But she was heartbroken. It was 5:45 a.m. when they left the studio and the sun was coming up.

Steve Sanders and George Sunga spoke about the money Judy would have received, $30,000 per show, but out of that she would have to pay her manager, etc., so her take was not that much. George talked about how the series had taken on a life of its own. Judy now had 26 one-hour musical episodes to add to her legacy of music, along with her movies and recordings.

Asked about the favorite guest star, George said it had to be Barbra Streisand. "Judy had no ego, she just wanted to help—she was so special—Barbra was 19 (actually 21) at the time and soon going to Broadway to do a new musical, *Funny Girl.* Their famous interpolated duet -- Judy's "Get Happy" and Barbra's "Happy Days Are Here Again" (inspired in part by Barbra's then

current hit with that tune on her first LP)-- was conceived by Judy. She could hear it in her head. Mel was not involved. Judy demonstrated how it could be done, worked it out on the piano, and Mort did the arrangement. This arrangement is now included in many music schools. Here are Catharine Kay and Erin Long performing the duet under the guidance of Edrie Means Weekly at Shenandoah Conservatory in 2012.

After our tour of the studio, Eleanor Lyon showed us where she and the other members of the Bench Wenches as they were called, waited for Judy to arrive and depart. Over time Judy became acquainted with the young people and brought them into the studio whenever she could. One early afternoon Judy arrived (wearing orange capris and a beige pullover sweater and clips in her hair and little make-up except lipstick) she asked the group, "Do I look glamorous enough for television?" Somebody asked her if the group could go in with her. She hesitated and said, "All right, come on!" The lucky group was able to watch Judy pre-record a complicated football number, and they understood the difficulties of getting of the technical aspect perfect. [3]

We all felt such sadness that the series had ended. I particularly felt such regret that I had not tried to contact Judy

during the time we were both working at the same television studio. Firm directives had come down from management that no one was to go near Judy's dressing room or try to talk to her. Most other performers were seen in the cafeteria and around the studio from time to time, but never Judy. She was kept away from everyone. I felt sorry I had not written to her through the internal mail system, reminding her of our meeting in London, but I was a new girl and very conscious of being a foreigner. I assumed she had all the friends she needed, and what could I have added? Sadly, she did not.

We retreated to Farmers' Market for lunch where I used to go every day fifty years ago. This was such a special day shared with Justin Sturge, Gary Horrocks from the UK club and Eleanor Lyon and Ruth Turner.

Later that evening we had dinner at Matteo's one of Judy's favorite places and celebrated the joy and genius of Judy Garland.

Judy in Hollywood April 2013

A second gathering of Jan Glazier's Judy Family group was planned for April 2013 to celebrate the 50th Anniversary of The

Judy Garland Show spearheaded by Coyne Steve Sanders and Frank Labrador.

Sadly, in February we heard the dreadful news of Steve's passing and the whole Judy community was in shock, but the "show must go on" as they say. So, in April we met again in Studio 43 at CBS Television City and George Sunga reminisced  again about the series, with Frank taking Steve's place prompting George for these precious memories. And we lunched at Farmers Market with Lauren McShea joining Eleanor, Amelia Armijo and myself.

On another day, we met at the Hollywood Heritage Museum to hear presentations from Sam Irwin about his book on *Kay Thompson* and Christopher Finch's book, *Rainbow*.

We remembered Steve. Randy Henderson spoke sharing some words from Daniel Berghaus. Don Azars spoke and shared a video, I read a tribute by Gary Horrocks tribute and also read my own. Ruth Turner and Tracy Terhune (reading words from Charles Triplett) shared their memories of Steve. Frank Labrador finished by telling us about the documentary he was preparing combining Steve's audio recordings for his book; "*Rainbow's End*" and film clips.

Steve had the uncanny ability to reach out and be the friend many of us needed. Frank summarized it best  saying, "Steve inspired you to be better than you thought you could be." In my case, he encouraged my writing about Judy and responded positively to my blogs saying things like, "Joan is a force of nature."

Sad though the occasion was losing Steve, it was also a joyous time remembering his love for Judy and his great contribution to the Judy Family.

We later have a tour of Warners Brothers studio and visit many of the locations where the 1954 version of, *A Star is Born* was filmed. Then the evening entertainment began. We rolled out on the LA freeways to Oil Can Harry's to see the fabulous Judy impersonator, Peter Mac. I don't usually like Judy impersonators, Jim Bailey is the only person I could tolerate, but Peter is actually more than an impersonator and there are moments when I actually felt he *was* Judy. Between the songs, he comments, as Judy, on her life and his facts are accurate. A truly gifted performer!

Our final evening is a dinner at Matteo's one of Judy's favorite places, and George Schlatter, producer of the first five episodes of Judy's CBS series was one the guests. Other

guests included Margaret O'Brien and Judy's son Joe Luft. After dinner, George Sunga and George Schlatter were the "floor show"-- Schlatter is the comedian and Sunga the straight man. They reminisced about the series and Schlatter repeated many of the stories, in Sanders' book, "Rainbow's End", but when he tells them, they are in glorious Technicolor with many embellishments. A night to remember!

My blog jcoulson4judy.blogspot.com "Judy in Hollywood" April 2013 has more details.

Chapter 19

June 1964–Australia and London

After the finish of the CBS television series, Judy left with Mark Herron to Hawaii for a vacation. Judy had several romantic  involvements while making the television series, including a real estate man and Glenn Ford, but when the series ended Mark Herron seemed to be her primary friend and companion. Mark had ambitions in the acting field and appeared in a couple of Federico Fellini movies. There was often talk of Judy and Mark appearing together in a play, but nothing came of it. As with other men  involved with Judy, being with her was a full-time job. After their split in 1966, he disappeared from the scene. The years with Mark gave Judy stability; they seemed to be fond of each other and Judy looked well, happy, and incredibly beautiful during this time. Lorna Smith met him many times while Judy was in England in 1964 and thought he was a charming young man and very attentive to Judy.[1] Wayne Lawless, another long time Judy fan, met him several times in Las Vegas and concurred.[2] It was a shame that the relationship ended. Mark continued to work in the acting field after their break, sometimes in summer stock. He died on January 13, 1996, in Los Angeles.

Shows in Australia were next on the agenda. On May 11, Judy and Mark arrived in Sydney along with conductor, Mort Lindsey, and others. There was a large press reception at the airport and Judy seemed relaxed and happy. In the evening, she gave a press reception at the Hilton hotel for about forty reporters, including interviews for radio and television.

On Wednesday, May 13, she gave a successful concert for 10,000 people at the Sydney Stadium and on May 16 she gave an even more successful concert, performing for more than 90 minutes singing 23 or 24 songs, including "The Man That Got Away," "Swanee," "When You're Smiling," and "As Long as He Needs Me."

If any of the young fans want to understand Judy's relationship with her audience, they should find a recording floating around the fan base one of the shows in Sydney. This captures the atmosphere and excitement of a live Judy show. See

my blog jcoulson4judy.blogspot.com for this subject.

We can tell Judy is feeling great and in a very happy mood. Some business with tangled mike wires comes up -- it often does! "Now, next!" she says firmly and launches into "Almost like Being in Love" followed by "But This Can't Be Love" (more applause). She takes a big breath and finishes with "When you are Smiling."

Next comes a very sweet "Do It Again," and the crowd reacts. They obviously have listened to the Carnegie Hall LP many times.

Then Judy talks about the early days of movies and how important music was, even before the talkies, and how all the great composers came out to Hollywood -- "Wherever that is!" —Cole Porter, Irving Berlin, and George Gershwin. She says she was lucky enough to sing some of these songs in her movies. Then she goes right into the melody starting with "You Made Me Love You" -- great response from the crowd -- "For Me and My Gal"—"Sing it with me," she says, and they do. I never heard an audience do so with such enthusiasm. "Clang, Clang, Clang…" -- the audience is out of their minds!

Judy says, "Don't know if any of you saw *The Pirate?*" (They did!) She chats with the audience. Judy thinks someone is the publicity agent for the Beatles! Then she goes into "Love of My Life."

A trumpet wails, and the crowd knows from the first note that it is "The Man That Got Away."

Time for a chat, maybe Judy is talking about it being warm because she takes off her jacket and says, **"Now We Can Go."** "I never will forget Jeannette McDonald"…cheers…the song about my hometown "San Francisco." Then it is time for a break.

After Intermission, Judy starts with "That's Entertainment" which she often did after the interval. A stop half way and it sounded as if some water had been spelt, "Somebody come up…" fits of giggles…"Oh Boy I don't know what the hell we were doing. I think we should forget that…." But Mort starts again and she finishes "That's Entertainment" changing many of the words.

Now it is old home week and a free for all. "We can sing anything we want" Judy says. People call out different songs but mostly "Swanee" so Judy says "Let's do it….they (orchestra) have to switch charts." "If I forget the words just throw things at me" she says as she goes into "Swanee" How she loves this song they cheer nearly all the way through the number.

The crowd calls out "sing anything….I know that!" she retorts. Tells them she got paid during the intermission and was happy and so the next song was "Make Someone Happy" and then "Just in Time." A discussion about the play *Oliver* and then she sings her song from that show. Then comes "As long as he needs me," "By myself" and "Rock bye." More discussion about what she should sing, they or Judy decided to sing "Chicago" and she ended with "Rainbow."

Judy had many joyous nights with her fans and this one must certainly be up there with the tops.

A train took the party to Melbourne on May 19, which was probably a mistake, and Judy arrived exhausted. She attempted to give a concert the next day but it was not a success because she was unwell although she managed to get through fifteen songs.

The *Melbourne Sunday Herald* reported on May 20, 1964 how kindly the staff at the hotel thought of her. They presented her with a toy koala bear and card from maids to manager, saying, "A very small Australian mascot, but a lot of good wishes." They found her quiet, polite and agreeable and when she left, she told assistant supervisor, Mr. Clarry Crew, "I really appreciate what everyone has done for me. I think you've all been wonderful. I've never had service like it anywhere in the world." These comments are important because they show how kind and charming Judy was when she received kindness.

Judy and Mark flew back to Sydney the next day and on to Hong Kong on May 22. On May 27, a typhoon struck Hong Kong. Sometime in the night, Mark found Judy unconscious and she was taken to a Catholic hospital where she was in a coma for 15 hours. She had pleurisy in both lungs and her throat and heart was damaged. The doctors told her she could not to sing for a year.

In early June, Judy first saw Peter Allen perform with his brother in their act. They continued traveling and arriving in London on June 30, 1964.

London

Judy tried to severe her connections with Fields and Begelman, and while in England, she was managed by Harold Davidson

Ltd. On August 6, Judy recorded two songs from Lionel Bar's new musical *Maggie May*, and two more songs on August 14.

In 1997 when I met up again with Lorna Smith, we reminisced about our time with Judy. Lorna told me about the six months when Judy lived in England in 1963 and gave me copies of the Rainbow Reviews from 1964 onwards. I was thrilled to have this material and I wrote a long piece about this six-month period when Judy lived in London. Judy was an avid theatregoer and would often talk with fans when she met them; some fans also attended the rehearsals and the Judy/Liza concerts, and a private party at the Mayfair Hotel with Judy. Many attend the Jack Parr show and finally there is an in-depth report with photographs of the club meeting attended by Judy, Mark Herron and others in her party. This article was published in Rainbow Review in 1999.[3]

Upon arrival in London Judy rented an apartment in Kensington with Mark Herron and appeared to settle down, for a while that is!

The annual midnight charity show, a fundraiser for the Actors' Orphanage and named *"Night of a Hundred Stars"* occurred on July 23, 1964. Judy had been admitted to hospital on July 20 and so had not been expected to even appear. But she discharged herself on July 20 and took everyone by surprise.[4]

Now, her doctors had warned Judy that she should not sing for a while after her illness in Hong Kong. Instead of being sensible, she could not resist the calls for her to sing.

The first half of the show had all the well-known actors and celebrities performing in sketches with other celebrities watching from side tables. Judy, wearing an orange-pink full-length dress, and Mark Herron were in the audience. Celebrities acted as emcees and announcers; the Beatles led them to their tables, but when it came to Judy's name, cheers from the audience blurred the second part of her name and chanting began, "Welcome home, Judy!" Judy bowed and went over to her table. The show could not continue because everybody in the theatre began to chant out and call out her name. She took another bow and returned to her seat. Shirley Bassey was the final act. Shirley sang, Noël Coward's "If Love Were All," and blew a kiss to Judy. After Shirley finished singing, a chant started "Sing Judy", Richard Attenborough led Judy to center stage, and the audience responded wildly. Judy whispered, "It's nice to be home again." "All right" she said. "What do you want to hear?". "Well, you discuss it among yourselves, while I talk to the piano player." (Billy Ternent) . . . "Does anyone know what key I sing in?" . . . After some discussion, Judy sang: "Somewhere over the rainbow" gently and wistfully. She discussed the tempo of "Swanee" with Ternent and tore into it. [5]

The Daily Mail reported July 24, 1964s Judy's comments about the evening:

> Judy said afterwards, "It left me speechless and so terribly grateful. Because these people were taking the trouble to show me that, to them, all the things that have happened in the past, all the things that have been said about me, didn't matter. They wanted me to know that they really cared. It was as if they were sending a great wave of love across to me. London has always been like home to me. Now it's more than ever home. I don't know what happened there at the Palladium or why the people should have shown such emotion towards me. I guess it's something which just happened. And believe me, the most exciting thing in the world." [6]

The people who acclaimed her were fellow professionals and people who had paid high prices to see this charity show. _The Listener_, which is a BBC publication and quite conservative in style talked of how celebrities are now classified as stars, instead of this title being given to someone who has earned it by theatrical performance and so the word 'star' is devalued. They felt it was good to be reminded what a star is; and the magic which justifies the fame.

> Such a reminder was provided last week, when Judy Garland walked on to the stage at the London Palladium . . . Miss Garland was just one of a host of artists gathering on the stage to watch a cabaret . . . But she has long had a special place in the hearts of London audiences, and on this occasion they knew she had recently been in hospital. What they did not know was that her doctors had forbidden her to sing, and as soon as she appeared they interrupted the show with cries of "We want Judy." Eventually. . . the audience won. With a touch of theatrical genius, Miss Garland exploited the

fact that she had had no rehearsal, asking the audience if they knew what key the accompaniment should be in, interrupting her song to tell the conductor to play five e times faster, and finally completing SWANEE virtually unaccompanied. . . Miss Garland's magnificent voice fully deserved the cheers which eclipsed any that had gone before in this genuinely starry story." [7]

Judy was an avid theatregoer and took every opportunity when in London to go to the theatre. In September, she attended the

opening of Maggie May with Mark Herron. Noël Coward and Rex Harrison were in the Audience and they chatted in the interval.[8] Also the opening night at the National Theatre of *Hay Fever* on October 27. She went to see a performance of *Giselle* on October 28 at Covent Garden. Then there was another

opening on November 3 Judy when she went to see Noël Coward's *High Spirits* with Mark, Liza, Peter Allen and Coward.[9] Judy asked Liza to come to London to perform with her.[10] Judy asked Mark to produce a show for them at the Palladium. The first show was on November 8, and as tickets sold out quickly, a second show was planned for midnight on November 15/16. Capital recorded these shows and issued a LP.

The Daily Mail reported:

"History was made last night at the Palladium, when Judy Garland and her daughter Liza Minnelli sang together for the first time on any stage. History was made too, by a frenzied mob of fans who gave Judy the ovation of a lifetime...To talk about Judy Garland rationally is about as difficult as describing magic. Apart from still being the greatest of them all, through every routine it was apparent that she also is an accomplished actress. And if, to the very critical, the voice is no longer always what it used to be, she still has that elusive 'star quality,' which makes her the most-loved performer in the world today."[11]

Judy was to appear on the Jack Paar show on November 25, and Judy arranged for the club to received sixty-five tickets for the telerecording. Judy had a long and close relationship with Jack Paar, so she knew he would encourage her to tell outrageous stories about show business—which she did, of course. The Marlene Dietrich "applause recording" story, for example, has gone down in classic Judy history. Sam Irwin explains this recording in his fine book on *Kay Thompson*. In Irwin's book he relates how Marti Stevens, reports on a party at Noël Coward's place in Switzerland in 1962 where many friends were gathered. Coward and Thompson were playing pianos and having a fine time, but no one was paying any attention to Marlene and she left. "Unfortunately, sometime later, she came back and in her hand she had some records. She interrupted the evening we were simply adoring to say, 'Here, you must play this. These are my applauses.' Records of applause! There was no music on them. Just the applause. And she was determined that we should hear it." [12]

Lorna Smith invited Judy to attend a club meeting to be held on Sunday November 29 at the Russell Hotel and she came with Mark, Snowy (Judy's nurse from Hong Kong Mrs. Slowda Wu), Peter and Chris Allen and another  young man. Lorna told me about this club meeting.[13] Judy wore a light gray woolen dress with a red chiffon scarf at the neck and a large green ring on her ring finger, and that she looked very well. Judy enjoyed seeing all the scrapbooks on display and thought they were marvelous; and they watched the movies, *Gay Purr-ee* and *The Harvey Girls*!

At one point, in answer to a question, Judy told the fans that she liked *Meet Me in St. Louis*, *The Clock*, and *For Me and My Gal* even though she knew it was corny!

Judy's humor came out during the showing of *The Harvey Girls*, and the print they had was terrible and kept jumping in places. Judy's charm, humor and kindness were very apparent on this occasion, making a difficult situation funny and tolerable.

At one point she said "I never knew what it was all about. No one ever told me anything. I'd walk into a scene without knowing why I was doing it . . . In the picture I always seemed to be having rows with Angela Lansbury, who is a very nice person and whom I liked, without knowing why. . . . .There were seven writers and they each had their own plot. . . . Marjorie Main is a dear, kind soul.

Just before she left she sang a couple of songs for members. What treat this must have been for those present. Everyone sat on the floor or nearby chairs to listen. Judy gave a beautiful rendering of "Make Someone Happy" and then sang "I Wish You Love" with Peter and Chris. Both songs were recorded for club posterity.

Then she was asked if she would please tape a message for the club. "Good-bye and God bless you all. I thank you so much. I couldn't have imagined a sweeter or nicer thing than today and I'm terribly and eternally grateful."[14]

Chapter 20

1965 to April 1966

When Judy returned to the States, she continued to work hard for the next eighteen months. There were many social functions, concerts and several television guest appearances; she looked beautiful and happy. She flew back and forth from New York, to Los Angeles, and Las Vegas. She performed well but had occasional health problems. There ought to have been enough money earned to support the family, but it seemed that it was not so. It was always becoming difficult to keep Judy's health stable. However, there were great shows and we rejoice in them.

On February 2, 1965 Judy taped her first TV appearance in New York since her television series, *Broadway Tonight*, that had ended in 1964. One could tell how popular she was by the long lines of fans outside the studio to see this show. The opening number is Judy with the Allen Brothers singing "I Wish You Love." Wayne Lawless told me that Judy looked beautiful and was in good voice-she sang four songs, plus one with the Allen Brothers and looked ravishing. [1]

Then Judy filled in for Nat King Cole at the O'Keefe Center in Toronto with the Allen Brothers, February 8 – 13. The first show on February 8 went well according to another fan. Judy came on after the Allen Brothers and Nipsey Russell at 10 p.m. and started with "When You're Smiling," "Almost Like Being in Love/This Can't Be Love," "The Music Makes me Dance," "Smile," "Swing Low, Sweet Chariot." There was a break when the Allen Brothers came back, and then she sang several more songs including a funny version of "Chicago," using the Canadian city of Oshawa in place of Chicago. On February 9, Judy changed the order of the songs and included "Just in Time" with Mort Lindsey. She missed one show on Wednesday, February 10, because she was ill. However, she was back and performing well on Thursday, Friday, and Saturday.

I am always pleased when I can find someone who was present and can give me first hand comments. A longtime Canadian fan, Gordon Stevens, told me about something which happened to show Judy's sensitivity. He and his friends had met with Judy several times during this engagement. When they saw Judy, Mark, and others going into a supper show, they did not want to intrude, but Judy beckoned them over and they talked. Someone suggested going in, but a girl was singing, and Judy refused to go in until the song was finished. This shows Judy's sensitivity and consideration to the fellow artist. [2]

Judy then went down to the Fontainebleau Hotel in Miami, and the reviews were excellent. Frank Meyer of *Miami Beach Daily Sun* said on March 12, 1965:

> Miss Garland switches keys with ease, at one time making four key changes in two sentences. She uses her musicianship for the ultimate effect....She turned in a beautiful rendition of "What Now My Love," a song which is handled only by singers who have the guts to try it. It's a difficult number and the audience caught their breath, then exploded with applause when she reached for, hit and sustained the final note....If you can get in, go see Judy Garland. This is one of those delightful show business experiences which don't happen too often. When

208

they do happen, you just feel lucky you were able to be part of it. Judy's back, and may she be around a long, long time.

Judy told him "I have three beautiful children. I'm a good cook. Life has been very good to me. There is nothing tragic about my life, I enjoy it....I have great respect for an audience. They pay their money. They take time away from things they have to do at home.... **And then I sing to them individually.** Not as a whole audience. There's the change I think." When asked about the Garland-audience rapport, she said "I know I'm a craftswoman of showmanship. I know – I THINK I know – how to handle an audience. You do it with love – through songs, through telling stories, through making mistakes. I forget lines. Or I trip and fall or the mike goes off. Usually these mistakes are important. They make people out there realize I'm no different than they are." [3]

Jean Wardlow of the *Miami Herald Sunday Magazine* captured the essence of Judy in her article on March 14, 1965, entitled "Judy":

The hands keep time to the music when they move. But the body – small, nervous, tense – keeps its own time. And when she moves, the steps are long – semi-circled cat-like if the skirt is long and tight – but usually sudden-stopped, short like dance steps not quite danced – "I move around a lot, but I don't even realize when I move that."...But it's the face you watch as you hear the voice – the face brushed with spotlights – many or one; white or blue; full length or centering only on the clear, asking eyes of Judy, America's "Eternal Waif," the woman in her early 40's who seems destined always to be the Child Dorothy following the yellow brick roads, searching for hearts and wisdom and courage. . . ."You don't listen to Judy," one rehearsal musician said thoughtfully about her. "You experience with her. It's something that happens, you feel it. You know when it's there. You know when it's over. But you don't know what to call it. You simply know she made it happen. [4]

On April 5, Gene Kelly introduced Judy at the Academy Awards ABC-TV, where she sang a complex melody of twelve of Cole Porter's songs.

Judy and Mark went to Hawaii for a vacation with Lorna and Joe. *The Honolulu Advertiser* reported on April 15, 1965, that a fire had broken out in their rented house.

Judy went to Charlotte to sing at the Mecklenburg Democratic Gala on April 23 at the Charlotte Coliseum, then on to Chicago on May 7 at the Arie Crown Theatre, and the fans loved it

Liza's debut on Broadway in *Flora, the Red Menace* was on May 12, 1965. Judy and Mark were there, reported *Life* Magazine: "Leading the cheers was Judy herself, wearing diamonds, black chiffon and wet eyes. She rushed back-stage, weeping, to embrace her daughter."

On May 19 the divorce from Sid became final. *New York News* reported on May 20, 1965, that Judy's 13-year marriage to Sid Luft was over.

Judge Edward asked her: "Is Mr. Luft working?"

"I don't believe he is. I don't know," said Miss Garland.

"I don't know why he should be relieved of supporting his children," the judge said, ordering Luft to pay $150 monthly support for each child. I was awarded this same amount in 1975 by the judge in my divorce settlement.

Judy caught a virus and could not complete her show on May 29 in Cincinnati. She returned to Los Angeles and entered UCLA for treatment. However, by June 14 she was present at a party Peter Lawford threw for her at his Malibu beach house with about 100 of her friends. John Carlyle was amongst the guests; he had been in and out of Judy's life since he had a small part in the movie, *A Star is Born*, sadly lost on the cutting room floor. He'd also been an usher during Judy's 19 week run at the Palace in 1951 and was a great admirer.

Judy left UCLA on June 15 and went straight to Las Vegas where she appeared at the Thunderbird from June 15 – 28. She did not miss any shows, getting rave reviews and standing ovations. Chris and Peter Allen opened for her. Wayne Lawless were there. My friend, Jack Wood, was also present and told me how amazing her performance was:

> people were literally standing on tables, jumping up and down, dazzled by her talent. Betty Grable was there one night and Alice Faye the next, right down in front standing, yelling and screaming with the rest of us.[5]

On July 9 she was a guest on the *Andy Williams Show* which screened September 20, 1965. Judy was not in good voice, but this did not stop her from giving an excellent performance.

She performed an excellent show on July 17 at Forest Hills and my friend Kenneth Young (one of Judy's gang) was there and reported that Judy was anxious about being so far from the audience so she broke the tennis stadium rules and came out on the green to be close to the audience. The audience stomped and clapped for over 30 minutes. Kenneth says this day is indelibly embedded in his emotional psyche.[6]

> *Billboard,* July 31, 1965 Garland Displays Her Old Form at Concert by Robert Sobel
>
> Judy Garland gave an energetic, frenetic and peripatetic 90-minute performance that was pure magic at the West Side Tennis Club in Forest Hills…It was indeed difficult to judge her on voice alone, although for the most part it had power, control and stayed on key. She simply is one of the rare artists who can transfix an audience by sheer personal magnetism.[7]

On August 12, Mark and Judy were in San Francisco where Judy performed from August 31 to September 5 at the Circle Star Theatre. Jack Wood commented on the "magic" of that evening. [8]

One evening, Judy mentioned on stage that she and Mark Herron would be married and named the date. Wayne Lawless was there, went out the next day, and bought a silver charm and had it engraved with their names on one side and the date on the other. He gave it to Judy the next evening as she arrived at the theatre with hair in rollers and wearing a bathrobe, and she quickly thanked him. Later that evening Wayne found the couple in the bar after the show and after the other fans had left Mark called Wayne over and Judy said, "You are so sweet" and gave him a kiss on the lips. What a lovely memory! [9]

On 3 September 1965, the *San Mateo Times* reported:

Judy Garland in Better Voice
by Barbara Bladen.

> Judy Garland gave a tremendous performance last night. She sang the ceiling off Circle Star Theatre and left her fans clamoring for more. Rested, smiling, and in excellent voice, she sang a dozen numbers without forgetting a single word and bantered jokingly with her capacity audience.[10]

After the last show in San Francisco, reports emerged that excited fans knocked Judy over and she hurt her knees. On September 6 she was back in Los Angeles.

September 13 Judy opened at the Greek Theatre in Los Angeles. On the 14th, she fell and broke her arm but managed to do the second show with the help of Mickey Rooney, Johnny Mathis, and Martha Raye. The rest of the shows were cancelled.

Judy appeared on the *Ed Sullivan Show,* telecast on October 3.

> Judy was great tonight…better than she's been since her return from London.…She looked great and for the first time in a year-and-a-half of TV appearances her timing (both in songs and in movement) was like the Judy of old. Gone were the half-spoken notes and the tentative gestures. Her voice was strong and the tremolo well under control.…Judy started "Come Rain or Come Shine" in the wrong key. She sang the first time and then switched to the correct key without any clue from the orchestra. I certainly breathed a sigh of relief when the orchestra came in with the bongos mid-way and they both hit

the same note smack in the middle. Actually I think what 'threw' Judy is the one note she's given at the start of the song. She came in on this note, but it wasn't the one she was supposed to start on. It appeared to me that either the wrong note was struck for her or else she was supposed to come in a third step ABOVE the note. At any rate, she apparently realized the error and corrected it without any prompting, which I thought was astounding. [11]

Wayne Lawless shared with me his experience of going to the taping of the Hollywood Palace show on October 15/17, 1965 (shown November 13). He mentions that the theatre is still there and is still called the "Palace," located on the west side of Vine Street, just north of Hollywood Boulevard.[12]

As with most of these television shows at that time, there were two tapings: a dress rehearsal in the afternoon and a formal taping in the evening. The show ran through in sequence except for the middle segment, which was done last. Judy started with a stirring rendition of "Once in a Lifetime." Judy had with her on this show three guests from her television series: Jack Carter, Chita Rivera, and Vic Damone, presumably all old friends. Wayne reported that Judy watched all their acts, sitting on the left side of the stage. She laughed so hard at Jack Carter's comedy that she spilled her drink.

The middle segment was taped last, presumably to give Judy time to get into her tramp outfit. She did the "Couple of Swells" number and sat down on the edge of the stage, commenting about being hot in men's clothes and saying, "I wouldn't be a *man* for anything." She then sang Cole Porter's "I Loved Him But He Didn't Love Me."

While my friend Wayne was waiting for Judy to come out from her dressing room after the show, he wandered out onto the stage. He saw Judy's mark and stood there for a while, imagining what Judy would have seen while performing.[13]

On November 6, Judy sang for Princess Margaret, whom she had met several times in London. Then on November 14, she was finally married to Mark Herron in Las Vegas.

She went on to do shows at the Sahara Hotel for two weeks, November 30 through December 13. On the last night Judy sang "Liza" in honor of her daughter, who was the next headliner.

On December 17, she was at the Astrodome in Houston for a concert. Judy, Mark and the children spent the holidays at her home in Los Angeles.

February 2 through 10, 1966, Judy was at the Diplomat Hotel's Café Crystal, and the reviews were good. Pat Mascola of the *Hollywood Sun-Tattler* said on February 4:

> The unpredictable Judy Garland electrified her opening night audience at the Diplomat Hotel with enough current to lift them off their seats for the first standing ovation seen this year along the strip. Miss Garland is, without question, the queen of phrasing and can get more out of the lyrics of a song than most pros. [14]

On February 12, Judy was at the Children's Hospital Miami Florida, and on the 14 she flew to New York to tape the Perry Como Kraft Music Hall for NBC to be shown on February 28. Bill Cosby was also a guest. This show got universally good reviews. The *Pasadena Star News* said on March 2, "Miss Garland's numbers were gay and off-hand. The hour, which sometimes moves very slowly, zipped by."

Judy went on to do an excellent show for the *Sammy Davis, Jr. Show* for NBC on February 27, shown on March 18, 1966. Judy sang some of her greatest hits and performed in Tramp costumes with Sammy Davis, Jr. She was in great voice.

The next *Sammy Davis, Jr. Show* was taped on March 6 and shown on 25. She had laryngitis; she couldn't sing, but she clowned most effectively in a hobo-costumed duet with host, Sammy.

Judy flew home to Los Angeles on March 7 and was to be on the second episode of *The Andy Williams Show* but had to cancel because of laryngitis. That day the sheriff put an attachment on her Rockingham house because of unpaid mortgages.

On April 1 Judy hosted a *Hollywood Palace* show with Van Johnson. The final two numbers, "Comes Once in a Lifetime" and "By Myself," were taped on April 3. This latter number was very suitable for the occasion because this, I believe, is when Mark Herron left the studio, marking the end of their relationship. It was shown on May 7, and Sonny Gallagher gave a good review. However, this ended Judy's television appearances for a while.

When a separation from Mark Herron was announced on April 15, John Carlyle became Judy's companion for a few months before Tom Green became Judy's publicist. Carlyle continued to be a friend for the rest of Judy's life.

She flew into New York for a cancer benefit for The American Medical Center in Denver on May 15 in honor of Judy Holliday.

Chapter 21

Clutching at Straws

April 1966-December 1968

I started this chapter with some trepidation, knowing of the details of the Group V contract, but one cannot count Judy out; there were some more exciting moments in her life, and she gave some excellent performances.

Judy separated from Mark Herron April 15, 1966, and apart from a cancer benefit for Judy Holliday on May 15, Judy did not work much in the next few months, because the IRS would just take her earnings.

In July, Luft came up with the idea of a new production company, Group V, as a way to evade the IRS. He told Judy that Group V meant "Judy, Sid, Liza, Lorna and Joey." However, in reality it meant Raymond Filiberti (a man who had spent years in the federal prison for taking stolen securities across state lines) with Judy and Sid being employees. According to Frank [1] Luft as president and producer would receive $1,000/week. In effect, Judy would sign over all her earnings to Group V. Here is another example of her reverting to being a little girl of seven years old and not dealing with business matters as an adult. She apparently only read the first page and signed with Group V and the unbelievable terms of the contract: she would be paid $1,000 per concert ($1,500 after 25 concerts) with Group V covering all living expenses. The IRS could take $300 per concert from her pay, $100 from Luft, but Group V would take the rest of the proceeds. Judy gave these details of the contract to the London court in a deposition on December 29, 1968. These details are in Anne Edwards' book *Judy Garland*. [2]

Tom Green came into her life at that time, as a publicist, and seemed to be her constant companion. As with most men and managers in Judy's life, she became emotionally involved with him. They went to Mexico on August 14 to do fourteen shows at The El Patio Nightclub, receiving cash payment, so the IRS

could not trace her earnings. She received rave reviews, but because of laryngitis, Judy cancelled the engagement after three shows and only earned enough to cover expenses.

In September 1966, Mrs. Chapman, Lorna and Joe's governess, left her employment, presumably for financial reasons.

On October 5, 1966, fans Nancy Barr-Brandon and Lynda Wells spent six hours with Judy at the Rockingham House, reporting this visit in a fan magazine called *Judy*.

Nancy has also talked on an internet site about how she became involved with Judy. She spoke also at the *Judy in Hollywood* function in April 2010 about her interactions with Judy. She said she was a fan and got to know Judy by following her from city to city. She felt that her own wacky sense of humor, giving high-end gifts especially for every holiday to Judy and the children, and helping her pay her bills and doing funny or touching pranks, brought her into Judy's life. Tom Green may also been helpful in getting her into Judy's circle. However, I believe when Barr helped get Green out of jail, Judy turned on her.

I met Nancy at the Judy Celebration in New York in 1998 when I was with Sonny Gallagher, (who had been a longtime friend of Nancy's) and we talked briefly. She said to me, helplessly, "I tried to help, but I was not a trained psychologist."[3]

When I became friends with Sonny in 1998, I asked him about those years when Judy was performing on the east coast and how well he knew Judy. He replied that although he drove the children, Lorna and Joey, to and from places and accompanied them swimming, he did not get involved with Judy personally the way that Nancy had.

On October 11 Judy and Sid sued CMA for $3 million, charging that they "deliberately and systematically misused their position of trust so as to cheat, embezzle, extort, defraud, and withhold monies from [Judy]." Luft, Vernon Alves, Bobby Cole and his wife, Delores, seemed to be the people accompanying Judy during this time.

Judy spent time with Tom Green's family at Christmas in Massachusetts,
and in January she was in New York. At the end of February, she flew back to Los Angeles.

On March 3, 1967, Liza married Peter Allen and

became Mrs. Woolnough. Judy, Vincente, Sid, Lorna, Joey, and Peter's family from Australia were there. Nancy Barr-Brandon was invited and she told me it was a small affair with just close friends and family present.[4]

Judy appeared on *What's My Line?* a popular Game Show in the 50's and 60's hosted by Charles Daly on March 5. This is the first time we hear from 16-year-old, John Fricke, who gives the *Rainbow Review* his comprehensive appraisal of the show.[5] Later in this same magazine, Fricke goes on to analyze an article in an earlier edition on the Palladium/Palace 1951/52. Here we see the beginnings of the great historian and writer that Fricke will eventually be on all things to do with Judy.

A couple of days after *What's My Line* Judy did an interview with Barbara Walters with the two younger children.

In March, there is a press announcement about Judy having a small role in the movie, *Valley of Dolls*. She completed wardrobe tests but extracted herself from the project. Judy is left with is a couple of pantsuits which she wears in upcoming concerts.

It was during this visit to New York that Judy first met Mickey Deans, the night manager at Sybil Burton's new discotheque, "Arthur."

The *Los Angeles Herald Examiner* reported on April 12, 1967, that Judy was divorced from Mark Herron. At the same time, Judy changed her name officially to Judy Garland (before that time Judy's official name was still Francis Gumm, despite being known as Judy Garland).

On May 14, 1967, she was a guest on the *Jack Paar Show*, but Judy did not look well.

In May, Luft sold Judy's Rockingham house for $130,000, but after taxes Judy received $15,000. From then on Judy would not have a permanent home. She would wander the globe, entertaining her audiences. Being a Gemini, as I am also, I know there is a certain amount of excitement for us around new people and new places. However, there must have been some regrets for not having a home base for her children and possessions. The constant need to keep traveling to perform to support her family plus the accumulation of years of prescription drugs in addition to shock treatment in 1948 left her health vulnerable.

On June 9, Judy took off for the east coast with Tom Green. I thought back to the time when I visited Grand Rapids in 1997 and Sid, Lorna, and Joe talked about those exciting days when the summer concerts started. Judy worked consistently during this summer for Group V: someone had made a lot of money from these concerts, but it certainly was not Judy. However, she was working well and happy as the following reviews confirm.

The start of the summer tour was at the Westbury Music Fair in New York from June 12 – 18, 1967.

Richard Hammerich of *The Springfield Massachusetts Union* wrote about her performance:

> Her impact on the audience is electric, magical, indefinable, and probably unexplainable. One thing is sure. She puts out all of herself in tremendous physical effort in an obvious attempt to perform for her listeners. She doesn't hold back. Judy looks fragile but is still explosive. In person, two or three feet away, in casual conversation, she is little, slight, fragile, her face is exceedingly mobile and her manner warmly gracious.

John S. Wilson of the *New York Times* reported on June 16, 1967:

> When she picked up a hand microphone and burst into the opening words of "I Feel a Song Coming On," the applause

rose in another immense wave. Then she reached back for one
of her old familiar, belting climaxes – and she found it, all of it.
It came through in an electrifying burst of power that brought
the eager audience to its feet once more. "We love you, Judy!"
someone shouted. "Oh I do, too," she called back, her eyes big
round pools.

My dear friend Bill Seibel, and his wife Carolyn, whom I first
met at Grand Rapids 1997, shared with me photographs he took
at the Camden County Music Fair, New Jersey, in July 1967, and
at the Garden State Arts Center, New Jersey, in June 1968. He
told me about the party he attended after one of the shows when
Judy sang around a piano.

The concerts at Storrowton Music Circus, Springfield,
Massachusetts, on June 26 and July 1, were also excellent. On
June 27, 1967, Sam Hoffman of the *Springfield Daily News*
reported:

> Never in the nine years of theatre-in-the-round on the West
> Side, or in any of our
> recollection, anywhere, has a
> performer – any performer –
> received an audience's
> complete surrender as was
> witnessed last night. Miss
> Garland captivated some
> 1500 patrons with a program
> of songs billed "An Evening
> With Judy Garland" and
> their response was standing
> ovations by the
> armful....Miss Garland is all
> professional. The stage was
> her home, the audience her
> family and she poured it on
> with one song after
> another...

Wayne Robinson reported in *The Philadelphia Bulletin* on July
11, 1967, about the Camden County Music Fair, New Jersey
concerts on July 10 - 15:

She walks down the red carpet on high heels – a slim, bob-haired Judy Garland in a sequined gold and green mod suit, green neckerchief, green earrings. On stage, she circles and smiles. Her left hand flutters nervously to her mouth, her brow....She chats a while, a queen being informal with her subjects at a garden party. "I must say theatre in the round is very peculiar," she tells them. "I never like to turn my back on an audience. Maybe if I just stood still, you could move around me!" Laughter. Applause.

The highlight of the summer was Judy returning to the Palace for the third time. This run started on July 31 and lasted until August 26. The children, Lorna and Joey, were with her and sometimes Liza as well. John Bubbles was also performing with her. After opening night old friend, John Carlyle, escorted her to El Morocco. Carlyle reports that Sid Luft asked

him to be "companion" to Judy for five hundred dollars a week, but the offer was declined. [6] The newspapers were full of reports of the show.

Earl Wilson reported in the *New York Post* on August 1, 1967 under the heading "It Happened Last Night – Garlands for Judy":

I've covered the Judy Garland cult for years. It's at its best at the Palace. There's nothing like it in the nation. She's the greatest Personality, where else can you get two shows —Judy, and the Audience? You are sitting there enjoying the artistry and timing of this 95-pound shrimp in rust brown bell-bottom trousers with silver dust in her hair. She ends a song which you found delightful. Suddenly you are almost hurled from your seat. From 20 – 30 people -- not kids -- but adults – leap up around you and start screaming "BRAVO! BRAVO!" From the balcony comes a thunderous roar, "We want Judy!" They've got Judy. What are they yelling about? They are blowing kisses to Judy. One young man on the front row seems to be shaking at 500 miles an hour. "I'm leaving here," says a friend near you. "This is either voodoo or a riot." And the same thing happened after the next song....

Sonny Gallagher told me how difficult it was to describe Judy's last night: "he said that she was in peak 1967 form on the final two performances at the Palace. Aside from the voice, Judy was a total person again. Gone are the fuzzy or tentative gestures. In their place were sporadic dance steps interspersed with the music (you can't hit a moving target). Judy uses every trick at her command to take attention away from the voice. Her personality is bright, alive, and vivid. She appears to know 100% what she is doing – where she is going. It's a new phase, a new outlook.[7]

Just recently, I found a new Judy friend, Jon Perdue, who shared with me his memories of taking a bus with his mother from Burlington, Iowa, to New York to see Judy at the Palace. He must have been a very young man then. Liza was in town on the night he saw the show and danced to "Chicago" as Judy sang. However, his exciting moment came after the show. Sid, Lorna, and Joey left the theatre, followed by Liza and her husband, Peter Allen. Finally:

> Two hours after the concert ended, Judy emerged from the theatre. It was a magical moment. The Lady, the Voice, the Legend in our midst. She stopped and just stood outside the theatre doors for a moment with her escorts. It seemed as if she were slowly allowing us to drink in the moment, and prolonging her exit so she could absorb all the love that was being directed towards her. I looked at her carefully so as to forever remember her appearance. The garish stage makeup had been scrubbed off. The gold glitter had been brushed from her hair. I was reminded of the scene in *A Star is Born* where James Mason scrubs off the excessive makeup to reveal Judy's

natural beauty, and then applies just the right touch of makeup. Judy had changed into her famous "Garland" outfit — a black skirt, black sequined top, and heels.

Slowly she moved towards her limo, graciously acknowledging the crowd. She was treated reverently – no pushing, no shouting, no popping flashbulbs. Judy knew that we were her loyal fans and she responded accordingly. Our crowd just naturally seemed to form into two parallel lines, stretching from the sidewalk to the curb, and she slowly walked between them smiling, shaking hands, thanking everyone, and receiving kisses on the cheek....And then my magic moment...I leaned down and kissed her cheek, noticing the softness of her skin and the smell of her face powder and perfume...Judy eventually made her way to her limo...Judy twisted around to her right so she could look out the back window. She beamed a radiant smile and waved to us as her limo pulled away. [8]

On the final night, Judy and the children went to *Arthur's* and met Mickey Deans. According to Deans, Judy would often drop in to the club when she was in New York.

Judy separated for the first time from Tom Green at the end of August.

The *Boston Herald Traveler* reported at an August 31 press conference these comments Judy made about her children:

It's wonderful how different my kids are. Liza and Joey are the most like me -- outgoing, affectionate and want to be liked. But Lorna! I call her the 'cruise director.' Mind like a whip, a born comedian and independent! Liza and Joey go to people, instinctively. Lorna sits and lets people come to her. And they do!

On August 31, 1967, there was a big concert in Boston with 108,000 (depending which review you read) people present. The mayor of Boston gave Judy a silver Revere bowl,, saying "Judy, we have taken you to our hearts; I think that is the sentiment of all of us. God bless you."

On September 1, she visited a VA Hospital in Boston. On September 4, she was at Paragon Park in Nantucket Beach with Joey.

On September 5, Judy gave an interview to Glenna Syse of the *Chicago Sun Times*. I feel this piece in Judy's own words helps explain her relationship with her audiences. It also explains how happy she was to be back at work, even if she was not collecting much money. Perhaps Luft did the right thing by making a dreadful deal for Judy. It gave her a lift to be singing again:

> Adoring audiences like I do, to have them give back that sort of affection, suddenly I feel it's absolutely marvelous to be Judy Garland. I'm so proud to give people even just a moment of fun, to take their minds off their worries. Frightened? I used to be frightened on stage until I finally realized the only time I have an enormous amount of fun is when I'm on stage...All I know is whether I sing to 8 people or 108,000, I do sing to each person. I believe what I'm singing, and we have an electric current going back and forth. They call out lovely things like 'We love you, Judy!' They wrap me up in cotton batting. They don't want anything to happen to me. They want me to know they love me and I want them to know I love them. Everything changed about 12 weeks ago. If you ask me why, it's because I got a job. I went back to work. They had missed hearing me and I had missed them, too. My career has had its ups and downs like a roller coaster. And I am hoping...I am hoping...it will stay on top.

On September 7, she arrived in Maryland with Lorna and Joey. The next two days she performed at the Merriweather Post Pavilion in Columbia, Maryland, and reportedly grossed $45,000 for the two nights. Or rather, Group V received the most; Judy got the usual amount and her expenses. From September 14 to 16, 1967, she was at the Civic Opera House in Chicago.

Michaela Williams of the *Chicago News* reported on September 15:

> In the 30-some years of the Opera House, nobody has put on a performance quite like that of Judy Garland Thursday night. More 'love' was exchanged during the three-hour celebration (there is no better name for it) than the Flower People ever hallucinated about....It was more than a performance; it was a mystical experience. Judy Garland keeps being reincarnated, but somehow manages to come back every time as herself....It's more than just a lyric when she goes back into "What Now My Love" – Afterwards she says to this theatre full

of people, who certainly seem to care: "You know I wouldn't leave you. I'd die first, and I'm not going to die. When my number's up, I want a new one."

While in Chicago, she visited Great Lakes Naval Training Hospital on September 17.

Judy did a concert on September 27 at Kiel Auditorium, St. Louis, and my new friend, Jon Perdue, was there again. He reported:

> The auditorium was an awful cavernous structure. She had done 60-odd performances and was near the end of her tour with six more to go. She seemed exhausted and was, understandably, in weak voice. When she came to "Over the Rainbow," she asked two young people to come up on the stage to help her out. Even though her voice was not up to par, it was still a good show, which reached the tone of an old-time revival by the time it was over. [9]

I had often thought that as much as we never wanted to leave Judy at the end of a show, perhaps she did not want the evening to end, either. Something happened at the end of the show Jon attended which confirmed that. During her final bows, she said, "Why don't you all come with me to my dressing room?" A couple of dozen people climbed up to the stage, including Jon, and he tapped her on the shoulder. She turned her big brown eyes on him and said, "Yes baby?" He was speechless. What a lovely memory!

She went on to Detroit to perform at the Cobo Hall on September 29. Don Newman of the *Macomb Daily*, Mt. Clemons, Michigan, on October 30 tried to explain what happens when Judy performs:

> [Y]ou can read about this magic rapport she has with the audiences and still never understand it until you actually witness it. Not that you understand it then, but you get a clearer picture

of why this wisp of a woman has had such a prolonged, if bumpy, career in show business. In the eyes of her friendly loyal fans she can do n wrong. Sure, the voice has given way to time. She doesn't always reach the notes she strives for and more than once there was a crack in her voice. Judy goes on because her fans encourage her. They overlook the flaws to see THEIR Judy. And she does belong to her fans more than any other star in show biz.

Variety reported on October 11 that after a two-night stint at Butler University Clowes Hall in Indianapolis on October 1 and 2, Judy grossed $33,940, making Raymond Filiberti a very rich man.

Judy went on to do a show on October 7 at Veterans Memorial Auditorium, Columbus, Ohio. By that time she was completely exhausted after over sixty shows all over the country.

On October 8 she returned to New York, then flew to London on October 11 for a holiday with Raymond Filiberti, and returned immediately when Filiberti and his wife became involved in an argument.

The intense pace continued. Judy made a personal appearance on October 16 at an ASCAP salute at Lincoln Center in New York City. She did shows on October 20 - 21 at Bushnell Auditorium in Hartford, Connecticut.

On November 3 and 4 she was at Sexton Hall, South Orange, New Jersey, and made a personal appearance on November 15 at a party following a Lincoln Center ASCAP tribute. On November 21, daughter Lorna spent her 15th birthday at Trader Vic's.

Judy performed at Caesar's Palace in Las Vegas from November 30 to December 16. Wayne Lawless told me how ironic it was that at this time of her life, when she was supposed to be at her worst vocally and health-wise, he found her looking so beautiful. Her skin glowed, and she was very healthy-looking, sang for 2½ hours without stopping, and did "Chicago" three times because they ran out of arrangements. He walked back to her room with her companions, including Tom Green. Along the way Judy decided to stop in at the linen cupboard and collect some more towels. Wayne found himself alone with Judy in the room, helping her collect towels from a high shelf. She thanked him sweetly. Wayne had met Judy on several occasions and was included in her inner circle of trusted fans. [10]

During the run on December 4, the news came of Bert Lahr's death; Judy did not perform that evening. Gene Palumbo was her conductor. To Palumbo, Judy was "the kindest, dearest, sweetest person to work for." [11]

She went on to the New Felt Forum in Madison Square Garden from December 25 to 31. She developed laryngitis and bronchitis and could not perform the last three shows.

Judy had performed nearly eighty concerts in seven months with only four shows being canceled; the tour grossed nearly a million dollars, but as we know she received very little of this money. Even with all these performances all over the country, the management of many theatres still considered her unreliable!

Angela Lansbury was leaving *Mame* on Broadway. Judy went to see her and expressed the desire to do the role. [12] She wanted the part of Mama Rose in Gypsy.

Judy met the producers, Fryer, Carr, Harries, and Bowab. Bowab remembered:

> She sang everything in the show and put us away....It was beyond comprehension what she did with the score. When she sang, "If he walked into my Life," "My Best Beau" and "It's Today," it was simply devastating.[13] Herman stated at the time, "To have seen even one performance of *Mame* with Garland would have been worth off the risks." Although later he realized the producers were protecting his show, Herman told Citron that he owed Garland a tremendous debt and said he heard her singing "It's Today" when I was writing it. She has had a deep effect on my life and my work since I keep her voice unconsciously in my brain, and her sound often will influence my choice of a word or a note." Interview with Herman 20 August 91. [14]

Judy heard in January 1968, that Janis Paige was to replace Lansbury, and she was heartbroken.

Nevertheless, she went on to perform at the Civic Center in Baltimore, Maryland, on February 18, 1968 (not a good show), but by the show at Philharmonic Hall, Lincoln Center on February 25 she was in great form. Her spirit was amazing. Judy had received so many knocks in her life time: losing *Annie Get Your Gun*; not getting an Oscar for *A Star is Born*; having CBS throw her to the dogs, but always she put on a bright face and got on with life. She visited Ray Bolger during his gig at the Waldorf.

On March 18 she hurt her shoulder in a slip in the bath. Tom Green took her diamond and jade ring and the pearl ring and pawned them for $1000 at the Provident Loan Society at Park Avenue and 25th Street to pay for medical charges. Judy was admitted to St. Claire's hospital at 3.30 p.m. Judy filed a report at a police station saying that the two rings vanished March 19.

March 30 was Joey's birthday, and they celebrated at Tin Lizzie restaurant in New York with Tom Green

On April 8 Tom Green was arrested for stealing these two rings, valued at $110,000, but he was released and they continued their relationship.

Things were beginning to unravel. On May 16, 1968, Judy found she was locked out of her two-room suite, as she owed St. Moritz Hotel $1,800, even though Group V should have paid her living expenses. Her possessions were confiscated, so the next week or so she stayed at Charles Cochran's apartment as Mickey Dean's roommate.

On May 17, an additional strange thing happened: Luft and Filiberti sold Judy's contract, as security, in exchange for a loan of $18,750 to two businessmen, Leon Greenspan and Howard Harper (whose real name was Harker; he had a police record). These two men got the exclusive use of Judy's services for the next year with the payment of only $1, along with both the screenplay of the still unmade *Born in Wedlock* and certain coal deposits located in the counties of Grundy, Sequatchie, Bledsoe, and Cumberland in the State of Tennessee! [15]

On May 24, Judy performed at the Back Bay Theatre, Boston, and was in good voice, singing on until midnight. The consequence was that she was too exhausted to sing the second night in her two-night engagement.

Luft hired Wesley M. Fuller, professor of music at Clark University in Boston, to be artistic advisor to Judy in early June.

Here is Bill Seibel's photograph from this gig. On June 24, 1968, Judy appeared on the *Johnny Carson Show,* plugging her show at the Garden State Arts Center, Holmdel, New Jersey, on June 25-29. She appeared fragile and confused. Carson was to say to his next guest, Bennett Cerf, commenting about Judy: "Basically she's a very shy person, but once she gets started she's marvelous."

Jonathan Kwinty of the *Evening News* reported June 26, 1968:

> Miss Garland stayed on stage an hour and 35 minutes and sang nineteen songs. Her voice has lost nothing with the years. She still can control that slowly pulsating vibrato so breathtakingly she could well be suspending the rhythm of waves breaking against the shore....[16]

Presumably, because Judy was not receiving any money from Group V, she insisted that Luft pay her $1,200 for each performance at 4 p.m. before every show. On June 29, she ill and taken the hospital.

Safe in Peter Bent Brigham hospital, Judy went through withdrawal and came out prescription drug free. Here is another occasion when Judy realized she needed help and tried to get it. The second Judy felt well she discharged herself and jumped right back into the performance arena and the cycle perpetuated itself. Unfortunately, as we know now the treatment for drug addiction is a long process and a week in hospital is not sufficient. The effects of the shock treatment in 1948 and years of different prescriptions drugs left her nerves on edge and she often was difficult with those around her. Resolutely though she managed to hide these problems while performing. However, as we see from the Apted study what a child is at seven years is what the adult will be. Judy was a performer then and it was impossible for her to change.

Luft took his Joey back to California; Lorna went to stay with friends.

Wesley Fuller was still escorting Judy.

She went on to do a concert on July 20 in JFK stadium in Philadelphia. This would be her last concert in the USA, and it was a magnificent show. She was medication free and in strong voice going from one song to another. Samuel L. Singer of the *Philadelphia Inquirer* said on 21 July:

> The crowd of 20,000…gave her a standing ovation on her entrance and an ovation at the close of her program….Her voice had that distinctive throb and resonance, and she sang with her practiced ease….It was a love affair from first to last. [17]

From July 31 until August 7, 1968, Judy took a trip to Los Angeles, staying with John Carlyle and later his friends, Tucker Fleming and Charles Williamson. She went with Joey to The Factory discotheque; this would be the last time she saw her son.

Judy appeared on August 9 on the *Mike Douglas Show* with Peter Lawford.

On Sunday, August 18, Judy appeared at Cardinal Kennedy Memorial Hospital; Tom Green gives a full write-up of that occasion is in the chapter "Entertaining Troops."

In September, Judy posed for photographer Richard Avedon in New York and received a mink coat.

On September 7, Judy, with new attorney Benjamin A. Freeman of Boston, reached an agreement with CMA to end her disputes with them and signed a new three-year management contract with them. This was probably so that she could receive $8,000 in back royalties from CMA. She went ahead, rented an apartment for $265.00 per month in Boston at 790 Boylston Street, and appeared to settle down for a time.

Judy wanted Lorna to join her, but the child was exhausted from trying to help her mother, so Sid arranged for Lorna to live with them in California.

On October 24, 1968, Judy met John Meyer, who was working as a pianist in the club called *Three* on East 72nd Street.

Meyer and Judy met at an apartment of some mutual friends, and Judy enjoyed some of his songs. Judy and Meyer went off together that night and ended up at the apartment of Meyer's parents, Herbert and Marjorie. Leo, Meyer's grandfather, also lived there. John got Judy occasional work for $100/night cash at his club starting on Saturday, October 26.[18]

Meyer has documented the next couple of months of their activities in his book, *Heartbreaker* and in a show by the same name that he has been working on for several years based upon his time with Judy. He informally recorded many of the music arrangements they worked on and conversations he had with Judy. He captured her speech patterns.

Mr. Wong, the IRS agent who was hounding Judy, visited her at the Meyer home. Meyer met Harold Arlen, whom Mayer is in awe of, but Arlen wanted to talk about the price of New York apartments, not music. Judy was in the hospital having treatment for a sore foot, and Harold Arlen paid her bills so that she could appear at the   Lincoln Center on November 17. The event was a great success and Richard Rodgers was present. Judy sang "The Man That Got Away," "It's a New World," "Get Happy" and "Over the Rainbow" with Arlen at the piano. It must have been a great night!

Meyer met Luft and tried to negotiate with David Begelman. Judy had just dropped her suit against CMA and wanted to work.

On November 19, Judy and Meyer flew to Boston to her apartment.[19]

Judy realized she could not work in the United States, so she contacted Harold Davison about working in London. He had been her agent in the past.

On November 30, Judy checked herself into Peter Bent Brigham Hospital again after losing control and banging her head against a wall.[20] So Judy knew when she needed help, but the constant need to keep on working ruined any hopes of her getting drug free.

Meyer reports that he arranged for three TV shows—Merv Griffin, Johnny Carson, and Dick Cavett.[21] On December 13 Meyer accompanied Judy on the piano on the The Dick Cavett show. Judy introduces John as "a marvelous songwriter by the name of Johnny Meyers." Note the "s" at the end of Meyer's name. We can see how funny Judy was then, also how romantically she sings Meyer's song. She ends with the prayer song "God Bless Johnny" John composed in Boston.

One can tell how difficult things were for Judy from Griffin's book: *Merv: An Autobiography*.[22] Judy called Merv from the hospital in Boston and said she needed to work. She said Sid had her musical arrangements. Griffin suggested she do his show because Mort Lindsey, his conductor, was familiar with her arrangements. He arranged for Christian Dior to make a gown. Judy told him she had enough money to get a train to NY. (This does not gel with Meyer's book; he says they drove in.)[23] Griffin made reservations for her at the American, but when she arrived, they refused to register her because of past bills.[24] The next day Griffin found her at the studio in tears. He booked her into the Hilton and sent cash over so she could have her hair and nails done. By show time, Judy was magnificent, and Griffin suggested she do his show while he was away for Christmas. Margaret Hamilton and Moms Mabley joined Judy.[25]

The next day Judy went to Arthur's and met Mickey Deans. They went back to his place. Charlie Cochran was there.[26]

On December 16, Meyer had the Hong Kong flu. Judy called him on 17 and 18.

Judy appeared on the *Johnny Carson Show* on December 17, 1968. She told everyone about a coming gig in London, and she sang Meyer's songs "It's All for You" and "Til after the Holiday."

Judy needs someone with her, but Meyer is ill and unavailable. She calls him every day but he has the flu.

On December 19 Judy taped "I'd Like to Hate Myself in the Morning" for the *Merv Griffin Show*. Later that night Merv rented out Sybil Burton's Arthur discothèque for his staff Christmas party. He asked Judy to join them for the evening. That evening Judy became engaged to Mickey Deans.

Chapter 22

Return to England for the Last Time

Talk of the Town

Many of the young Judy fans have told me that they are unable to finish reading many of the books about Judy because her last few months were too painful. I do not want them NOT to read this chapter. It is sad, of course, but anything to do with Judy has magic in it, and so read on!

When Judy came back to London in December 1968, she had very few clothes with her. From the previous chapters we can see that many of her possessions were impounded by hotels for nonpayment of bills which Group V was supposed to cover.

Judy and Deans arrived on December 28 and were served with a writ preventing Judy from performing in London. Harper and Greenspan were behind this as Luft had assigned the Group V contract to them. Detailed information about the contract is in Anne Edwards' book, *Judy Garland*. Luckily Judge Magarry threw the case out of court and made them pay court costs. [1]

When Lorna Smith and other fans met Judy when she arrived, they asked her if there was anything they could do for her. Judy replied that Lorna could help her get ready for the show and help with dressing. Lorna agreed, warning Judy that she was not necessarily "good at things like that." Smith stayed with Judy through the five weeks of *Talk of the Town* and documents this time in her book, *Judy, with Love: the story of Miss Show Business*. Lorna noticed that the large photographs she remembered of the children in leather frames did not seem to be evident, and Judy only had small photos of the children. Judy had two copies of the pantsuits from *Valley of the Dolls*, but the sequins kept coming off these and had to be repaired.

Lorna Smith told me a funny story about the pink dress, which was a favorite and had been worn many times. Judy had it on one night before the *Talk of the Town* show, but Lorna could not find matching shoes, only two rights or maybe two lefts.

Lorna implored Judy to change her gown, but Judy retorted, "Don't tell me my business!" and hobbled out on to the stage telling a hilarious story about the missing shoe, then kicking them off. This brought the house down. People backstage said to Lorna, "How could you let her go out like that?" All Lorna could do was to roll her eyes. [2]

Opening night was December 30 -- Ginger Rogers, Zsa Zsa Gabor, David Frost, and Danny LaRue were in the audience. Judy sang, "I Belong to London," "Get Happy," "The Man That Got Away," "I'd Like to Hate Myself in the Morning," "For Once in My Life," "You Made Me Love You," "For Me and My Gal," "Trolley Song," "Just in Time," "San Francisco," "Rainbow," and "Chicago." The reviews were excellent.

On January 4, 1969, the British Film Institute was showing *A Star is Born* and Judy and Mickey Deans attended and Judy answered questions from the audience in-between the two showings. My friend, John Theaker was there and said how thrilled the audience was to learn Judy was present. Judy gave John one of her beautiful smiles as she left the theatre which he would remember forever.[3] In the interval Brian Baxter, Press Officer for the British Film Institute, commented:

> We invited Miss Garland to a screening of 'A Star is Born' and she came down to talk to the audience for half an hour. So overwhelmed was she by the reception that she asked to come back to introduce the second performance. This time she stayed even longer and brought her husband Mr. Deans on stage. I have never seen her happier. She could not stay for the show because of a cabaret engagement—but instead brought friends to a private late-night screening of the film. Her only other 'reward' was a small bouquet of flowers.[4]

On January 9 Judy and Deans had a church blessing because their marriage had to be delayed.

On January 19, Judy subbed for Lena Horne at the Palladium and sang "For Once in My Life," "Get Happy" and "I Belong to London." This was her last appearance at the Palladium.

On January 21, Judy had the flu but went to see Johnny Ray

perform. Her doctor advised her to cancel her performance, but she insisted on going on. On January 22, John Meyer arrived from the States, went to the show, and joined Judy on stage. She was sick on January 23; according to Anne Edwards, Deans insisted that she perform even though she felt ill and was crying. She was late for the performance, and there was some unpleasantness with the audience. Later Judy was horrified to learn that no one had reported that she was sick. She had a few days rest and was back on January 27, when Meyer rented a portable recorder. Meyer was on stage with her again the next day. Meyer and Deans recorded several of Judy's performances, which are now available. Her last show was on February 1 and it went well.

In early February, Judy and Deans moved into Johnnie Ray's London home in the Belgravia district of Chelsea. Judy's divorce from Herron became final on February 11. Judy and Mickey Deans were married on March 15 at the Chelsea Registry Office. Lorna Smith and other fans attended the wedding along with lots of press and a few big name stars. One can see newsreels of the couple arriving and leaving the Office, and it is apparent how frail Judy has become.

On March 18 Judy flew to Stockholm to give a concert on the 19th; she was in great form. Deans contracted with Swedish producer, Arne Stivell of Music Artists of Europe, to make a documentary film to be called, *A Day in the Life of Judy Garland*. Cameras were installed around the hotel, upsetting Judy; she felt

she was being recorded everywhere. The whole project came to nothing. She managed to get through the performance on March 24 in Copenhagen but was becoming frailer every day. The last concert was at the Falkoner Center Theatre. On March 27 Mickey and Judy flew to Torremolinos, Spain, for a holiday, but Judy was not well.

In early April, Judy and Deans went to Hazelmere in West Sussex with Judy staying on until the middle of the month. As I come from West Sussex, it was nice to think that she spent a few of her last days in this pretty countryside.

Judy was still in close contact with June Allyson, and in one of their last conversations, Judy said to her: "If I ever die, Junie, make sure they put me in a white casket—and that everybody wears white and yellow." Judy had called her from London saying, "Now I can try my hand at playing housewife and taking care of my little nest and a man,…I'm even cooking." [5]

Then there comes some craziness with Judy and Deans flying to New York on May 21, returning on May 29, then flying back again the following week, and staying until June 17. Deans was trying to set up a chain of theatres, which did not materialize. They stayed at the apartment of Charlie Cochran, where Judy spent her birthday on her own with just a call to John Carlyle. On June 15 Judy, Deans, and Cochran went to see Anita O'Day and Judy performed with her.

Lorna Smith visited Judy in London on June 16, and she was worried about how frail she appeared. On June 18, Judy and Deans went out; Judy was in good spirits. On June 20, Judy told her publicist, Matthew West that she wanted to go back to work, and she went to a dinner party that evening. Saturday June 21 was a quiet day at home. West called her from the theatre during intermission; she was feeling happy talking about the children.

Charlie Cochran had flown out to spend a few days with John Carlyle in Los Angeles and while talking of Judy, they decided to call and speak to her at 10:40 a.m. When they called Deans he awoke and found the bathroom door locked, so he climbed out of window of the dressing room, walked over the roof and looked through the window of bathroom. He saw Judy sitting on the toilet with her arms on her lap and head resting on her arms; sometime between 2:30 and 4:40 a.m. Judy had passed away.

Dr. Derek Pocock at Westminster Hospital reported on Wednesday, June 25, that Judy had died from an accidental death from an incautious overdose of barbiturates: ten 1½ grain Seconal sleeping tablets were in her system and no food. Her system had closed down, liver had completely shut down, she was dehydrated, and eating had become painful.

"Accidental death by an incautious dose of barbiturates," said the coroner, Gavin Thompson, at the inquest.

> This is a clear picture of someone who had been habituated to barbiturates in the form of Seconal for a very long period of time…and who, on the night of June 21-22 -- perhaps in a state of confusion from a previous dose, although this is pure speculation — took more barbiturate than her body could tolerate.

He added, "I think one should bring it out publicly there was no question of alcoholism." [6]

Judy returned to New York and was laid to rest at Campbell's in a white casket. She had requested "Battle Hymn of the Republic" and that everyone wear pastels. Twenty thousand people passed by her coffin continuously for 14 hours Thursday and until 2 a.m. Friday. [7] Judy wore the gray chiffon gown she wore at her wedding. Mayor John V. Lindsay was there along with Mickey Rooney, Betty Comden, Adolph Green, Patricia Kennedy Peter Lawford, Kay Thompson, Lauren Bacall, Ray Bolger, and Marc Rabwin supporting her children, Liza, Lorna, and Joe.

Excerpts from the eulogy by James Mason on June 27, 1969, try to explain "this lady's greatness" for those who will discover her in years to come:

> I traveled in her orbit only for a while but it was an exciting while and one during which it seemed that the joys in her life outbalanced the miseries. The little girl whom I knew who had a little curl right in the middle of her forehead, when she was good she was not only very, very good, she was the most sympathetic, the funniest, the sharpest and the most stimulating woman I ever knew.

> People took from her what they most wanted. Had I ever been in a position to take what I wanted from her it would have been a long program of funny movies since I firmly believed that she was the funniest girl in the world. But she was so touching that she was invariably in demand to do the purely emotional thing. It was this very touching quality that made her such a great comedian. In these great funny films that I dreamed of she would have developed a line of whacky comedy which would have been the more effective being played without a trace of emotion in the framework of a harrowing plot…

I think that I have a hint for the Judy Garland student yet unborn. Her special talent was this: she could sing so that it would break your heart. What is a tough audience? A tough audience is a group of high-income bracket cynics at a Hollywood party. Judy's gift then was to wring tears from men with hearts of rock. [8]

After I made contact with the U.K. Fan Club and had several conversations with Brain Glanvill, he wrote to me the following letter:

I last met Judy the night her *Talk of the Town* engagement ended early in February 1969. I gave her a goodbye hug and walked back happily to Ealing, not realizing, of course, that I would never see her again. I did however speak to her on the phone only 6 days before she died. A lady who worked on the costumes for [Chekov's play] *Uncle Vanya* at Chichester in 1962–Beatrice Dawson–was also working on Judy's *I Could Go On Singing* at the same time–and in 1969 she thought I might be good for Judy. It was arranged with Judy that I phone her on her return from New York, which I did, but also fate decreed otherwise! [9]

Chapter 23

Since Judy has left us

At the time I am writing this in 2013, Judy has been gone from this planet for forty-three years, but it seems like only a few months ago that I witnessed her many concerts and triumphs. Many of her long-time and devoted fans who wrote about her and shared their information have also gone; the few who come to mind are Mark Harris, Frances (Sonny) Gallagher, Dana Dial, and my dear friend, Coyne Steven Sanders. But Judy has not entirely gone from this planet; she is still very much with us in the enormous body of work she left for us to enjoy. Perhaps because of this, Judy will be a part of our culture for 100, 200, and even 500 years in the future. She is perhaps as important now as she was when alive because of her artistry, music, and the pure joy of living and entertaining her public and fans that continues in her movies and recordings. Young people hear her voice or see a glimpse of her on television, and they are captured; they want to learn more about her, and so it continues.

There has been a great resurgence of enthusiasm for Judy in the last few years. There are number of websites, festivals, and fan clubs devoted to her artistry. Performing arts universities regularly study and perform her work.

The Wizard of Oz was one of Judy's earliest movies, made in 1938—and for which she received a Juvenile Academy Award. Perhaps because universal themes appear in the movie, it has become a part of our culture. Each generation of new children is introduced to the good and bad witches and the three unique characters who help Dorothy find her way home. The themes from this movie are referred to repeatedly in other movies and television programs. Everyone knows the dialogue in the same way the words of Shakespeare decorate our lives. The National Film Preservation Act classified the movie as a National Treasure in 1988. The Recording Industry Association of America chose the song "Over the Rainbow" (Arlen and Harburg) as the "The Song of The Century" in March 2001. It was also rated No. 1 song in January 2005 (out of 100) of the 20th century by the American Film Institute. Other winning Judy songs were "The Man that Got away" #11, "The Trolley song" #26, "Have Yourself a Merry Little Christmas" #76, and "Get Happy" #61. Just recently, Judy's blue test dress from the Wizard of Oz sold at audition for $1,119,000 and a pair of ruby slippers sold for $627,000.

But Judy Garland was more than the character she played in this movie. Judy made nine short movies in her early MGM career, and thirty-four full-length movies, depending how you categorize them. Most of these movies were musicals and entailed long rehearsals, and be found on DVDs and shown regularly on television. She left a vast body of recordings done through the years with Decca, Capitol, Rhino, and other companies, and they are constantly being re-issued. Her concert years are captured on recordings and on film clips, and her many fans share these moments with others who love to listen and learn the magic of Judy.

Judy performed for 45 years of her 47-year life — ten years in vaudeville and fifteen at MGM under the guidance of musical and dance directors making movies. She was perfectly at home in comedy or dramatic work. Although not trained in a classical ballet field, she received dance lessons from an early age, and with her photographic memory, could watch a dance routine and immediately be able to reproduce it. She was talented and versatile—she could sing, dance, and shine in comedy routines— in addition to acting naturally and showing vulnerability, which made audiences love her. Her whole presence lit up the screen in a movie, and she was one of the most popular actresses of that era. June Allyson once commented, "If MGM could have put her into every movie they would have done so." The next nineteen years she spent in concerts halls, television studios, and nightclubs performing over 1,100 times. She continued to record and made several more movies.

Judy received a Tony Award for reviving vaudeville to the Palace in 1951. She received Academy Award nomination for best actress in *A Star is Born*. Although she did not receive the award, she did receive the Golden Globe and Look Magazine awards for her performance in this movie. Judy also received best a supporting actress nomination for her role in *Judgment at Nuremberg*.

Her album of the famed Carnegie Hall concert won five Grammy awards. A documentary called *Stay All Night* is in development about fans who attended Judy's April 23, 1961, Carnegie Hall performance. Rob Epstein and Jeffrey Friedman are executive producers and Steve Lippman directs "a documentary film about memory and a time." http://www.stayallnightthemovie.com/

Judy was exquisitely beautiful. Unfortunately, she did not realize it. Once when she saw Jim Bailey doing his impersonation of her, she said to him afterwards, "I didn't realize how pretty I was!" One can only assume the negative remarks from her mother and references in early MGM movies to her being plain, along with Louis Mayer's comments that she was his "little hunchback," could not be erased. It was not just her perfect skin, enormous magnetic brown eyes, pretty nose, perfect profile, warm generous lips, and beautiful long legs, it was how dainty she was; she was incapable of moving ungracefully—every movement in her body, as she turned and twisted, particularly her arms and shoulders, was perfect. Even with a blacked-out tooth, fright wig and dirty face in an old tramp costume with ugly big shoes, she was exquisite. In addition, everything about her was musical including her speaking voice with its hesitations and lifts which nearly go into a song. I once commented on this to Sid Luft, who agreed, adding, "Even when she coughed, it was musical." Along with this, Judy just was warm and loving from inside. She had a great soul. She spent hours entertaining the servicemen during World War II and later would visit them in veterans' hospitals around the country. Her other great concern was for sick children; she often donated proceeds from many concerts to children's hospitals, along with visiting as many as she could.

MGM produced a movie called *That's Entertainment* in 1974, shown in movie houses and on television, and a LP record was issued at the same time. This movie captured the magic of the MGM years; it was so successful that *That's Entertainment, Part 2* followed in 1976 and *That's Entertainment, Part 3* in 1994. These movies made known to the public just how important Judy was to the MGM studio.

PBS produced "The Concert Years" in the Great Performances series as well as many other special programs about Judy.

Pioneer Entertainment and Classic World Productions have issued DVDs of CBS's *The Judy Garland Show.*

The United States Postal Service issued a First-Day-of-Issue Commemorative Postage Stamp for Judy Garland on June 10, 2006, under "Legends of Hollywood". She was twelfth person to be so honored. Art director Ethel Kessler designed the stamp using a portrait of Garland by Tim O'Brien.

In 1975, the Judy Garland Rose was developed by R. Harkess & Co. in England, and now it's available in the States. There is a Judy Garland Rose Garden overlooking Manhattan and the Statue of Liberty, arranged the NY Parks & Recreation with around 200 rose bushes "In celebration of Judy Garland, 1922-1969."

There were two big Judy events in the summer of 2011 in New York City, one a comprehensive retrospective of Judy Garland's career on television. This event was coordinated and produced in association with the Film Society of Lincoln Center. The Center also presented complete and comprehensive retrospective analyses of her movies. They screened 31 titles -- all but two films were presented in 35mm, with the two exceptions (*The Wizard of Oz* and *A Star is Born*) presented in 4k digital restorations. Another presentation of short films and rarities was hosted by John Fricke, noted historian and authority on Judy Garland and *The Wizard of Oz*.

RESOURCES

appendix

Much information can found in the dozens of books have been written about Judy—some good and some bad—they are all listed in my bibliography. John Fricke's many books are to be recommended, along with Coyne Steve Sanders' book, *The Judy Garland Show: Rainbow's End,* about the CBS Television series, and Lorna Smith's *To Judy, with Love.*

WEB SITES

Some of the web sites you have to join to participate in discussions; others are free to view.

The Judy Garland Experience (created in 2006) is a source for Judy information and rare audio recordings (including unofficial concert recordings referenced in this book) One has to join the Yahoo group to participate, but it has many great features. New rare Judy concerts are posted every week, many photos; there is lots of discussion by members every day. It offers contests and trivia:
http://movies.groups.yahoo.com/group/thejudygarlandexperie nce/

Also the Judy Live Performances site (created in 1995) is great for information on her concert and TV career, many newspaper articles from back in the day are re-posted here: http://rainbowz.deltacomm.com/

The Judy Room (founded in 1999) offers great info on all her vinyl and CD albums and many photos: http://www.thejudyroom.com/

The Judy Garland Message Board (founded in 2005) is a place to discuss all aspects of Garland's life and career, related performers and events. http://jgmb.judyandfriends.de/

www.thejudygarlandpage.com Michael Siewart collection

www.judygarlandcostumes.com Charles Triplett collection

thejudylist@googlegroup.com Steve Jarrett, Administrator

www.judygarlandmuseum.com Grand Rapids, Judy's birthplace, has a festival each June.

www.btinternet.com/~judyin.london/judyil1.htm

www.judygarlandclub.org The International Judy Garland Club based in London and administered by Gary Horrocks and Dr. Justin Sturge has over 300 members worldwide. This club is the contemporary version of the same Club Garland endorsed as led by Lorna Smith, during Garland's lifetime and has become the source of information for researchers over the years. The Club hosts social events and publishes two magazines per year. In 1970 the club dedicated a plaque to Garland on the Wall of Queens' staircase leading to the Royal Box at the London Palladium. (it may be in a different location now) Sir Richard Attenborough commented that Judy "changed the manner of our profession for all time—she brought something that no one has ever equaled."

Finally, we must not forget Judy's three children. We are lucky enough to hear her voice when her two beautiful daughters--Liza Minnelli and Lorna Luft—sing. Her son, Joe Luft, graces many of the Judy functions, and talks with fans about his mom. And we have a legacy of her many movies and recordings to keep us happy.

NOTES

Preface
[1] Coulson, Joan M. Beck. Daughter of the Landlord: Life History of a Chinese Immigrant. A Thesis presented to Department of Social Sciences, San Jose State University M.A. degree, 1989
[2] Kluckholm, C. (1945). "The Personal Document in Anthropological Science" The Use of Personal Documents in History, Anthropology, and Sociology, Bulletin 53, New York: Social Science Research Council, 112.

Chapter 1-Carnegie Hall
[1] Fadiman, Clifton. Excerpts from "Party of One", New York: Program Publishing Company, undated

Chapter 2-The Early Influences
[1] Apted, Michael. *56UP–A film by Michael Apted, DVD 2012* www.firstrunfeatures.com
[2] Apted, Michael. *49UP-A Film by Michael Apted*, DVD 2006 www.firstrunfeatures.com
[3] Apted, Michael, edited by Bennett Singer. *42 Up* (New York: The New Press, 1998)79
[4] Dahl, David & Barry Kehoe. *Young Judy* (New York: Mason Charter, 1975) 38

Chapter 3-Parents and Vaudeville
[1] Levine, Lawrence W. *Highborn/Lowbrow: The Emergency of Cultural Hierarchy in America* (Cambridge, Harvard University Press, 1988) 21
[2] Tosches, Nicholas. *Where Dead Voices Gather* (Boston: Little Brown & Co. 2001) 11
[3] Shipman, David. *Judy Garland: The Secret Life of an American Legend* (New York: Hyperion 1993) 2
[4] Dahl, David & Barry Kehoe. *Young Judy*, 7 & 12
[5] *Ibid.*, 3
[6] Clarke, Gerald. *Get Happy: The Life of Judy Garland* (New York: Random House, 2000) 9/10
[7] Dahl, David & Barry Kehoe. *Young Judy*, 18
[8] Clarke, Gerald. *Get Happy: The Life of Judy Garland*, 5
[9] *Ibid.*, 7
[10] Dahl, David & Barry Kehoe. *Young Judy*, 22
[11] Burns, George. *Gracie: A Love Story* (New York: G.P. Putnam's Sons, 1988) 60

Chapter 4-Grand Rapids
[1] Dahl, David & Barry Kehoe. *Young Judy*, 25
[2] Itasca County Independent newspaper, March 24, 1917
[3] Dahl, David & Barry Kehoe. *Young Judy*, 15
[4] Shipman, David. *Judy Garland: The Secret Life of an American Legend*, (New York: Hyperion 1993)10
[5] Frank, Gerold. *Judy* (New York: Harper & Row, 1975) 12/13
[6] Stringer, Chris. *Lone Survivor: How we came to be on the only Humans on Earth* (New York: Times Books, Henry Holt & Co. L.L.C. 2012) 172
[7] Shipman, David. *Judy Garland: The Secret Life of an American Legend*, 13
[8] Frank, Gerold, *Judy*, 18
[9] Dahl David & Barry Kehoe. *Young Judy*, 7
[10] Itasca Independent Newspaper, June 1924
[11] Dahl David & Barry Kehoe. *Young Judy*, 100
[12] *Ibid.*, 59

Chapter 5-Los Angeles & Lancaster
[1] Dahl, David & Barry Kehoe. *Young Judy*, Appendix 229-238
[2] Frank, Gerald. *Judy*, 23-26
[3] Dahl, David & Barry Kehoe. *Young Judy*, 80
[4] Clarke, Gerald. *Get Happy: The Life of Judy Garland*, 40-43
[5] Dahl, David & Barry Kehoe. *Young Judy*, 79
[6] Clarke, Gerald. *Get Happy: The Life of Judy Garland*, 28
[7] Dahl, David & Barry Kehoe. *Young Judy*, 93/94
[8] *Ibid.*, 79
[9] *Ibid.*, 100
[10] *Ibid.*, 127
[11] Dahl & Kehoe. *Young Judy*, 136
[12] Shipman, David. *Judy Garland: The Secret Life of an American Legend* (New York: Hyperion 1993) 33.
[13] Schechter, Scott. *Judy Garland, The Day by Day Chronicle of a Legend* (New York: Cooper Square Press, 2002)23
[14] Finch, Christopher. *Rainbow: The Stormy Life of Judy Garland*, 31
[15] *Ibid.*, 55
[16] Schechter, Scott. *Judy Garland, The Day by Day Chronicle of a Legend*, 26
[17] Frank, Gerald. *Judy*, 44/45
[18] *Ibid.*, 44
[19] TJGS CBS-TV episode 7 taped Sept. 20, 1063 aired September 29, 1963.
[20] Finch, Christopher. *Rainbow: The Stormy Life of Judy Garland* 59/60
[21] *Ibid.*, 64/65
[22] Frank, Gerald. *Judy*, 57

[23] Finch, Christopher. *Rainbow: The Stormy Life of Judy Garland*, 72/73

[24] Shipman, David. *Judy Garland: The Secret Life of an American Legend*, 44/45

[25] Dahl, David & Barry Kehoe. *Young Judy*, 214

[26] Clarke, Gerald. *Get Happy: The Life of Judy Garland*, 59

Chapter 6-Early MGM movies

[1] The Observer, 1951

[2] Montgomery, Elizabeth. *The Best of MGM* (London, Bison Books Ltd. 1986)10

[3] Clarke, Gerald. *Get Happy: The Life of Judy Garland*, 70

[4] Montgomery, Elizabeth. *The Best of MGM*, 12

[5] *Ibid.*, 10

[6] Eames, John Douglas. *The MGM Story: The Complete History of 57 Roaring Years* (New York: Crown Publishers, Inc. 1979) 8/9

[7] New York Times Review quoted Di Orio, Al, Jr. *Little Girl Lost* (New York: Manor Books, Inc. 1975) 36

[8] Clarke, Gerald. *Get Happy: The Life of Judy Garland*, 128

[9] *Ibid.*, 134

[10] Rooney, Mickey. *I. E An Autobiography* (New York: G.P. Putnam's Son, 1965)84

[11] Frank, Gerold. *Judy* (New York: Harper & Row, 1975)108

[12] Clarke, Gerald. *Get Happy: The Life of Judy Garland*, 87

[13] Frank, Gerold. *Judy*, 21

[14] Vare, Ethlie Ann. *Let's Get Personal: Revealing Intimate & Intriguing Details about Judy Garland*, Modern Screen October 1940, A Star-Studded Tribute to Judy Garland, Boulevard Books, 1998, 4

[15] Fordin, Hugh. *M-G-M's Great Musicals: The Arthur Freed Unit* (New York: De Capo Press Inc. 1975) 1

[16] Fordin, Hugh. *M-G-M's Great Musicals: The Arthur Freed Unit*, 8

[17] Lahr, John. *"The Lemon Drop Kid"* The New Yorker, 9/30/96) 70/73

[18] Fricke, John & Jonathan Shirshetan. *The Wizard of Oz: An Illustrated Companion to the Timeless Movie Classic*, (New York: Fall River Press, 2009)

[19] Edwards, Anne. *Judy Garland. A Biography* (New York: Simon & Schuster, 1975)

[20] Irwin, Sam. *Kay Thompson, From Funny Face to Eloise, A Biography* (New York: Simon & Schuster, 2010) 72/73

[21] *"There'll Always Be Another Encore"* McCalls Magazine, Jan-Feb 1964

[22] Clarke, Gerald. *Get Happy: The Life of Judy Garland*, 142

[23] Kimball, Kreugar, Day & Davis. *The Complete Lyrics of Johnny Mercer* (New York: Alfred A. Knopf, 2009)

Chapter 7-Marriage to David Rose

[1] Allyson, June. *June Allyson*, (New York: G.P. Putnam's Sons, 1982)42

[2] Lake, Veronica with Donald Bain. *Veronica*, (New York: A Bantam Book pub. arr. with Citadel Press, Inc. 1972) 83/84

[3] *Ibid.*, 85

[4] Wayne, Jane Ellen. *The Golden Girls of MGM* (New York: Carroll & Graf, 2003) 141/142

[5] *Ibid.*, 16

[6] *Ibid.*, 381`1

[7] Hirschhorn, Clive. *Gene Kelly* (New York: St. Martin's Press, 1974) 96/97,

[8] Irwin, Sam. *Kay Thompson, From Funny Face to Eloise*, 94

[9] Guiles, Fred Lawrence. *Tyrone Power: The Last Idol* (New York: Simon & Schuster, 1979) 67

[10] *Ibid.*, 160

[11] *Ibid.*, 161

[12] Baxter, Anne. *Intermission* (New York: Ballantine Books, 1976) 254

[13] Mankiewicz, Joseph L. *Interviews*, ed. Brian Dauth, (Jackson, University Press of Mississippi, 2008)60

[14] Shearer, Lloyd talks to Virginia Garland Thompson, *The Happy One in the Family*, Parade (The Sunday Newspaper Magazine, St. Petersburg Times, Oct. 4 1964). 4/5

[15] Mankiewicz, Joseph L. *Interviews*, 154/155

[16] Fordin, Hugh. *M-G-M's Greatest Musicals: The Freed Unit*, 95

[17] *Ibid.*, 140

[18] Irwin, Sam. *Kay Thompson, From Funny Face to Eloise*,

[19] Fordin Hugh. *M-G-M's Greatest Musicals: The Freed Unit*, 162

Chapter 8-Entertaining the Troops

[1] Schulman, Lawrence. Compiled and annotated. *Judy Garland Lost Tracks 1929-1959*, JSP Records 965

[2] Schechter, Scott. *Judy Garland: The Day-by-Day Chronicle of a Legend*, 80

[3] Liza. *Judy*, Screenland, June 1942

[4] Boston Record American September 11, 1967 12/13

[5] Wotton, Dick. Cleveland News, September 19, 1967

[6] Green, Tom. *Twenty years ago: The Legend: An Intimate Bio of Judy Garland. Sunday August 18 Cardinal Kennedy Memorial Hospital*. Rainbow Review June 1996, p12 reprinted from October 1977, The Judy Garland International Club.

[7] Smith, Lorna conversation with author October 10, 1997

Chapter 9-Marriage to Vincente Minnelli

[1] Shipman, David. *Judy Garland, The Secret Life of an American Legend*, 188

[2] Fordin, Hugh. *M-G-M's Greatest Musicals, the Arthur Freed Unit*, 33

[3] Minnelli, Vincente, with Hector Arce. *I Remember It Well*, (New York: Doubleday & Co., 1974) 163

[4] Photoplay, May 1945

[5] Frank, Gerold. *Judy*, 224

[6] McVay, Douglas. *"The Art of the Actor"* Films and Filming, September 1966

[7] *Judy Garland, Collectors' Gems from the M-G-M Years*, CD produced by George Feltenstein & Bradley Flanagan. 1996

[8] Shipman, David. *Judy Garland: The Secret Life of an American Legend*, 216

[9] *Ibid.*, 217

[10] Clarke, Gerald. *Get Happy: The Life of Judy Garland*, 38

[11] Fordin, Hugh. *M-G-M's Greatest Musicals, the Arthur Freed Unit*, 226

[12] Steiger, Brad. *Judy Garland* (New York: Ace Books, 2nd Ed. 1975) 61

[13] *Ibid.*, 62

[14] Anslinger, Harry J., & Will Oursler. *The Murderers-The Stories of the Narcotics Gangs* (New York: Farrar, Strauss & Cudahy, 1961)

[15] Pasternak Joseph. *Easy the Hard Way, The Incomparable Judy* (New York: G.P. Putnam,1956)

[16] Clarke, Gerald. *Get Happy: The Life of Judy Garland*, 253

[17] Smith, Lorna conversation with author October 10, 1997

[18] Hutton, Betty, USA Today newspaper, June 19, 2000

[19] Goode, James, *Show Business Illustrated*, Oct. 31 1961

[20] Hirschhorn, Cleve, *Gene Kelly*. (New York: St. Martin's Press, 1974)

[21] Unger, Arthur, editor. Daily Variety, June, 1950

[22] Curtis, Tony and Barry Paris. The Autobiography (New York: William Morrow & Co., Inc. 1993 (86)

[23] E. Y. Harburg talks to Catherine Stott. *"Judy Garland Death Blame on 'System'"* The Blade: Toledo, Ohio, 13 July 1969

Chapter 10-The London Palladium

[1] Judy Garland and Johnny Carson conversation on The Tonight Show NBC-TV June 24, 1968.

[2] Barber, John. *The Daily Express* April 10, 1951

[3] Extensive coverage Palladium 1951 show in Rainbow Reviews Issue 21, March 1998 and Issue 27, 2001, The Judy Garland International Club

[4] Daily Telegraph, April 10, 1951

[5] Baxter, Beverley (later to be Sir Arthur Beverley Baxter) *Evening Standard*, April 10, 1951

[6] Horrocks, Gary and Kathryn Leach, *At Long Last Here I am: Judy Garland in Europe—1951*, Rainbow Review, Issue 27 19, London: The International Judy Garland Club

[7] Horrocks, Gary. *A Toast to Miss Showbusiness*, Rainbow Review, issue 29/30, 2002 24, London: The International Judy Garland Club

[8] Smith, Lorna. *Judy, with Love*. (London: Robert Hale & Co., 1975) 81

Chapter 11-The Luft Dynasty

[1] Bogarde, Dirk. *Snakes and Ladders* (London: Triad/Panther Books, 1979) 194

[2] *Ibid.*, 96

[3] Crane, Cheryl with Cliff Jahr. *A Detour* (New York: Arbor House/William Morrow, 1988)   133-134

[4] Crane, Cheryl with Cindy De La Hoz. *Lana: The Memories, the Myths, the Movies* (PA: Running Press Publishers, 2008) 64

[5] Crane, Cheryl with Cliff Jahr. *A Detour*, 133-134

[6] Crane, Cheryl. *Lana: The Memories, the Myths, the Movies,* 179

[7] Sperber, A.M. & Eric Lax. *Bogart* (New York: William Morrow & Co. 1997) 280

[8] Allyson, June with Frances Spatz Leighton. *June Allyson* (New York: G.P. Putnam's Sons, 1982) 11

[9] *Ibid.*, 15

[10] *Ibid.*, 14

[11] *Ibid.*, 106

[12] Steketee, N.W. (January 2011). *"Dorothy Ponedel (1998-1979). "She Performs Miracles of Surgery with Grease Paint Instead of a Knife,"* Judy Garland: A Celebration (Issue 2 Winter 2011). London: The International Judy Garland Club, pp.16-25

[13] Irwin, Sam. *Kay Thompson: From Funny Face to Eloise, A Biography,* 27

[14] *Ibid.*, 95/113

[15] *Ibid.*, 134

[16] Bacall, Lauren. *By Myself* (New York: Alfred A. Knopf, 1970)119

[17] Haver, Ronald. *A Star is Born* (New York, Alfred A. Knopf, 1988)

[18] Bacall, Lauren. *By Myself,* 220

[19] San Jose Mercury, 7/15/83

[20] Reynolds, Debbie. *Debbie, My Life* (New York: William Morro & Co. Inc. 1988) 201

[21] *Ibid.*, 91

[22] *Ibid.,* 201/202

[23] Bacall, Lauren. *By Myself,* 504

[24] Reynolds, Debbie. *Debbie My Life*, 201

[25] Schechter, Scott. *Judy Garland: The Day-by-Day Chronicle of a Legend,* 202/203

[26] *Ibid.*, 205

[27] *Ibid.,* 205

Chapter 12-The Dominion, London

[1] Smith, Lorna. *Judy, with Love* (London: 1978) 48/49

[2] Schechter, Scott. *Judy Garland: The Day-by-Day Chronicle of a Legend,* 212

3 Jenkins, Gordon. *"Miraculous Person"* The Melody Maker, November 16, 1967

4 Smith, Lorna. *Judy, with Love* 65

Chapter 13 –Musicians in her Life
1 Jenkins, Bruce. *Goodbye: In Search of Gordon Jenkins*, Berkeley, CA: Frog Ltd., 2005)64

2 *Ibid.*, 68

3 McClellan, Dennis, Los Angeles Times, May 11, 2012

Chapter 14-1858-59 Back in the States
1 Schechter, Scott. *Judy Garland, The Day-by-Day Chronicles of a Legend*, 215

2 Wood, Jack conversation with author, July 20, 2013

Chapter 15-Judy comes back to London 1960
1 Shipman, David. *Judy Garland, the Secret Life of an American Legend*, 393

2 Bogarde, Dirk. *Snakes & Ladders* (London: Triad/Panther Books, 1979) 1978) 235

3 *Ibid.*, 235

4 *Ibid.*, 257

5 Coulson, Joan. *Harold Davison presents An Evening with JUDY GARLAND, Sunday, 28th August, 1960 London Palladium*, Garland Gazette January 1961, 14/16

6 Smith, Lorna. *Judy, with Love* , 81/82

Chapter 16-CMA
1 Shipman, David. *Judy Garland: The Secret Life of an American Legend*, 405

2 *Ibid.*, 407

3 Gallagher, Sonny. *Judy and Me,* date unknown, 4/5

4 Paglia, Camille, Professor of Humanities, University of Arts, Philadelphia, New York Times, June 13, 1998

5 Bogarde, Dirk. *Snakes & Ladders*, 245

6 *Ibid.*,

7 Goode, James. *Part I of the Garland Story*, Show Business Illustrated, October 31, 1961 86

8 *Ibid., Part III of the Garland Story*. Show Business Illustrated November 28, 1961 70

9 Stritch, Elaine, conversation with author, London: The Old Vic Theatre, October 17, 2002

10 Judy Garland and Noël Coward conversation, Redbook Magazine November, 1961

11 Wood, Jack, conversation with author July 20, 2013

[12] Eichelbaum, Stanley. *Another Sensational Evening with Judy!* San Francisco Examiner newspaper, September 15, 1961 25
[13] Schechter Scott. *Judy Garland, The Day-by-Day Chronicles of a Legend*, 237/8
[14] Stevens, Gordon, email to author June 5, 2008

Chapter 17-*I Could Go on Singing*
[1] Smith, Lorna, letter to author, May 8, 2013
[2] Neame, Ronald with Barbara Roisman Cooper. *Straight from the Horses's Mouth* (Maryland: Scarecrow Press, Inc. 2003) 185
[3] Smith, Lorna, letter to author, May, 8, 2013
[4] Smith, Lorna, conversation with author on September 10, 1997 in London
[5] *Ibid.*

Chapter 18-CBS Television Series
[1] Coulson, Joan. *Be my Guest*, Rainbow Review, Issue No. 31, Autumn 2004 38/40, reprints from Rainbow Review, and Garland Gazette 1963/1964
[2] Philipson, Judy. Miami Beach Reporter, March 11, 1965
[3] Lyon, Eleanor, email June, 25, 2001

Chapter Australia and London
[1] Smith, Lorna conversation with author London: September 10, 1997
[2] Lawless, Wayne, conversation with author Los Angeles: July 10, 1998
[3] Coulson, Joan. *I Belong to London: Recollections of Judy Garland in London 1964* Rainbow Review, 23 Spring/Summer 1999. The International Judy Garland Club.
[4] Smith, Lorna, letter to author June 30, 2013
[5] Shipman, David. *Judy Garland: The Secret Life of an American Legend*, 477/478
[6] The Daily Mail, July 24, 1964
[7] Shipman, David. *Judy Garland: The Secret Life of an American Legend* 478
[8] Smith, Lorna, letter to author June 30, 2013
[9] *Ibid.,*
[10] *Ibid.,*
[11] The Daily Mail, November 9, 1964
[12] Irwin, Sam. *Kay Thompson, From Sunny Face to Eloise, A Biography* 2010) 341
[13] Smith, Lorna conversation with author London: September 10, 1997
[14] The International Judy Garland Club.

Chapter 20-April 1965-1966
[1] Lawless, Wayne, conversation with author, Los Angeles, June 20, 1998
[2] Stevens, Gordon, email June 23, 2013
[3] Meyer, Frank. Miami Beach Daily Sun newspaper March 12, 1965
[4] Wardlow, Jean. *Judy* Miami Herald Sunday Magazine, March 13, 1965
[5] Wood, Jack, conversation with author, San Francisco, April 8, 2003

[6] Young, Kenneth, conversation with author, FB, August 18, 2013.

[7] Schechter, Scott. *Judy Garland, The Day by Day Chronicle of a Legend*, 2002) 306

[8] Wood, Jack, conversation with author, San Francisco, April 8, 2003

[9] Lawless, Wayne, email to author March 8, 2001

[10] Bladen, Barbara. *Judy Garland in Better Voice*, San Matteo Times, September 3, 1965

[11] Gallagher, Sonny, letter to author, November 18, 1998

[12] Lawless, Wayne, letter to author March 15, 2002

[13] Ibid.

[14] Mascolsa, Pat. Hollywood Sun-Tattler, February 4, 1966

Chapter 21-Clutching at Straws

[1] Frank, Gerold. *Judy*, 584

[2] Edwards, Anne. *Judy Garland: A Biography*, 227/230

[3] Barr-Brandon, Nancy conversation with author June 16, 1998

[4] Barr-Brandon, Nancy email to author July 11, 2013

[5] Fricke, John. *Appraisal of "What's My Line"* - Rainbow Review June 1967, 9

[6] Carlyle, John. *Under the Rainbow, An Intimate Memoir of Judy Garland*, (New York: Carroll & Graf Publishers, 2006) 211

[7] Gallagher, Sonny letter to author, November 18, 1998

[8] Perdue, Jon, email to author July 18, 2012

[9] *Ibid.*

[10] Lawless, Wayne, email to author, March 14, 2001

[11] Frank, Gerold. *Judy*, 99

[12] Citron, Stephen. *Jerry Herman* (New Haven & London: Yale University Press 2004) 153

[13] *Ibid.,* 154

[14] *Ibid.,* Interview with Jerry Herman, 153

[15] Edwards, Anne. *Judy Garland: A Biography*, 248/9

[16] Kwinty, Jonathan, Evening News June 26, 1968

[17] Singer, Samuel L., Philadelphia Inquirer, July 21, 1968

[18] Meyer, John. *Heartbreaker*, New York: Doubleday & Co., 1983) 35/36

[19] *Ibid.,* 129

[20] *Ibid.,* 176

[21] *Ibid.,* 192

[22] Griffin, Merv with Peter Barsocchini. *Merv* (New York: Simon & Schuster, 1980) 151/152

[23] Meyer, John, *Heartbreaker*, 213

[24] *Ibid.,* 221/222

[25] Griffin, Merv with Peter Barsocchini. *Merv* 151/3

[26] Meyer, John. *Heartbreaker*, 241

Notes

Chapter 22 Return to England-Talk of the Town

[1] Edwards, Anne, *Judy Garland: A Biography* (New York: Simon & Schuster, 1975)

[2] Smith, Lorna, conversation with author, October 10, 1997

[3] Theaker, John, email to author, June 13, 2013

[4] Baxter, Bruce, British Film Institute, January 5, 1969

[5] Allyson, June with Frances Spatz Leighton, *June Allyson* 239

[6] Shipman, David, Shipman, David, Judy Garland: The Secret Life of an American Legend,(New York: Hyperion, 1992) 508

[7] San Jose Mercury 6/28/1969

[8] Di Orio, Al, *Little Girl Lost* (New York: Arlington House, 1973) James Mason Eulogy

[9] Glanvill, Brian letter to author August 13, 1997

BIBLIOGRAPHY

Allyson, June with Frances Spatz Leighton. *June Allyson*. New York: G.P. Putnam's Sons, 1982.

Anslinger, Harry J., & Will Oursler. *The Murderers: Stories of the Narcotics Gangs*.
New York: Farrar, Strauss & Cudahy, 1961.

Apted, Michael. ed. Singer, Bennett. *42 Up*. New York: The New Press,1998.

Bacall, Lauren. *By Myself*. New York: Knopf, 1979.

Baxter, Anne. *Intermission: A True Story*. New York: Ballantine Books: G. P Putnam's Sons, 1976.

Bergan, Ronald. *Glamorous Musicals*. London: Octopus Brooks Ltd., 1984.

Bergreen, Laurence. *As Thousands Cheer: the Life of Irving Berlin*. New   York: Viking Penguin
a division of Penguin Books USA, Inc., 1990.

Bogarde, Dirk. *Snakes and Ladders*. London, Triad/Panther Books,1979.

Burns, George. *Gracie: A Love Story*. New York: G. P. Putnam's Sons, 1988.

Carlyle, John. *Under the Rainbow*, New York: Carroll & Graf, 2006

Clarke, Gerald. *Get Happy: The Life of Judy Garland*. New York: Random House, 2000.

Citron, Stephen. *Jerry Herman*. New Haven & London: Yale University Press, 2004.

Coleman, Emily R. *The Complete Judy Garland*. New York: Harper & Row, 1990.

Crane, Cheryl with Cliff Jahr. *A Detour*. New York: Arbor House/William Morrow, 1988.

Crane, Cheryl with Cindy De La Hoz. *Lana: The Memories, the Myths, the Movies*.
Philadelphia PA: Running Press Publishers, 2008.

Curtis, Tony and Barry Paris. *Tony Curtis, The Autobiography*. New York: William Morrow, 1993

Dahl, David, and Barry Kehoe. *Young Judy*. New York: Mason Charter, 1975.

Deans, Mickey, and Ann Pinchot. *Weep No More, My Lady*. New York:Hawthorn Books, Inc. 1972.

DiOrio, Al. *Little Girl Lost*. New York: Arlington House, 1973.

Eames, John Douglas, Roaring *The MGM Story: The Complete History   of 57 Years*,
New York: Crown Publishers Inc. 1979

Edwards, Anne. *Judy Garland: a Biography*. New York: Simon & Schuster, 1975.

Farmer, Steven. *Adult Children of Abusive Parents: a Healing Program for Those Who Have Been Physically,
Sexually, or Emotionally Abused*. New York: Ballantine Books, 1989.

Bibliography

Finch, Christopher. *Rainbow: the Stormy Life of Judy Garland*. New York: Grosset & Dunlap, 1975.

Firman, Julie and Dorothy Firman. *Daughters and Mothers: Healing the Relationship*. New York: Continuum 1989.

Fisher, John, *The Legends*, New York: Stein & Day, 1976

Fordin, Hugh. *Great Musicals: the Arthur Freed Unit*. Cambridge, Mass.: 1996.

Frank, Gerold. *Judy*. New York: Harper & Row, 1975.

Fricke, John. *Judy Garland: World's Greatest Entertainer*. New York: Henry Holt & Company, Inc., 1992.

Fricke, John. *Judy Garland: a portrait in Art and Anecdote*. Bell Finch Press div. of AOL Time Warner, 2003.

Fricke, John and Jay Scarfone & William Stillman, *The Wizard of Oz   The Official 50th Anniversary Pictorial History*, New York, Warner Books, Inc. 1989

Fricke, John & Jonathan Shirshekan, *The Wizard of Oz An Illustrated Companion to the Timeless Classic*, New York, Fall River Press 2009

Furia, Philip. *Ira Gershwin: the Art of the Lyricist*. New York: Oxford University Press, 1996.

Goode, James. "*Judy*." Show Business Illustrated, 42-45, 50-52, 61-62, 68-69, 70-71, 86-87, October 31, 1961

Griffin, Merv with Peter Barsocchini. *Merv*. New York: Simon & Schuster, 1980.

Guiles, Fred Lawrence. *Tyrone Power: the Last Idol*. New York: Doubleday & Company, Inc., 1979.

Haver, Ronald. *A Star is Born*. New York: Alfred A. Knopf, 1988.

Heilbrun, Carolyn G. *Writing A Woman's Life*. New York: W.W. Norton, 1988.

Hirschhorn, Clive. *Gene Kelly*. New York: St. Martin's Press, 1974.

Irwin, Sam, *Kay Thompson: from Funny Face to Eloise, a Biography* New York: Simon & Schuster, 2010

Jenkins, Bruce, *Goodbye: In Search of Gordon Jenkins*. Berkeley, CA: Frog Ltd., 2005.

Jenkins, Gordon. "Miraculous Person" Melody Maker, London: November 1957.

-----Garland, Judy. "There'll always Be An Encore," McCall's, New York, January 1964

Juneau, James. *Judy Garland*. London: W.H. Allen, 1976.

Keylin, Arleen & Suri Flesischer, edited *Hollywood Album*, New York:The New York Times Co., 1977

Kimball, Robert, Miles Kreuger, Barry Day, & Eric Davis, *The Complete Lyrics of Johnny Mercer*. New York: Knopf, 2009.

Kluckholm, C. "*The Personal Document in Anthropological Science*" The Use of Personal Documents in History, Anthropology, and Sociology, Bulletin 53, New York: Social Sciences Research Council, 112.

Lake, Veronica with Donald Bain. *Veronica.* New York: A Bantam Book pub. arr. With Citadel Press, Inc. 1972.

Mankiewicz, Joseph L. *Interviews,* edited by Brian Dauth, Jackson: University Press of Mississippi, 2008.

McArthur, Dorothea S. *Birth of a Self in Adulthood.* New Jersey: Jason Aronson, 1988.

Markel, Howard. *An Anatomy of Addiction.* New York: Pantheon Books, 2011.

Meyer, John. *Heartbreaker.* New York: Doubleday & Co. 1983.

Middleton-Moz, Jane. *Children of Trauma: Rediscovering Your Discarded Self.* Deerfield Beach, FL: Health Communications, Inc. 1989.

Miller, Alice. *The Untouched Key.* New York: Anchor Books, Doubleday,1990.

Miller, Alice: *The Drama of the Gifted Child.* New York: Basic Books, Div. of Harper Collins,1997.

Minnelli, Vincente, with Hector Arce. *I Remember It Well.* New York: Doubleday, 1974.

Montgomery, Elizabeth Miles, *The Best of MGM.* London: Bison Books Ltd. 1986

Morella, Joe, and Edward Z. Epstein: *Judy: The Films and Career of Judy Garland.* London, Leslie Frewin, 1969.

Neame, Ronald with Barbara Roisman Cooper. *Straight from the Horses's Mouth.* Maryland: Scarecrow Press, Inc., 2003.

Parrish, Dee Anna, *Abused: A Guide to Recovery for Adult Survivors of Emotional/Physical Child Abuse.* New York: Station Hill Press,1990.

Quirk, Lawrence J. and William Schoell, *The Rat Pack: the Hey-Hey Days of Frank and the Boys.* Dallas, Texas: Taylor Trade Publishing Co. 1998.

Reynolds, Debbie with David Patrick Columbia. *Debbie: My Life.*. New York: William Morrow & Co. Inc. 1988.

Rooney, Mickey, *I.E.: An Autobiography.* New York: G. P. Putnam's Sons, 1965.

Rosenfeld, Richard, editor.*Hollywood 1940s.* New York: Multimedia Publications(U.K.) Ltd., 1985.

Sanders, Coyne Stevens. *Rainbow's End: the Judy Garland Show.* New York: William Morrow & Co.Inc.,1990.

Schechter, Scott. *Judy Garland: the Day-by-Day Chronicle of a Legend,* New York: Cooper Square Press, 2002.

Shelden, Michael. "Sid Luft Talks: 'I Couldn't Stop Judy Falling Apart.'"*Daily Telegraph.* London, January 6, 2001.

Shearer, Lloyd. "*Judy Garland's sister. The Happy One in the Family*" Virginia Garland Thompson. *Parade,* The Sun Newspaper Magazine, S. Petersburg Times, Oct. 4 1964

Smith, Lorna. *To Judy with Love: the story of Miss Show Business.* London: Robert Hale & Co., 1975.

Bibliography

Smith, Lorna. *My Life Over the Rainbow.* New York: Vantage Press, Inc.,1987.

Shipman, David. *Judy Garland: the Secret Life of an American Legend.* New York: Hyperion, 1992.

Spada, James. *Judy and Liza.* New York: Doubleday & Company, Inc., 1983.

Sperber, A.M and Eric Lax. *Bogart.* New York: William Morrow & Co.Inc., 1997.

Steiger, Brad. *Judy Garland.* New York: Ace Books, 2nd ed., 1975.

Stringer, Chris. *Lone Survivor: How We Came to be the only humans on Earth.* New York: Times Books, Henry Holt & Co., L.L.C., 2012.

Taylor, John Russell. *1940's Hollywood,* New York: New York Gallery Books, 1985.

Tormé, Mel. *The Other Side of the Rainbow.* New York: Oxford University Press, 1991.

Vare, Ethlie Ann. *A Star-Studded Tribute to Judy Garland.* New York: Boulevard Books, 1998.

Watson, Thomas J. and Bill Chapman. *Judy: Portrait of an American Legend.* New York: McGraw-Hill, 1986.

Wayne, Jane Ellen. *Lana: The Loves of Lana Turner.* New York: St.Martin's Press,1995.

Wayne, Jane Ellen. *The Golden Girls of MGM.* New York: Carroll & Graf, 2003.

Wilson, John Morgan. *Inside Hollywood: a Writer's Guide to Researching the World of Movies and TV.* Cincinnati, Ohio: Writer's Digest Books, 1998.

Woodman, Marion. *Addiction to Perfection: The Still Unravished Bride.* Toronto, Canada: Inner City Books, 1982.

INDEX